Not Just Any Body

NOT JUST ANY BODY

Advancing Health, Well-being and Excellence
in Dance and Dancers

The Ginger Press

Design by Lori Ledingham
Cover photo of Desmond Richardson by Antoine Tenpe, for the Holland Dance Festival

National Library of Canada Cataloguing in Publication data

Main entry under title:

Not just any body : advancing health, well-being and excellence in dance and dancers

Based on a conference entitled Not just any body : a global conference to advance health, well being and excellence in dance and dancers, held simultaneously in Toronto and the Hague, in Nov. 1999.

ISBN 0921773-56-0

1. Dance – Congresses. 2. Dancers – Congresses. 3. Dance – Health aspects – Congresses. 4. Dancers – Health and Hygiene – Congresses.
I. Jowitt, Deborah.

GV1594.N67 2001   792.8   C2001-930314-9

"Not Just Any Body" was initiated and co-produced by Canada's National Ballet School, Theater Instituut Nederland, The Dutch Health Care Foundation for Dancers and The Holland Dance Festival.

Published by
The Ginger Press, Inc.
848 Second Avenue East
Owen Sound, Ontario
Canada N4K 2H3
www.gingerpress.com

Printed in Canada

Contents

This book began as an event. "Not Just Any Body: Advancing Health, Well-being and Excellence in Dance and Dancers" (NJAB) was a remarkable conference for hundreds of presenters and participants in The Hague and Toronto as well as a dozen satellite and Internet sites. This book is intended to preserve that experience and extend it beyond the confines of the original conference.

Dancers dance. Choreographers choreograph. Dance teachers teach dance. They do not often write about dance. This book will act as a sourcebook for readers who want to measure the state of the art by finding out what dancers, choreographers and dance teachers are thinking about, doing and planning. *Not Just Any Body* is a primer on the issues concerning the dance world today.

The process of converting the many sessions, discussions and demonstrations at the conference into print required editing hundreds of hours of transcripts, then sorting them thematically from both sites and presenting them in a way that would be useful to readers. This book is organized into chapters that reflect the original event. Chapters One to Three are transcribed chronologically from satellite presentations and discussions that took place simultaneously in Toronto and The Hague. Chapters Four to Nine are transcribed from sessions that happened in both sites; the selected material is organized thematically. The Afterword is a reflection, written one year after the event, on what happened at the Not Just Any Body conference. Appendix One is a summary of the workshops at both sites and Appendix Two contains brief biographies of the contributors.

The Steering Committee for the NJAB conference wishes to thank project coordinator Mary W. Rowe and the dozens of staff and volunteers on both sides of the Atlantic whose work made it possible to bring together the rich ideas explored in this volume.

INTRODUCTION

At the beginning of every project lies a need and a dream. In the early spring of 1998, a handful of people in Canada and The Netherlands, inspired by a shared vision, joined forces across two continents to develop what became one of the largest events in dance, reaching people around the globe. Never in our wildest dreams did we imagine that we would capture the interest of so many. We soon found that topics we considered vitally important were also relevant to a large number of people around the world. With their support and their interest we were able to build "Not Just Any Body, A Global Conference to Advance Health, Well-being and Excellence in Dance and Dancers."

This was the first time the dance community was linked by satellite technology. In the two principal conference sites, Toronto and The Hague, and downlinks in several international centres, the dance community convened by satellite in daily plenary sessions. In addition, con-

ference participants in Toronto and The Hague had the opportunity to exchange and discuss ideas through a wide variety of site-specific workshops. We never envisaged dramatically changing the dance world in just three days, but rather it was our goal to serve as a catalyst to highlight the key issues challenging our community. Discussions revealed both a shared determination to effect change and the enormous complexity of contesting the status quo in a productive fashion.

The Hague (on screen) and Toronto (on stage) in a joint satellite discussion during NJAB.

In retrospect, very much like the nature of dance itself, the three conference days seem but a fleeting moment. Therefore, during the planning stages of NJAB, priority was given to capturing the spirit of this unique event by creating a legacy. You are holding that legacy in your hand. This book is pertinent to all members of the dance community whether or not you actually attended the conference. You will be touched by the information, vision and thought which informed this momentous November 1999 event.

This book, like the conference, reflects the passions of an extended dance community, vibrant with tremendous potential, strong in vision and full of hope. Dance holds a unique position in our world and in our time, with its gift of boundless communication and its propensity for evolution. However, much still remains to be accomplished and explored. It is up to each and every one of us to carry on the work to manifest our needs and dreams. May we all be encouraged and rejuvenated by the spirit and integrity of NJAB and its legacy in this volume.

Paul Bronkhorst
Career Counsellor
Theater Instituut Nederland

Margot Rijven
Chair
Dutch Healthcare Foundation for Dancers

Anuschka Roes
Head of Teacher Training
Canada's National Ballet School

Robert Sirman
Administrative Director
Canada's National Ballet School

Mavis Staines
Artistic Director
Canada's National Ballet School

Samuel Wuersten
Artistic Director, Holland Dance Festival
Artistic Director, Rotterdam Dance Academy

Clockwise from top right: Samuel Wuersten, Mavis Staines, Paul Bronkhorst, Anuschka Roes, Robert Sirman and Margot Rijven (centre).

Focus on Excellence

Photograph on previous page:
Dancers: Jillian Vanstone and Matthew Kwasnicki
Ballet: *Four Last Songs* by Rudi van Dantzig
Photographer: Jeannette Edissi-Collins

CHAPTER ONE
FOCUS ON EXCELLENCE

DEBORAH JOWITT

As a critic and historian, I am a living example of a fairly fortuitous career transition. And, I'm one of the walking wounded as a result of a long-ago, ill-advised cartilage operation.

If all were well in Western theatrical dancing today, theorists and practitioners would not be gathered on two continents to ponder the connections between artistic excellence and creativity, on the one hand, and health and spiritual well-being on the other. We sense that something is wrong. Among dancers, as among all people, struggle to achieve a goal may be desirable. Challenge quickens the senses, helps one to strip away the non-essentials, and focus on the task of the moment—whether that is beating a mayonnaise just to the point when it might separate, or performing a difficult balance. But these sorts of challenges may prove most fruitful for individuals with a healthy (and I use that word with caution) sense of their own present abilities and future potential in relation to the feasibility of the task, as well as a capacity for courageous thoughts and actions. Not every dancer has the presence of mind of the young Merce Cunningham who, taking daily classes with Martha Graham and also studying at the School of American Ballet to remedy a rather late start, went off by himself, after classes, to practice and analyze all he'd been given in order, he said, "to discover how I did that." And when an individual crumbles—her confidence undermined by ill health, injury, private grief or cruelty in the workplace—she can no longer translate adversity into challenge.

We gather these three days, both actually and virtually, as a community; and, the implication is that we hope to ascertain without doubt—and spread the word—that sane and humane practices in the classroom, rehearsal hall, and the day-to-day functioning of dance companies are not antithetical to artistic excellence, but in fact promote it.

Not Just Any Body focuses on Western theatrical dancing. Perhaps we need to consider its goals, values and contradictions in relation to the larger dance picture. In many societies, dances promote acculturation, that is, educate a given age group into that society's values and their role in it. In Paul Spencer's analysis, the dances performed by boys of the Samburo of North Kenya during the period prior to their circumcision ceremonies unify them as a group and gradually bring out in them the assertiveness embodied in those dances and songs—the boldness that tells everyone they're ready to enter a new stage of life. On a professional level, the nine female Javanese court dancers performing the mesmerizing *bedhaya* are taught that they must feel themselves dancing as one, that no dancer should strive to excel above the others or to make herself stand out in any way.

In Western culture, however, dance has lost almost all its connections with rites of passage and, indeed, with any other religious rituals. A corps de ballet dancer wishing promotion would naturally laugh at the idea of trying not to excel or, within limits, call attention to herself. What we have on stage, I think, are illusory

3

communities, generated by a choreographer's imagination and skill, and the dancers' interpretation of what is produced in rehearsal. But to what degree do those dancers feel that they are contributing members of that community? The choreographer, however enlightened, may come to think of the dancers as instruments rather than collaborators; the dancers do not need to be privy to the choreographer's struggles and doubts, or even to know what the dance is to be "about." Dancers who enter the profession in part because they find the structure of being told exactly what to do comforting, a relief from life's frequent chaos, will not mind this, as long as it is benign. A psychologist might wonder, however, if masochism plays a role. (Marie Taglioni noted that she fainted frequently during daily practice sessions decreed by her father when he was struggling to get her up to snuff for her debut in Vienna. She endured three sessions of two hours each per day, one of which was supposedly devoted entirely to balance. "Put your leg à la seconde. Now hold it there for a hundred counts. All right, other side." But, she never complained of this or rebelled–at least, not publicly.)

Other dancers will find unquestioning obedience oppressive. This may be in part because we, unlike some other cultures, place great value in all the arts on originality and individuality. Today, we see the struggling artist as a cultural icon. However, this concept only gained currency beginning in the 19th century. The renaissance painter wasn't deeply offended if a patron stipulated a certain amount of lapis lazuli in the Virgin Mary's robes. If that patron was willing to pay for expensive pigments, like lapis, to enhance his prestige, and dictate how the colours should be deployed, a painter like Ghirlandaio didn't storm out of the room muttering about his integrity being compromised.

Johann Sebastian Bach, slaving to support twenty offspring, also worked for hire, not feeling it beneath him to tailor this oratorio or that collection of keyboard pieces to a particular need. The image of the composer staring out the window awaiting inspiration arrived with Beethoven. George Balanchine allied himself with earlier artists' lack of hubris when he announced that only God creates, man assembles. And he showed himself no snob when he composed a ballet for elephants and showgirls.

The difficulty in this concept of the elite "creator" lodges in a fact we all know: While a composer or a painter or a writer can work in private (pulling out hair, taking long breaks, indulging in dangerous substances) a choreographer works largely in public, surrounded by eager or bored "materials," sometimes with agendas of their own. And, because the instruments dancers play are not violins or paintbrushes, but their own perishable bodies and souls, they are especially vulnerable to criticism. Their vulnerability interacts, sometimes explosively, with that of the choreographer groping to fulfill a still shadowy idea. So, tradition casts the choreographer as an autocrat, expecting from the dancer silence, disciplined skill, approval and self-sacrifice, so that nothing will derail his fragile focus on whatever it is he is trying to "assemble." Even progressive choreographers who view their dancers as collaborators must have the last word and dancers who make creative contributions to choreographers are both more invested in the work and more vulnerable when their ideas are rejected.

Dance class, too, is structured like a dictatorship, however benevolent, and many choreographers and teachers carry their power to an extreme believing that contentment is anathema to excellence, convinced that keeping dancers on edge, in doubt and in competition with one another produces more exciting performances. Is this really true? Provable? And more important, what is the cost?

If I may carry the musical instrument analogy a little further, a violinist makes sure that violin and bow are maintained in excellent condition–protected from extremes of temperature and humidity, from shock and so on. But dancers' instruments are often compromised by inadequate nutrition, lack of sleep, and performing while injured.

Dancing, at its best, is a transformative experience for the dancer. Let us hope we discover some clues to minimizing the sacrifices and enlarging the scope and duration of those amazing peak moments that make dancing not just a job but a way of life.

Deborah Jowitt has been principal dance critic of the Village Voice *since 1967 and published three books. She has lectured and conducted workshops at universities, festivals and museums in the U.S. and abroad, and has been on the faculty of New York University's Tisch School of the Arts since 1975.*

★　★　★

MARION WOODMAN

Theatre was once a sacred place. Audiences went there to experience their own depths, hoping that the god and goddess would make their divine presence felt. As Matisse so profoundly revealed in paint, and Eliot revealed equally profoundly in words, "without the point, the still point," there is no dance in which divine and human meet.

Like every other art, dance comes from the eternal depths of Being. Dancers touch that place in themselves and release it in the souls of the audience. That place of Being is populated with images common to every culture, in every period of history. The precise images differ, depending on the specifics of time and place; the magnetic force that the images carry does not change. For example, images of Mother and Father are not the same in 2000 as they were in 1950. Such images are called archetypes. They are the life blood of every culture.

Dance is archetypal energy. Without words, without clay and without paint, the body becomes the image. Through the rhythm and glory of the music, the dancer's central nervous system is activated. The instinctual unconscious is released, accompanied by images that are the embodiment of that energy.

So long as a culture is disciplined enough to open itself to the energy of the eternal world, it thrives. If it cuts itself off, the divine images shrivel into stereotypes like old-fashioned Mickey Mouse cartoons. In other words, when the divine spirit ceases to ignite the human bodysoul, both the culture and the individuals within it disintegrate. The dancer must be in touch with those vital inner images that carry the creative fire of individuals within a culture.

Body makes soul visible. If the body is exhausted or unhealthy through prolonged starvation (as so often happens with dancers), the instincts are betrayed and connection to the natural flow of being is eventually lost. Loving discipline is one thing; whipping a pedigreed animal into submission is another. While our culture admires pedigreed animals, it does not generally honour forcing the natural rhythms, the good food, the rest, the psychic health–those essentials that underlie grace and beauty. Too often we are incapable of listening to soul until the soul, cast into exile, eventually erupts in symptoms that shriek out its anguish.

As artists, dancers dare not collude with that collective suicidal drive that so often looks like genuine yearning for perfection. Perfection can be a deadly killer. On the stage or in life, if we dance to escape who we are–to escape from life, failing to love ourselves as human beings subject to laws of nature and balance–we will find ourselves dancing around a hole at the centre, a volcanic hole. Our rejected instincts will eventually erupt to notify us that they are determined to put us back in touch with soul.

It seems to me that a genuine dancer, like a genuine human being, develops, with infinite patience and discipline, a container strong enough and flexible enough to receive the penetration of divine spirit. However disciplined the muscles, however perfect the technique, without the spontaneous opening to transcendent power, the dance is dead.

In 1952, I saw Margot Fonteyn dance what was intended to be her last performance. Her technique was flawless but she was not alive in the moment. She was not in deep soul connection. Fonteyn was a magnificent diamond, brilliant and cold.

Nine years later, Nureyev arrived and a new Fonteyn was born–a Fonteyn connected to her own soul. The woman and the dancer were one, not only with herself, but also with Nureyev and the audience. Fonteyn and Nureyev danced as one body, filled with presence. The audience was captured in what I would describe as a mystical experience. When it was over there was a long silence. The dancers were as still as we were. Then the audience burst into tears, into applause, into the aisles, and out into the foyer to gather daffodils from the jardinieres to throw onto the stage. For twenty minutes, Covent Garden was like a yellow waterfall with daffodils splashing from the boxes and the galleries. Fonteyn was a luminous pearl and Nureyev was every inch a man–part animal, part divine. New life was born that night. The stereotype that had been so deadly perfect was filled with new and vital energy.

I suggest to you dancers, professional and non-professional, that a new dance lies ahead in this new millennium. The body filled with soul will dance and audiences will recognize its radiance because they will have learned to honour the sacredness of matter both in their own bodies and in Earth. Dancers, you are the priests and priestesses of bodysoul. Your bodies speak the universal language that can be understood by every citizen of this planet. Ultimately there is one music, one dance. As W.B. Yeats put it in "Among School Children:"

O body swayed to music, O brightening glance,
How can we know the dancer from the dance?

Marion Woodman is a Jungian analyst and author of Addiction to Perfection: The Still Unravished Bride. *A pioneer in the study of eating disorders and compulsive behaviors, she is a renowned lecturer and workshop leader, affiliated with the University of Southern California (Berkeley).*

* * *

MIHALY CSIKSZENTMIHALYI

For over thirty years, I have been studying those optimal moments which make the rest of life worth living. I became interested in these peaks of experience as a child growing up in Central Europe. I was ten years old when the war ended. As I experienced the collapse of the society I had assumed would last forever, or at least my lifetime, I was taken aback by how unprepared people were for what was happening. I realized they had no clue about what life was about. Most of the adults around me were winging it, trying to make sense out of life, but they had very little idea of what made life worth living. When they lost their jobs, their property, their money and their status, they felt completely empty and lived, from then on, in what was essentially a shadow of what life should be.

Given those experiences, I became fascinated with these questions: How can we make a life that is better than the one most of us have? How can we perfect life into a work of art, as a very few people seemed to be able to do even during and after the war? After trying different things for a while—I painted, exhibited and wrote stories for newspapers as well as *The New Yorker* and other magazines—I decided to study human nature a little more systematically by becoming a psychologist. I wrote my doctoral thesis on the subject of creativity because I thought that by studying creative people who produced something out of nothing, I would discover how it is possible to make a kind of life that is worth living.

I had experienced creativity in my own painting and writing, and wanted to understand that creativity better.

One of the things that really struck me when I observed the visual artists' performances was how they would begin with a blank canvas and slowly get involved with the process of painting; within an hour, they would be so taken by the activity that if you talked to them, they wouldn't hear you. They would forget to eat or sleep. Sometimes this state lasted for a few hours, sometimes days. And yet, what was so fascinating was that as soon as the painting was finished they looked at it, said, "Not bad," put it against the wall and forgot about it. All they wanted was to start on a new canvas.

At that time, psychologists assumed that you expend energy in order to get a product that you use or exchange or consume. But this is not what happened with these artists. They were not painting in order to have a painting; in many ways the finished canvas was only an excuse so they could paint. This contradicted most of the theories on what motivates people to act.

After completing that initial study, I started talking to other creative people—musical composers, dancers and even those outside the arts because I eventually realized that athletes, for example, experience their sport in the same way that artists experience their work. For many runners, winning the race is simply an excuse or an opportunity to experience the body in motion, to experience optimal physical potential.

Experiences can be either intrinsically motivated—in which the motivation is not to get something at the end, but to actually do whatever you're doing—or extrinsically motivated—in which the motivation is to do something for the pay cheque at the end of the week. The extrinsically motivated work may be boring and alienating, but one does it nevertheless to get the reward afterwards. The intrinsic motivation which artists have is found in many other activities. My students, colleagues and I interviewed people in the arts and we found that when a dancer described how she or he felt in the best moments of the dance, their account was not really different from that of a painter or a composer describing how it feels to create a work of art, or a chess player describing a tournament, or an athlete involved in the physical exertion of a sporting event.

It was intriguing to discover that the more people we talked to in the U.S., Japan, Korea, India and Europe, the more similar their internal experiences seemed to be, even though the activities that produced them were extremely different. Using consistent interview methods, we discovered that the best moments in many creative respondents' lives happened when they felt that what they were doing was worth doing for its own sake.

My colleagues and I have collected over eight thousand interviews from around the world, each one roughly twenty pages in length when transcribed. One response, from a musical composer, encapsulates many of the common themes. First of all, this man says he is in an ecstatic state when the composing is going well. You may think that ecstasy—a strange, mysterious term—is induced by chemicals, drugs, or something bad, but it is actually a very simple psychological phenomenon. The ancient Greeks knew about it; to them it meant to stand to the side of something. Occasionally we are able to step outside our conventional daily routines—getting up in the morning, washing, dressing, going to work, working, coming home, cooking, eating—all those things we have to do to live. Every civilization has found ways to escape temporarily from those routines.

We could call those moments ecstasy—when we enter an alternative reality which exists partly in objective reality, but mostly in our own consciousness, in our own minds. If you think about it, in the great ancient civilizations—Egypt, Greece, China, America, India—we know much more about their ecstasies, found in their temples, theatres, sport arenas and the art they created, than their everyday lives. Thus, civilizations are defined by their ecstasies not by their daily routines.

Baboons in the jungles of Africa have to get up, groom, get food and travel back and forth to the food: their survival is very predictable and biologically determined. Humans, on the other hand, step outside the everyday to create ecstasy, the defining feature of our human nature and our culture in history. Ecstasy is a powerful and important part of our lives.

The musical composer says that when he is in an ecstasy he feels as if he almost doesn't exist. This is what nearly everyone involved in this deep, intrinsically motivated experience identified: that they forget themselves. Although this sounds like an excessively romantic notion, it has a rational explanation based in human neuro-physiology, namely that we cannot process more than approximately 120 bits of information every second. This may seem like a lot, but it is not.

For instance, to understand the words I am saying a listener would have to use about 40 bits of information processing per second, which means he or she could not listen to more than three conversations at a time. In fact, two concurrent conversations are all that can be followed. While involved with a creative process, as a composer is when he is writing music, individuals cannot process information having to do with their bodies. The composer, working with notations and sounds, does not have room in his mind to process anything else.

Dancers, working on a different modality of experience—the physical—process information about their bodies and the space in which they're moving. This fills their process information capacity, leaving no room to think about anything else such as their name, address, and bank account (or lack thereof).

The musical composer says that his hand is devoid of himself and he doesn't have to direct it or force it to go in one way or another. It goes by itself. I'm sure dancers feel this: their bodies, after years of practice, seem to dance on their own. Of course, developing the skill is essential. I could watch my hand for two weeks and I wouldn't feel any awe or wonderment because I don't know how to write music. It just wouldn't come out. "Flow" is a metaphor to describe how creative individuals felt when they were fully engaged in what they were doing. I use it to describe the whole quality of the experience.

One of my former students in Los Angeles has written a best-selling book based on interviewing some of today's prominent poets and authors. In it, one of the writers describes how it feels to move from the ordinary reality of everyday life into a kind of ecstatic moment, getting so involved with the words he is putting together that his contact with the everyday world is lost and he begins to inhabit this new world of his creation. This is a very vivid and precise, although flowery, description of the process. The poet writes about entering this world: you can't force the door open, all you can do is create the circumstances that may allow you to suddenly find the handle.

One of the things individuals have to do is somehow distance themselves from the gravitational pull that is trying to keep them in the world of everyday life. Physicist Albert Einstein, when describing how he was thinking when he began to formulate his theory of relativity, said he saw great shapes moving like clouds in space; they would combine themselves like huge pieces of a puzzle as he tried to fit them together.

An Olympic figure skater, interviewed by Australian sport psychologist Susan Jackson, describes how it feels to do well in a program: "You don't have to think about it. You are on automatic pilot. You merge with the music. You are not separate from what you're doing. You're at one with what you're doing." Her comments are consistent with those of the thousands of individuals my colleagues and I interviewed.

The condition that is necessary for an individual entering the state of flow is concentration, an intense focus on what he or she is doing. In our studies in everyday life situations, we find that people usually don't concentrate on what they are doing: their mind and body are divided. If there are thirty students sitting in front of a teacher, he or she might believe they are equally paying attention. What we have found is that perhaps two are listening to what the teacher is saying. The other twenty-eight minds have separated from their bodies; they are in the future or in the past, wherever; they're not with the teacher in the classroom.

In a way this is a great feature about human beings: we can detach the mind from the body, giving us tremendous flexibility. But the price we pay is that often we feel we are not together working in holistic harmony, which is what happens when we are in flow–we feel completely present and 100 percent involved.

The condition of focused concentration usually occurs when an individual knows moment by moment what it is they have to do. If they're playing an instrument, they know what note they want to play, what chord they want to hit and they know immediately whether they actually did what they wanted to do. They can correct themselves. They can improve. They can speed up or slow down. And, in order for them to know exactly how well they are doing, they get a constant stream of feedback.

Think about any sport. Let's say an individual is playing tennis. He or she always knows where they want the ball to go and can see immediately whether it ended up there. This constant abil-ity to direct moves and get instant feedback is an essential component of concentration. Because if there was delay, the player would sit back, relax and lose concentration.

Another feature of activities that use complete involvement–flow–is that there is a balance between what needs to be done or could be done, and what can be done. There is not too much to do and the challenge is not too high for the individual's level of skill. If the challenge is too high compared to skills, the participant feels increasingly worried and anxious. If the challenge is too low, boredom and apathy can result. In everyday life, we don't know what we have to do moment by moment: we have too many goals; we don't get feedback; and the challenges are either too high or too low. Keeping a fine balance between what can be done and what one is capable of doing is one of the components of the system of action that produces flow.

One of the things people forget when they are in this state of flow is themselves. Our studies show that thinking about yourself is about the worst thing that happens to ordinary people like us. If you look in a mirror or see yourself reflected in a store window as you walk down the street you see your reflection. Generally, what that produces is complete depression, at least temporarily. You may think: "Oh my God, my tie isn't right." "My hair is all wrong." "I'm getting fat." "I'm getting old," etc. We have to constantly protect this image we have of ourselves from others. We're always monitoring how we come across. Are we smart enough? Are we presentable enough? This is a big burden on our psychic resources. We are always diverting part of our attention to protect ourselves from others. So people's moods plummet when they are made aware of themselves.

One of the advantages of the flow experience is that you don't worry about yourself. Why? Because you don't have the information processing capacity. If you begin to think about yourself while you are playing the violin, you will hit a wrong note. If you are climbing a rock face and you start worrying about how you look, you will fall three thousand feet. There is no capacity to process your self-image during a flow experience and that's a big relief. Paradoxically, we find that self-esteem increases after an episode of flow because during an experience of deep concentration an individual often accomplishes something he or she did not think they could. They have pushed the envelope of life experience a little bit further and feel better about themselves than they did before. Thus, forgetting yourself is a prerequisite for feeling better and more connected to the world around you.

Another element that those involved in intense creative activities mention is that time seems to shrink or disappear during a flow experience: a long period of time may pass in what seems to be just a few minutes. Although there are all kinds of examples of this from around the world, unfortunately we are not timeless here, so I have to go on.

Whenever you feel all of these dimensions of experience, whatever you are doing becomes intrinsically motivating; that is, you want to do it again because it feels good. You could be dancing or writing poetry or skating or climbing mountains or doing your job or playing with your children or having a good conversation with your significant other or spouse. The beauty of the flow experience is that it is not limited to art or sports, although that's where you see it in its full potential. Art, dance, music, etc., are activities that exist only because they produce flow. There was no reason for them to survive historically except that they made us feel this ecstasy of a different way of living. And, if you want to see flow in its pure state, you turn to the arts or sports that exist purely for giving you this experience.

However, I think it's a great mistake to divide life into times when you occasionally experience the ecstasy of the aesthetic, and times when you deal with your family and your job, thinking you should suffer through. The real challenge is to integrate the joy you get from flow into everyday life, so that jobs, school and family also provide this feeling.

We use a watch to do our studies, giving it to participants to wear for a week. The watch is programmed to go off at random moments between eight in the morning and eleven at night. Whenever it goes off, participants write down where they are, how they feel and their level of happiness and creativity. We have about a quarter million responses collected from around the world, allowing us to see how people feel on a daily basis. We can actually measure where each person's average level of skill and average level of challenge is during a week. Given that, we can predict very clearly how participants will feel as they move away from that average. If the challenges are very high and the skills are low, participants feel anxious. If the skills are very high compared to the challenges, participants feel bored. The flow experience exists in the balance between challenges and skills. The point is to try to achieve that balance in whatever a person is doing.

One way to achieve flow is to start from a skill level which is higher than your challenges. You feel comfortable and in control. You feel pretty happy. But you don't feel very excited. You are not really concentrating because it's too easy. To move to flow, you have to find new challenges. People who feel anxious feel that their skills are so far below what it will take to get into flow that they don't even try most of the time. If you are anxious, often you will try to avoid, ignore or obliterate challenge from your consciousness by taking drugs or alcohol. This subjectively makes the challenge disappear, but you actually fall into apathy rather than move into flow. Relaxation is the state when challenges are quite low but your skills are high; that is a good place to be when you eat, read a good book and visit with friends. It's a positive state but it's not very exciting. Boredom, often a negative state, usually accompanies housework, cleaning and other routine maintenance work. Apathy happens when all systems go down. You feel sad, drained and passive; people spend a lot of time there especially while watching television and sitting in the bathroom, places that are roughly equivalent in terms of demands on cognitive capacity. Worry happens when the challenge begins to outstrip your skills, usually when you are dealing with people (bosses, colleagues, family) who are creating problems for you. The task we have is to try and transform more of our everyday experiences into flow experiences, so that the whole life can begin to resemble a work of art.

Mihaly Csikszentmihalyi is author of the groundbreaking book Flow: The Psychology of Optimal Experience *as well as thirteen other books. He is professor and former chair of the Department of Psychology at the University of Chicago.*

* * *

HEALTH, DANCE AND ILLNESS
PATRICIA DE MARTELAERE

In some cases, the difference between health and illness seems only too obvious: illnesses have symptoms such as fever, exhaustion or headaches; health could then be defined as the absence of symptoms. Only this definition doesn't seem to work. We know of lethal illnesses which show no symptoms whatsoever until just before their final blow; we also know of symptoms which are really indications of strength and health—the organism's defensive reaction against the illness.

So what is illness after all? Clear-cut, easily recognizable diseases such as the measles, the flu, cancer and AIDS have specific symptoms with specific patterns allowing for specific prognoses for either recovery or the total decay of the organism. But not all diseases show a clear-cut clinical picture with an identifiable, unambiguous cause. There are secret, invisible, festering diseases which hardly disable the organism; there are also terrible pains and disturbances which may point to no disease whatsoever. Of some diseases, one can be the carrier, and even infect others, without ever developing them oneself.

Is it enough to speak of a disease as soon as one knows certain physical germs are present, even in the total absence of any symptoms? Or should any kind of pain or dysfunction, even without an organic basis, be labelled an illness? Some illnesses are said to be psychic, showing symptoms with vague, often unconscious, repressed or utterly inexplicable causes. Wouldn't it be better to call them psychic disturbances, rather than illnesses, because of their vagueness and unpredictability? But then, what exactly is the difference between an illness and a disturbance?

Matters get even more complicated if one turns to health in search of a definition. Obviously, health cannot be identified as a subjective feeling of well-being, neither physical nor psychic, for in both cases the most convincing well-being can hide impending catastrophies. Neither can health be defined as a state of complete absence of all potential illness. A person who grows up in a completely sterile environment cannot really be labelled healthy, even though he or she has never contracted a single disease. The same applies to psychic matters: a person who painfully avoids the slightest conflict and, as a result, leads the most placid emotional life, would not be an example of good psychic health. Both of these examples would surely collapse at the very first undesirable intrusion from the outer world.

Health, so it appears, cannot be considered the absolute opposite of illness; rather, health is the ability to resist and progressively build up resistance against the assaults of disease. In this sense we need not be surprised to find Beckett's character Molloy praising himself for his exceptional health, allowing him to stay alive even though he is crippled, deaf and blind. Health is not an unalterable state or an inherited property; it can only be measured by the degree to which an organism is capable of successfully dealing with various germs or disease. Of course, no organism can ever be called absolutely successful in this respect. Even the strongest power of resistance ultimately meets with total defeat. And yet it is not always through illness that an organism, at the end of its life, is defeated: it sometimes happens that it dies as if from within, all by itself, from a natural but invincible aging process that has nothing to do with illness in the usual sense of the word.

In search of a more pragmatic definition of health and illness, I consulted my doctor. But even he could not help me. Medicine, the pride of Western science, cannot provide us with a coherent view on the exact nature of either illness or health. An interesting attempt to do so comes from the 19th century German physiologist Rudolf Virchow, who described illness as "a way of living under altered circumstances," and thought of recovery as a return to the previous, so-called "normal" circumstances. Every illness affects fundamental changes on the organism, which is either weakened or reinforced by it and made more or less susceptible to similar or totally different germs. Illnesses are not temporary catastrophies that succeed each other in a haphazard way with no inner connection. Illnesses, just like the people who are afflicted by them, build a history—a meaningful interplay between chance and necessity—in which a past condition is never arrived at for a second time. Every illness permanently alters the so-called normal circumstances in which an organism lives.

This leads to other questions: What circumstances of an organism should be counted as fully normal? Do organisms not live perpetually in changed and changing circumstances, from their birth to their death, and even beyond? Doesn't this make Virchow's interesting definition synonymous with that of health or even with that of life? When do we ever meet with circumstances that do not change? The very act of living seems to be a permanent succession of illnesses.

Apparently this interpretation carries us too far. It must be possible to find a pragmatically useful description allowing us to decide which kinds of change or alteration are normal and which are pathological. Wherever definitions do not satisfy, statistics can offer a solution. Normality could then be equalled with the properties and characteristics of the majority with all due respect, of course, for slight and acceptable deviations. Another option would be to call the moment the harmonious functioning of an organism or a mind is disturbed beyond control abnormal, but here again, what is harmonious functioning? And what is control? This would allow us, for example, to call a person healthy who could keep his illness or miserableness limited to the weekend, functioning and feeling perfectly well on all other days. We could also say that Doctor Jekyll remained basically normal as long as he could autonomously decide the exact time and duration of his transformation into the hideous Mr. Hyde. In other words, whoever succeeds in limiting his abnormal behaviour to secret and exceptional situations can be counted as fully normal. Or, as Ovid remarked, "Whoever can counterfeit sanity, is sane."

But now, let us try and make matters a bit more specific, leaving the realm of definition and philosophical reflection and turning to the actual way people are treating specific questions concerning health and illness. Here we find two basic models of thought and behaviour: Western traditional medicine and the so-called alternative approaches–often Eastern in inspiration–such as homeopathy and acupuncture.

The West has traditionally thought of disease as either a visible and physical attack upon an organism by foreign intruders (bacteriums, viruses) or a physical lesion or injury of a part of the body. Attacks are dealt with by means of powerful counter-attacks through the administration of chemical substances. Lesions or physical defects from whatever causes–accidents or hereditary imperfections–are, if possible, treated with surgery. As soon as the intruders have been removed, the organism is said to be recovered or restored to its state of health.

It would be extremely simplistic to reject all the achievements of Western medicine because of its so-called aggressive approach. Despite its undeniable success, fundamental shortcomings are becoming ever more obvious. Many patients are heard to utter the same complaint when, not feeling well and having undergone countless inconvenient examinations, they are told by some extremely qualified specialist that no traces of physical defects have been found and that, therefore, they are perfectly all right. Should patients then be relieved that they are only feeling unwell–in some cases quite miserable or even in continuous pain–although, objectively, their state is that of a healthy person?

Western medicine is divided into two quite separate specialties that parallel the traditional division between body and mind. If physical symptoms are found to have no visible physical cause, they are treated as psychosomatic, but this is only a scientific attempt to hide the fact that their origin is unknown. Chances are great that the patient, healthy in all other respects, will simply have to live with the symptoms. The suggestion is made that it is his or her own fault if he or she stubbornly insists on producing symptoms of illness in the total absence of illness.

The Eastern approach is completely different; of course, it too has limits and imperfections. The Eastern belief is that an organism, even while being severely attacked by foreign intruders, continues to function in a healthy way. The severity of the symptoms is a possible indication of the organism's health. Should an organism function unhealthily, even in the absence of all physical defects, it will become more susceptible to disease in the narrow, Western sense.

In traditional China, people see their physicist/acupuncturist weekly for a regular treatment to keep them in health. If they fall seriously ill, they are treated free of charge because their physicist fell short of his or her original aim: to keep the body healthy. Treatment is a means of keeping the organism in a state of optimal functioning, similar to a motorcar being properly maintained so that accidental breakdowns may be avoided (see *Zen and the Art of Motorcycle Maintenance* by Robert Pirsig).

Western treatment is mainly negative. In mechanical terms, it is called for only after the accident has happened, when the car is quickly mended and sent back into full traffic.

Western art and dance are clearly heir to the Western approach of body and mind, health and disease, normality and optimal functioning. This is apparent in classical dance, which seems to aim at conquering the natural laws of gravity and the human body, causing many crippling injuries and distortions. Light and effortless though it seems, the performing of classical ballet is certainly not a health-improving activity: it only creates the illusion of lightness, masking a hidden struggle against exhaustion and pain. The dancing body is not really in harmony with its environment and neither is it, ultimately, in harmony with itself. It is continuously pushed towards ever more impressive and extreme performances, no matter how great the inner costs.

The same applies to Western sports and athletics, exclusively built on the competition model and set on breaking time or distance or weight records. If necessary, this is accomplished with the aid of either tricks, such as fasting or blood transfusions, or drugs, legally permitted or undetectable. Any possible harm done to the body is of no immediate concern: the car may break down much earlier than it should, but even if it runs fast only for a short time, the owner might make enough money to survive being crippled for the rest of his or her life.

I do not mean to suggest that the East is not interested in displacing the limits of natural human achievement. In fact, Eastern philosophy and Western curiosity and ambition are all explorations of extraordinary and extreme human conditions. The difference is that the East promotes inner control—not the suppression of natural tendencies, but rather the skilful and gradual displacement of them—while the West encourages outer appearance. The end result may be the same or, in the case of the East, even more impressive. Haven't we heard about yogi who control their own temperature so they can make the snow melt all around them? And don't we know about old Tai Chi masters who, while quietly smiling and barely moving, fend off the boisterous aggression of karate champions, making them turn against themselves? In a certain sense, the art of Tai Chi can be considered the most striking opposite of classical Western dance: it is said to be the art of inner movement and harmony, consisting of a controlled yet

effortless flow of energy. As such, Tai Chi considered by the Chinese to be both an exercise in health and a kind of practical medicine. Yet it does not rely on the passive acceptance of so-called naturalness and normality–its results are, to all standards, exceptional and most uncommon for human beings.

The advantage the Eastern way of exploring extremes has over the Western way is that it is less likely–or even totally unlikely–to have undesirable side effects or harmful drawbacks. It shows us that extreme health, too, has unexplored yet fascinating possibilities, whereas the artistic West still seems to be heir to the romantic misconception that health is synonymous with mediocrity and that, to be a genius, one has to pay the price of illness, injury or insanity.

Patricia de Martelaere studied philosophy at the Catholic University in Leuven where she graduated in 1984 with a thesis on the skepticism of David Hume. She is currently professor of Modern Philosophy and Philosophical Anthropology at the Catholic University in Brussels as well as professor of the Philosophy of Language at the Catholic University.

✳   ✳   ✳

FOCUS ON EXCELLENCE
A DISCUSSION BETWEEN MICHAEL CRABB, MIHALY CSIKSZENTMIHALYI AND MARION WOODMAN IN TORONTO AND PATRICIA DE MARTELAERE AND DEBORAH JOWITT IN THE HAGUE WITH QUESTIONS FROM BOTH SITES

MICHAEL CRABB: Deborah, you talked about the narrow confines of Western theatrical dance tradition and you also mentioned the way in which, in other societies, dance is more broadly integrated into society. Mihaly also alluded to the fact that, even in Western tradition, if you go back far enough, dance began in a more ritualistic, socially integrated way. Since we are looking at the possibility of change, in a sense drawing a new model, I would be interested to hear how much it is possible for dance to take a leadership role in remodelling itself, given the fact that society obviously has a pervasive effect on the way we think. There has always been a connection between external society and the nature of the dance. Whether it's in dance costuming or the hierarchical structure of dance companies, can dance change without society around it changing?

DEBORAH JOWITT: Society has to change and that's not easy. I think we have to help. Excellence seems to be very much a part of our goal for professional dance. But we also thrill at virtuosity which reflects our ability to defy the forces of nature, escape gravity, ignore dizziness, master our control of balance in a turning world and go beyond the normal limits of flexibility. I've seen pictures of a woman, supported by a man, with her leg past twelve o'clock. It looks pretty grotesque to me, but some people find it beautiful. I think what we've done is upped the ante beyond anything we've seen before. There are artists who have become involved in community-based work; of course, they are sometimes derided by those who think of themselves as connoisseurs of professional dance. We have to redefine excellence. In my role as a critic, all I can say is what I think true excellence is. Perhaps it's located in expressiveness and musicality; I think there are many people in the audience who appreciate that. I think it is the responsibility of both the press and the audience to insist on change. For example, we have to help redefine thinness; too often I've seen writers in influential positions fault a dancer, in print, for being overweight when it was a matter of only two pounds. This should be changed.

MARION WOODMAN: How can the concept of flow be incorporated in teaching young people?

DEBORAH JOWITT: There are possibilities for change that we haven't even tapped. Does everybody always have to face the front? Can't dancers face each other? Are there joint exercises that people can do together, even in a ballet class?

I think there are ways of creating physical exercises in the classroom for children which focus either on the "whole" or on dance as a communal experience. There is a constant separation of mind and body that occurs in our terminology. It would be so nice not to hear "the leg goes here" but "try to think about putting your leg here." Your leg has that intelligence fully embodied in it. We need to stop isolating body parts and separating them from the person. Margaret Jenkins says, "I try to

remember, when I teach adult beginners, that they may be beginning dancers, but they are not beginning people." This is appropriate for all students.

I think teachers are just beginning to explore that, but I'm not an expert in this field.

QUESTION: Mihaly uses only psychic terms to describe flow; I think that's dangerous because we have the subjective impression of attaining a flow which runs easily and we become addicted to it. The reality of the flow lies in the body and not in the psychic feelings one has.

MIHALY CSIKSZENTMIHALYI: The implication of flow for teaching children is very clear: if anything goes wrong, the student's self defenses will be activated. That is, whenever you make a person or child feel inadequate, you interrupt the concentration objective. A child who is criticized by a teacher at nine o'clock in the morning will spend the next five or six hours thinking about the teacher and what he or she said. That student isn't listening to anything else; new information just goes by and doesn't register because the student is so concerned with repairing the damage to his or her ego. No further learning takes place. I think one of the major ways teachers undermine learning is by invoking the self, attacking the self-esteem of the student, making them respond in the subconscious instead of allowing them to immerse themselves in the activity. Excessive praise of a student has a similar effect: it evokes self-consciousness and does not allow the student to focus on the learning activity.

MARION WOODMAN: When I was speaking to Mihaly between sessions here, he told me that what I meant by archetypal world is what he refers to as flow. I would like to weave those two words together so you can see that images underneath the conscious are the very images that move into the world of flow. How do you bring a young person into that world? I taught creative theatre in high school for years, working with poetry and allowing seventeen and eighteen year olds to bring that poetry into their bodies. If we were doing a poem like Blake's "The Tyger," I would give the football team a ball and let them throw the ball and work with it, allowing the connection between the body and the imagery to take hold, moving the body into a totally different state. And that happened when we were working with poetry in combination with dance, in combination with singing, and in combination with any of the other arts–painting, photography etc.

QUESTION: Mihaly, you spoke only of the individual. Is the same true for the group?

MIHALY CSIKSZENTMIHALYI: Yes. Some of my students have published books on flow in group performance, improvisations in theatre and jazz. Certainly, athletic teams that work well also produce these experiences through the interaction of different skills. Even surgeons who enjoy their work in an operating theatre say it's like a choreographed event where nurses, anesthesiologists and radiologists work together in a perfect harmony which lifts the performance of that operating team to a higher level. And this is typical of flow in the performing cultures where dance is part of everyday ritual. We don't know that much about it in the West because we have become more specialized; we don't experience this group flow very often anymore, but it is certainly part of our heritage.

MICHAEL CRABB: Mihaly, as a critic, I attend many performances every year. I think I understand better, from your comments and your speech earlier, that magic feeling the audience experiences when a dancer is having that special moment. You feel one particular performance radiating–not just among the performers on stage who somehow become a collective part of it–but it flows into the audience which enters into the whole expressive and communicative experience. I remember my very first performance experience in London in which Fonteyn and Nureyev danced *Romeo and Juliet* at Covent Garden–not a bad way to begin. I experienced a feeling of ecstasy as if I had been lifted onto a different level. There was a collective energy in the audience which seemed to feed back to the stage creating a whole cycle.

QUESTION: Marion, is the use of mirrors counterproductive to the search for profound inner self?

MARION WOODMAN: I do not train dancers, but I do know that in my work, in mirroring people in my office, for example, it is absolutely fundamental. I attempt to show them who they are in their own being; I'm not trying to make them into anything else. Many children are so trained to an agenda their parents hold for them, they have no idea who they are. So, I continually mirror. I

would think that that would be true in a dance studio where the student has to see herself or himself in the reality of the mirror.

QUESTION: Mihaly, if students are asked to focus on the mirror the majority of time, does it not prevent the acquisition of flow?

MIHALY CSIKSZENTMIHALYI: Yes, that's interesting. I've never thought about the mirror as part of training, part of the acquisition of skills, but I think it's important. I suppose if I was to train a dancer it might be to develop a kind of distance, which might be opposite to what you are trying to accomplish. You would like dancers not to feel threatened by the mirrored image; for most people the mirrored image is almost an attack on their self-concept because they don't live up to their inner image of who they are.

MARION WOODMAN: It requires immense honesty.

MIHALY CSIKSZENTMIHALYI: Yes, it requires honesty and perhaps a helping hand, which the teacher might provide, so students learn to live with themselves in a comfortable way instead of being threatened by their own image. I think it's a delicate issue–one that I haven't thought about before–that needs great understanding. Your image can be very threatening and you have to mediate that interaction somehow.

QUESTION: Mihaly, are you saying that when a person or a group is in flow, that they have less of a chance to become ill or injured?

MIHALY CSIKSZENTMIHALYI: If that were true, we would all get rich helping insurance companies to protect themselves. No, we don't have data about the physical repercussions of the state of flow and whether flow makes people rich or healthy or wise or something else outside the experience. If we want to improve the quality of life, we have to learn to live well in the moment and then the future, hopefully, will take care of itself.

DEBORAH JOWITT: All dancers know the experience of being in such complete flow that they come off stage and notice blood dripping from a hole in their foot: they were so completely focussed on the moment that all secondary thoughts drifted away or became peripheral. I think, as Mihaly has implied, that flow creates a sense of profound well-being; however, when the experience of being in flow drowns out physical discomfort the addiction to flow can become dangerous.

MARION WOODMAN: So, how do you control the flow? How

do you control getting addicted to it?

DEBORAH JOWITT: I suppose you need to be realistic about it: if you have torn a hole in your foot one night, you find flow in some other aspect of your daily life in dance until that wound has healed, if possible. I think you need to be aware that you are becoming addicted.

QUESTION: Deborah, excellence is defined by culture. As global culture has many cultures in it, where does one start to change attitudes and approaches to excellence: with the critics, the audience, the management or the dancers?

DEBORAH JOWITT: I think it can start in any of those areas. I'm more familiar with the critic's position because that's what I do. For instance, if I attend a Kabuki performance and point out that extreme refinement and subtlety indicate mastery rather than a great deal of large scale, out-in-space physical movement, and I can make readers aware of that, then I hope they will have a positive response. I think that program information and preperformance lectures and demonstrations educate an audience. I think we should expose dancers in the Western culture to dancers from other cultures and explain what's going on: give them master classes in belly dancing or Chinese opera so they get that experience in their body and they begin to appreciate these other artistic experiences.

MIHALY CSIKSZENTMIHALYI: I understand flow to be a form of energy which, like all forms of energy such as fire or nuclear energy, you have to learn to control. Some people might get flow from stealing at work or going to war and shooting at other people but this is not acceptable. There are all kinds of ways to have full concentration which are not positive; even if they are positive, there is the risk of addiction where a person becomes a workaholic. Flow is not a substitute for common sense.

QUESTION: Marion, what is your definition of soul?

MARION WOODMAN: Soul is that part that is living in us, that is eternal; it takes up residence in the body so long as we're on this earth. Blake said that soul is that portion of body perceived by the five senses so it reacts to the world through all of the senses, through all of the orifices of the body. We are continually working with that eternal part that is limited by the fact that it is in the body and yearns to express itself and grow. I think spirit is that glorious, fast, speedy fire that can touch the soul and quicken–bring to life. The dancer, for example, is working continually with technique, attempting to strengthen muscles and make the body as strong as possible but ultimately, the dance is when dancers are on stage, the music begins and the spirit either touches in, creating a moment of grace, or it doesn't. When I'm writing, I hope that the spirit will touch in and take over my pen and I, rather than my ego, will be writing. I do what I can in terms of preparing to make this as powerful as possible, to allow it to open. But I can only trust that the spirit will come in and greet the soul.

QUESTION: Deborah, why should we seek to minimize the sacrifice? A freely chosen cost is not extortion and the choice to pay it is a fundamental part of the dancer's credibility.

DEBORAH JOWITT: I think that sacrifice is part of dance–you make certain sacrifices for anything that you love and believe in, but we must recognize that there is a point at which sacrifice goes beyond what is reasonable. Dancers tend to defer the problem, saying "I'll think about that later. I'm not old yet. I can still dance on this ankle. Let me think about the next performance." They're making a small sacrifice, perhaps. But are they thinking about the bigger sacrifice they're making in terms of what will happen to them ten, fifteen, twenty years down the road? I would say there are degrees of sacrifice which are necessary in anything one loves; but there is also a boundary beyond which one shouldn't go in terms of health and eventual fullness of life.

QUESTION: Is that what you call the obsession, the idea of the struggling artist?

DEBORAH JOWITT: I don't know if the artist has to suffer although there is that feeling in the West. Dancers bear their wounds and cherish them because they show physical struggle. I'm not prepared to say that the point of this is fun and it should keep you laughing and sane, but at what point does it becomes unhealthy or obsessive?

QUESTION: A dancer's career is short and ends quickly, but the feeling and the skills remain. What about the excellence of the grown old body? Is it gone forever?

DEBORAH JOWITT: Nothing replaces the joy we get from seeing a beautiful, wonderfully strong, young person perform at peak capacity, but I've noticed in New York there has been increased interest in what the older performer can do. And we do have Netherlands Three, although those dancers look pretty damn fit to me. In the East there are venerated older performers. I'm interested in the resurrection in the West of appreciation for what the older performer can do. A few years ago I created an autobiographical, talking, moving solo called the "Body Imprint," which I have performed many times, lame as I am. People seem to like it, so that gives me some sort of encouragement that there is a place for the older dancer as long as that place is well chosen.

QUESTION: Is this part of the new definition of excellence?

DEBORAH JOWITT: Maybe it's part of the reaction by the general audience against the extremes of danger and virtuosity. "The Horse's Mouth"—a structured improvisation for all kinds of older performers who told stories about their experiences as performers, and interacted with each other—was performed in New York several times. Apparently it is a real high for the dancers, as well as the audience. This indicates that although nothing replaces youth, there is still something that older performers can tell us.

QUESTION: Mihaly, you've talked about the artist's flow. What about the audience? Do they attend theatre or sports events to experience flow vicariously? If so, they're experiencing either skill or challenge. How does this fit on the graph you showed us?

MIHALY CSIKSZENTMIHALYI: Yes, that's a very good question. For the audience, the experience of flow depends as much on skill and challenge as it does for the performer. You won't appreciate a performance or a sports event if you don't understand the rules or what the moves mean or what they could be like. You will be outside the interaction, the emotional bond, that is created between the audience and the performer. The more you know about what's happening, the more you can get caught up in the activity and participate, vicariously perhaps, in the event. You have to understand the skill in order to empathize with it, to visualize the skill, and interpret both the motions and what is happening on the stage. That's the skill of the audience and high level of performance necessary to really engage the audience in what's happening.

MARION WOODMAN: I think that in any of the arts, the audience is participating at the level of the creative imagination, so that they become, for example, the hero in the novel they are reading. Creative imagination is the giving over of the ego to enter into whatever's happening.

MICHAEL CRABB: In the case of dance, which isn't a specific language as is the spoken word, you can sometimes take someone who isn't prepared. I once took a soprano to see a dance performance and she looked at the bodies moving and said, "They're singing with their bodies." She had a wonderful time, even though she knew nothing about dance. But she had a way of evaluating it and absorbing it and experiencing it for herself, which I think is what is meant by "opening oneself to the imaginative experience." The problem is so many audiences turn to critics (like me) to prescribe their expectations.

QUESTION: Marion, could you comment on your way of being genuine and fully connected to yourself and your soul versus Mihaly Csikszentmihalyi's comment on losing yourself while you are experiencing a creative process?"

MARION WOODMAN: When I'm working with myself or with any artist, I try to make my ego container as strong as possible. It's a lifetime process, but I try to recognize my own strengths, build up my own disciplines, find out what my feelings are and recognize what my own imagery is so that a part of me can say "I am." That's the part—and here's where the paradox comes in—that surrenders to whatever this magnificent energy is that's coming in from underneath. I could say, "I won't go with that;" "I will not sit down right now and write what's coming through;" or I could say, "I will not fall in love at this moment." All of these things are coming in from deep, deep levels of the unconscious; for me, it's a question of building a container strong enough to allow this to come through and hold it. If you compare *Romeo and Juliet* with *Anthony and Cleopatra* you can see the additional years of Shakespeare's experience separating them. We have to honour where we are, but continue to build what I call the container, which is the ego, so that it does not break apart when energy comes through. Genius and madness are very close together.

QUESTION: Mihaly, is achieving a state of flow or ecstasy now a new pressure to put on ourselves in order to achieve artistic excellence?

MIHALY CSIKSZENTMIHALYI: I wouldn't worry about it. If you are trying to do something well, whatever it is, flow will come by itself. It is kind of guaranteed. If you are able to focus on what you are doing and forget yourself, you will feel flow.

QUESTION: Deborah, it seems that the urge to explore the extremes of performance is more an extrinsic motivation of the dancer than a wish or demand of the audience. What do you think about that?

DEBORAH JOWITT: The demands the dancer places on himself or herself go beyond the natural limitations of the body in terms of flexibility and the ability to jump and control balance. This is part of our tradition. I think the audience is complacent in pushing for extremes but the dancer has a natural wish to try to set new challenges which is part, I believe, of getting into flow.

Focus on
Dance

Photograph on previous page:
Dancer: Barak Marshall
At: Holland Dance Festival
Photographer: Gadi Dagon

RICHARD PHILP

During my thirty-year career with *Dance Magazine*–a long career for any journalist with a single publication–I have seen many changes in professional dance. The size of the audience has increased enormously. Techniques–once sacred territories that defined who a dancer really was–have been crossed-over, incorporated, modified, melded and sometimes butchered. There have been great advances in injury prevention and care. In fact, a whole new field of dance medicine has developed. Some anti-traditionalists in dance have gone out of their way to de-sanctify, vilify, reduce and humiliate the time-honoured traditions of our training style and manners. During this period, dancers have at last found their voices within the field, while opportunities for continuing education have increased. Wages have improved and health insurance has become available for performers.

Three years ago, *Dance Magazine* made a ground-breaking survey under the direction of Linda Hamilton who danced with the New York City Ballet for nineteen years and is now a magazine columnist as well as a very effective clinical psychologist whose practice focuses on performers. Beginning with questions generated out of my editorial staff's broad knowledge of the field, Hamilton wrote the survey and supervised the statistical analysis. The 53-question survey was completed by 960 dance students, professionals and ex-dancers. The average age of respondents was 24 years. We learned that the majority of dancers surveyed took 6 classes per week and had danced for 15 years. Of the 20 percent with college degrees, the majority ranked at the top of their academic classes. On average, women started training at age 7; much earlier than the average age of 17 for men. Ninety-seven percent studied ballet; 73 percent studied jazz; 60 percent, modern; 8 percent, ballroom. When there is trouble, dancers tend to blame themselves rather than make hard-nosed evaluations of their teachers. Our survey showed that men have an easier time finding employment than women–no surprise there. Men were also much more secure financially. On average, professional careers of male dancers last 8 years longer than women's careers. Dancers tended to be in better health than the general population, because of their ongoing concerns with diet, weight and exercise, and they enjoy their good health. Only 4 percent of respondents were dissatisfied, compared with 10 percent dissatisfaction in the general population. The majority of dancers, we found, loved their work. There are very few professions that can boast this kind of dedication. Very few dancers compared themselves favourably to the long, lean, so called Balanchine Ballerina currently so much in fashion. Two-thirds of our dancers 18 and over were sexually active, 13 percent lower than the national average. In terms of sexual orientation, 96 percent of the female dancers were predominantly heterosexual, with only point 4 percent homosexual. Forty-seven percent of the male dancers were heterosexual, 6 percent were bi-sexual and the balance described themselves as homosexual. Seventeen percent of the women and 6 percent of the men in our survey reported that they had, in their estimation, eating problems; however, only 4 percent of our female dancers actually met all the diagnostic criteria for specific eating disorders. The group most at risk, we found, was the older dance students. The most common injuries in dance occur from overuse, leading to chronic problems such as tendonitis and arthritis. Nine out of 10 dancers try to handle their injuries on their own. Almost half continue to work despite being injured. One out of 4 dancers reported that they had been expected to keep working even with a serious injury.

It is interesting to me that this kind of statistically valid study about issues of such importance to dancers had not already been conducted. Very little was known for sure about the participants in this fascinating journey called dance. How did this journey begin? Instead of going back to what little we know of dance in ancient cultures, or even as far back as Catherine de Medici in the sixteenth century, let's look at the desperate life of your average theatrical dancer at the beginning of the nineteenth century when, if you were a professional dancer, you were also probably female. You had to survive backstage fires, leaking gas pipes, starvation wages, untreated diseases, malfunctioning scenery, malnutrition, polluted drinking water, unsanitary and crowded conditions, and negative social stigma. Some would say that conditions for dancers haven't changed all that much, but a life in dance a hundred years ago was very different from what it has become in our much more enlightened era. Noel Coward's advice to Mrs. Worthington in the famous comic song, "Don't put your daughter on the stage" was sage in many ways. No wonder. By 1900, dance as a profession had slid to the bottom of everybody's heap, where it would stay well into the twentieth century. And when Sir Noel warned, seventy years ago, against putting your daughter on the stage, he knew very well that there was almost no place at all for your son. Certainly not in dance. The prejudice against men in dance has only been addressed in the past fifteen or twenty years. Until recently, the U.S. Department of Labour barely recognized dance as a profession; they lumped it under the heading of "Amusement and Recreation Services" and insisted that dance studios were actually dance halls. In order to copyright choreography, dance was officially marginalized in an odd category called "Dramatical Musical Compositions." This despite the fact that dance, as we all know, is too often neither dramatic nor musical in nature.

Not until the second half of the twentieth century would dance evolve in terms of public awareness to the point where it could take its place securely alongside other performing arts such as theatre, music, opera and the fine arts. Dance writing played a significant role in these changes. One hundred years ago, press coverage of dance by knowledgeable writers was almost non-existent. Specialist writers in the field were rare. Some of us feel that is still the case today. Serious dance didn't have a chance for review and what early writing there was came primarily from music critics. With the evolution of modern dance in this century came a need for better print coverage. Modern dance, which had been regarded as frivolous, began to carry a social message and that message required intelligent commentary in the media. Martha Graham often said that she preferred being reviewed by sports writers rather than music critics, because sports writers at least knew something about movement. The charge of elitism in dance has only recently been wrestled to the ground as a result of dance companies needing to make money by drawing larger audiences.

Twentieth century psychology, experimentation and politics have given dance a voice, techniques, discipline, repertoire and, perhaps most importantly, self-esteem. The art form that had been regarded widely as non-essential in the seventeenth, eighteenth and nineteenth centuries is now able to probe the deepest themes of our society. You cannot see a contemporary work today without looking for underlying meanings and agendas. This happened first with the moderns and post-moderns, and ballet soon followed suit.

Early in this century, Americans regarded ballet as an almost exclusively Russian art form. There were two major exoduses of Russian dancers and teachers to the West: after the 1917 Revolution; and after the fall of the Soviet Union in 1991. The Russian-born, St. Petersburg-trained ballerina, Anna Pavlova

(1881-1931) was a primary inspiration to a later generation of dancers and choreographers, most prominently Agnes DeMille, Anthony Tudor and Frederick Ashton. For decades, Pavlova toured the world, bewitching audiences everywhere. She was an utterly alluring trouper who never knew what it was to be still. She sailed on tramp steamers, rode camels which bit off people's hands, performed in roasting deserts and steaming snake-infested jungles, and won fans for dance around the world. She once danced for a wildly ecstatic crowd during a violent thunderstorm in a Mexican bull ring between bull fights.

In 1921, during one of her exhausting tours of North America–New York City, Milwaukee, Minneapolis, Chicago, Toronto–the legendary Russian ballerina found herself in Fresno, California accompanied by forty dancers. But there was a snag. Fire swept through Fresno's business district, cutting off electricity to White's Theatre. The audience, however, was so fired up to see the mythic dancer that they took carbide lamps out of parked cars, linked them to a portable generator and watched the dancer dance outdoors on a makeshift plywood stage, illuminated entirely by automobile headlights. After only two numbers, however, they hit another snag. The generator ran out of fuel.

Why is this story about ballet pioneering so charming? So compelling? It reminds us of the curiosity and hunger for art that generations of so-called pioneers carried with them in their wagons across the expanses of the New World. Those audiences were not composed of culturally deprived peasants, as popular movies and novels might portray; they carried with them culturally rich backgrounds from their homelands. These aggressive, successful people became founders of universities, libraries, opera houses, orchestras, theatres and, eventually, dance companies.

Right from the beginning, Russians taught us about the crossover from ballet to other techniques. Nureyev was perhaps the most visible in his day, but even Pavlova taught about dancing in silence, which of course the moderns would do later on. Pavlova expressed a wish to abandon the sometimes awful music she so often selected. She wanted to experiment with American jazz and blues, and New Orleans honky-tonk. Imagine Pavlova performing such jazz steps as a Dalton body-wave, deep knee-hinge variations, or buzzard glides!

Our culture has been dominated in this century by the concept of modernism, out of which various schools of painting, music, architecture, literature and modern dance have evolved. Modernism rejected the nineteenth century Victorian beliefs in the order of things such as class structure and religion, politics, gender issues, and "acceptable forms of self-expression." Modernists embraced the post-Darwinian view that nature was ruled by chance and constant change, things that Merce Cunningham would take up by mid-century. Many artists found these ideas to be powerful stimulants. But other more traditional people were uncomfortable and found the new art–including modern dance–threatening.

This battle of ideas continues today. Consider the debates in Washington over government funding for the modern arts. The arts have always had the ability to expose and this makes some people very uncharitable; that which ignorant people fear becomes a target for condemnation and persecution. This is one of the reasons why artists are often targetted by those who wish to silence dissenting voices. We need our artists for that very reason–because they can and do speak out. Perhaps we need them more today than ever.

The dance world of only fifty years ago would be unrecognizable to us. Audiences in 1950 were small and fragmented–devoted to segments of a growing, prejudiced, dysfunctional arts community. The words "starving" and "artist" were almost universally linked. Nobody was bothered much by the inequity–except the artists. Attitudes towards the arts sanctioned such inappropriate terms as "egghead" and "long-hair" and much, much worse for men in ballet–if they were mentioned at all. Since those days, the appearance of powerful male figures–Russian dancers such as Nureyev and Baryshnikov–have inspired generations of men and raised the standards of training for both men and women to today's high level. The controversial issue of Blacks in ballet, a taboo subject fifty years ago, has at least been addressed, although imperfectly. Blacks in modern dance were a different story, by-in-large, although Denishawn, the school formed by Ted Shawn and Ruth St. Denis in 1914, with branches all across America, allowed neither Blacks nor Jews.

Balanchine, a trained musician and choreographer, taught us

23

by example to take serious music even more seriously, elevating it to the same level on-stage as the dancing. As a result, dance and music are often equally important today, a fact that some musicians' unions have yet to understand. Thanks to their unions, musicians in America are still paid a great deal more for their work in the pit than the dancers are on the stage. This is another of those inequities that must be addressed.

Jazz music and jazz dance are truly indigenous American art forms that have become international in their influence and appeal. Only in this century, however, did jazz get a foothold in the mainstream. Although jazz does have roots in slave cultures, its origins, like so much that we are learning about African history today, were much further back. For example, we know that the Charleston derives from an African Ashanti Ancestor dance with truly ancient origins.

Since World War II, television has played a central role in developing audiences, not just for the small screen, but for live performance as well. PBS, CBC, BBC and European TV, among many, have given audiences everywhere a taste of the real thing. One of the earliest television pioneers in Europe was Sweden's Birgitt Colbert, whose belief in the power of the tube supported and defined its early development. As we all know, television has had a tremendous impact on our culture and has reached audiences never before dreamed possible. Its role in building dance is one of the most interesting recent chapters in the long history of this art form.

During the last two decades of the twentieth century, we have lost a number of our major figures–Graham, Balanchine, Tudor, Halley, DeMille, Robbins, Ashton, McMillan, Colbert and Nureyev, among many. How are we going to save the integrity of their works? Various foundations have been set up to protect and distribute the repertoires and so far this is working pretty well. But for a very long time, dance has been regarded as the most ephemeral of the arts. This condition has changed with the widespread availability of notation, film, video and computers for recording purposes. If choreographers or dancers forget the steps, they no longer just make up new ones as they once did. They can go back to the video–that universal aide-memoire–or now, to their computers. As a result it is possible to have a dance company in Seattle, Houston, San Francisco or Miami, with a repertoire of dance pieces that are recognized masterpieces.

Today, every city of any size has at least one dance company owing in part to the efforts of the regional dance movement a generation ago. Strong regional companies abound and opportunities for jobs in dance exist to a degree never before imagined. While many of us may still be struggling with the basics of the rapidly changing world of computer technology, Merce Cunningham's experiments in cyberspace have added a genuinely fresh and imaginative dimension to the way we look at dance.

There is an ocean of information about dance out there on the Internet–from dictionaries of dance terms to live dance chats, to critical commentary signed with monikers like Ballerina Baby, Nanachka, Flat Tummy or Hot Pants. Hiding behind these names–and I have never allowed unsigned, anonymous letters to be published in *Dance Magazine*–are websites that give wanna-be dance writers an opportunity to launch a lot of bile into cyberspace without any serious professional consequences.

According to a report published by the U.S. Department of Health, there is no substitute for a live performance. The "live" part of human contact affects every aspect of our well-being. Choreographer Bill T. Jones talks about the, "transforming experience of communication." Although our new technologies are a great advance, we are still creatures in need of the dynamic interaction with others that comes from direct communication.

There was a flourishing movement in dance in the 1960s that lasted into the 1970s, which was based in part on the idea that expressing ourselves as artists was all that mattered; traditional discipline and training were regarded with ambivalence. At its worst, painters worked without knowledge of techniques and materials; musicians did not know about scales, notation or melody; and dancers flung themselves about just for the hell of it without the obvious–to me–advantages of any training at all. A kind of instant performance dance happened with results that were sometimes colourful, but also had the potential to drive dance audiences away forever. We spent a lot of time in lofts and parks and construction sites watching and waiting for something significant to happen. Eventually we figured out that, life being short, time could be better spent.

Why is the idea of anything instant so attractive these days–it certainly isn't when it comes to coffee! We have become used to the idea of instant electronic access to an incredible abundance of information. And I suppose there has always been a seductive tendency to believe that it is no longer necessary to take time to pursue a subject–whether it is dance or painting or music or mathematics or beekeeping (I'm a beekeeper so I had to get that in there) or even gardening (I am also a gardener). Like dance, gardening shows us the value of time, preparation, patience and instinct. Unfortunately even gardening has undergone an instant revolution, with garden services that will transform your green environment in a matter of hours and thereby completely miss the point of taking time to nurture, love, care and watch things grow. You can't have something instantly just because you want it. Things that are worth having, take time–like learning to dance.

Today, a life devoted to dance is still hard–physically, emotionally and economically. To make one's way successfully requires tremendous persistence, dedication and passion. But there is another quality as well, something daft, a kind of madness that can propel an artist forward–a willingness to risk everything on the front lines despite the consequences. As with most aspects of the human psyche that sometimes surprise or mystify us, I suspect that this aspect of our nature–our artistry–has to do with the survival of our species. We need our artists and their contributions to keep the rest of us thinking along creative lines and adapting to a constantly changing environment. Playwright/critic George Bernard Shaw said, "The reasonable man adapts himself to the world. The unreasonable man persists to adapt the world to himself. Therefore, all progress depends on the unreasonable man." Shaw's aphorism embodies a general truth applicable to creative people everywhere–persistence of personal vision in the face of discouraging odds. Martha Graham's physician father expressed the same idea, but a bit differently. "Martha," he said to the strong-willed, probably obnoxious teenager, "Martha, you have always been a racehorse that runs best on a muddy track."

How many progressive, creative solutions have been found as a result of having to run on muddy tracks? Dancers know all about this. We should celebrate their uncompromising determina-

tion, because it is the very meat and potatoes of the creative individuals whose visions feed us and keep us full of life and looking to a future filled with hope. A few years ago, I happened to cross paths with Ming Cho Lee, the dean of American stage designers. Referring to a very strong anti-art rhetoric going on at that time, Lee said, "A country without art is a country without a soul. A society with no storytelling soon finds itself with nothing to pass along." A former chairman of the NEA in Washington, John Frohmeyer, reminded us of an old adage that goes to the heart of the matter: "If your vision is one year, you plant rice. If your vision stretches to ten years, you plant trees. If your vision stretches ahead to one hundred years, then you educate your children." A survey prepared for the American Council of Arts showed that an overwhelming majority of Americans believe that the arts should be a regular, required part of school curriculum. It also showed that 57 percent would cut spending on school sports programs before cutting the arts.

In the past, dancers have often been unfairly portrayed to the outside world as stupid because the years of necessary training beginning at an early age usually restricted their formal academic training. I believe that if you want to get a job done, give it to a dancer: who knows better how to manage time, learn quickly and be able to adapt on short notice? Dancers, as I have mentioned, now tend to rank at the top of their academic classes. Dance still has an image problem among educators. A relative newcomer to traditional education programs, dance was introduced as an accredited academic pursuit at our universities along with theatre and music and the fine arts only in this century. And in most cases, only in the latter part of this century. Mistakenly, dance was viewed primarily as the province of women and, because dance has never promised to make its practitioners rich, its value in a materialistic culture is viewed as almost negligible.

We found in the survey that the way a teacher teaches has a strong effect on the health of dancers. Abusive training from a dance teacher who verbally humiliates students, for example, or who asks that an injured dancer perform full out, results in a much higher level of stress and injury that can shorten a dancer's career. Hamilton suggested that dance teachers would benefit from courses in kinesiology and child psychology. I believe one of the most important recent developments in dance is the new openness in addressing our common problems and concerns. Only a generation ago, topics such as stress injury, abuse, bulimia, anorexia, weird diets, intimate health matters, homosexuality, bad teachers, bad training, AIDS and low wages were swept under the carpet. That has changed. There is a new freedom of expression in the dance world that will, I hope, eventually free us all for much greater things. This global conference is the perfect example of what I am talking about.

In conclusion, I do not want you to leave here thinking that I am opposed to computers. I am not. But I am seeing, with growing uneasiness, their dehumanizing effects on our culture. My belief is that there will be a backlash against computerization just as the Arts and Crafts Movement at the end of the nineteenth century was a rejection of Victorian industrialization. Part of that movement was the fresh air and health infatuations of the 1890s that eventually gave rise to modern dance. Something like that might happen again, and dance will play a simple, high-profile role. Isadora, at the beginning of this century, could see America dancing. I see a return to the values and colours and textures of our natures. We need to find the self within ourselves again and the joy of that search is my wish for all of us in the unknown times ahead. It is the journey, not the arrival that matters most.

Richard Philp is a writer, editor and journalist. He is currently Executive Editor of Dance Magazine *where his association dates back many years.*

* * *

FOCUS ON DANCE
A Discussion Between Richard Alston, Ivette Forster, Jiří Kylián, Moira McCormack and Jean-Claude West in The Hague and
Peggy Baker, Michael Crabb, Sorella Englund and Benjamin Harkarvy in Toronto
With questions from both sites.

Michael Crabb: Peggy, I know you are considered by some to be a late starter as a dancer. Yet you have become a great performer and now an incandescent teacher here at the National Ballet School (NBS). What are your feelings on the trade-offs (a pejorative phrase in itself) between being a healthy person and achieving artistic excellence and optimal performance?

Peggy Baker: First of all, I think that excellence is created by individuals in conjunction with teachers and other sources of stimulation. I think of good health as a pliable state of strength and flexibility–physical, emotional and mental–in which you can meet many different kinds of challenges and not be broken. You can have your anger raised without losing control, you can forgive a slight, you can apologize, you can exhaust yourself without destroying yourself, you can work hard over a very sustained period of time and instead of wearing yourself down you gain strength. Good health has natural peaks and valleys; I don't expect the same things from myself or my students every day. Part of the big task in teaching and learning is to get very quickly onto that level where you are in the moment: get into the groove; get into the grain of your own person. I think we each have this kind of grain, almost like wood-grain, and if we move with it we are more resilient and more faithful to who we are on the very deepest level.

Ivette Forster: Richard, you have been at the forefront of modern dance for over three decades now, working with companies around the world. What, in your experience, is the relationship between creativity and health and excellence?

Richard Alston: In the last thirty years, knowledge about training and well-being and health has made massive steps in the field of dance. When I started, it was perceived that you had to suffer to be creative, that you were tortured and went into your soul and came out with something wonderful. I think there are definitely creative artists in all fields, including dance, who feel they can achieve excellence by a buzz caused by stress. We all know the apocryphal stories about last-minute choreography and Martha Graham chopping up all the costumes just before the first night. Such notions are no longer necessary. Being open to creative ideas now comes from a sense of balance and being centred; in fact, if choreographers engineer a situation that works, it works not only for them as creative artists but also for their collaborators–the interpreters, the dancers. **Dance should be a fantastic conversation that makes you happy.**

MICHAEL CRABB: Sorella, there are many who have heard your story over the years–people who love you and love your career and have watched you struggle with the heavy toll that anorexia nervosa took on your life. When you went to your artistic director, he said, "My dear, you are performing at your best." Yours is an experience that should never happen to anybody in their dancing life. From your perspective as a teacher and a choreographer, how do you try to make sure that the experience you have been through doesn't happen to your students? How do you make them understand the dangers?

SORELLA ENGLUND: First of all, I don't think I was harmed intentionally by my director. We didn't even know the word anorexia when I was young. I think what is really important today, and it is happening in many places, is education: students are inspired to learn to take responsibility for their own lives and to shift the focus from how they look to how they feel. I think there will always be suffering associated with an artistic career. But I don't think we should glorify it. There is something wonderful in working very hard and achieving success. I may be a little bit overprotective with my pupils because I am so afraid they will be damaged. They have to be challenged but I am, of course, very much aware that we are all different: some need it softer; some need a little more spice. There is a huge pressure from society as well as the ballet world. I think it is so much more important to go into the inner voice in each of us, as human beings, as artists and as dancers. I am trying in my quiet way.

MICHAEL CRABB: One of the theories that always intrigues me is that some of the most interesting dancers I've seen–both ballet dancers and modern dancers–do not necessarily have the "ideal body." What has made them into artists, of course, is their realization that the body is only part of the process: it's what you have to say and how you allow the body to say it.

SORELLA ENGLUND: Because we are living in this fascinating technological age, I think we have gone to the extreme where we have tuned our bodies and our techniques but we never get to speak the language. The tuning has become the goal in itself.

MICHAEL CRABB: It is almost as if the objectives of sport are taking over the objectives of dance as an art form. The point in sport is to jump higher or run faster or whatever, but that shouldn't be the point of dance, in spite of what some young dancers may imagine based on what they see around them. I remember a dancer at the National Ballet asking, "Why wouldn't I do ten pirouettes if I could?" and I said, "Well, has it not occurred to you that four done beautifully might actually be nicer to watch?"

SORELLA ENGLUND: Yes, but it is also fun to do ten beautifully! I think dancers give you what you ask for. The responsibility is ours: if we don't start wanting to know what dancers have in their hearts and keep asking them to give the inside of their legs, that is what they will give. It is quite a complex thing, influenced by the whole of society.

IVETTE FORSTER: We need to think about the physical care and conditioning of the dancer. Moira, you are trained as a physical therapist, but you were a dancer until an injury sent you off the stage. How would you define health?

MOIRA MCCORMACK: Health in young dancers is a balance between how they exercise and the energy they take in (how much they eat) and how much goes out. This balance is a scientific and a spiritual thing. I work with pre-professional students and it is a joy to see that a few of them have found that balance. They know where they are going, but they are in the minority. A lot of the students I see are already injured. They suffer and have lost balance–maybe that is the reason they were injured.

MICHAEL CRABB: Jean-Claude, in your practice, do you think young dancers today are actually more tuned in about their health?

JEAN-CLAUDE WEST: Absolutely. Therapists now understand the movement quality and demands that dancers face–it is very context specific–and that treatment is not ended at the point of recovering from the injury. One thing I found really beneficial over the years is learning to respect a dancer's personal signature of portraying movement and not trying to change it but make it as efficient as possible.

MICHAEL CRABB: The dancer's perception of optimal performance and excellence is at odds with your clinician's perception of the mechanics of the body. What happens if you tell a dancer, "If you persist in dancing like this, you will return to me with this injury."

JEAN-CLAUDE WEST: Therapy has to take a very close look at what I call the inner unit of the body–the intrinsics of the body. A lot of the time it is the extrinsic joints that have the pathology, but the intrinsic unit is not addressed, although this is beginning to change.

MICHAEL CRABB: Yesterday I overheard someone say, "I feel as if ballet is on trial" and somebody from the ballet world responded, "You are right, and the truth is there is just as much damage done by poor education and inadequate training in modern dance." What is your experience with modern dancers?

JEAN CLAUDE WEST: I think modern dance is quite different because you are dealing with a spine that is more dynamic. Modern dancers have to rely on ballet class to keep them physically conditioned and in touch with their movement. When dancers go into modern choreography, they are not prepped. Injuries happen more frequently.

IVETTE FORSTER: I would like to ask Jirí Kylián to comment on the relationship between creativity and excellence. Jirí, when dancers are performing your choreography, what do you feel makes the difference between a so-so performance and a great performance?

JIRÍ KYLIÁN: Thank you for asking me this question, but I would like to say something else first. I particularly enjoyed Sorella Englund's very humane assertion of her feelings of what dancing is and what makes a performer perform at his best. I was quite taken by the fact that everybody speaks about education; it is an important factor in our lives, but I think we should speak also about the education of the educators which is at the core of the problem. It is wonderful to have a very efficient corps of physiotherapists, osteopaths,

surgeons, psychologists, gurus and so on, but if you don't have a child or a young dancer who is well equipped from home and from school, then you are at a dead loss. I think you should equip children with a self-protective system to start them off right. Then, if things go wrong, you still have all these wonderful experts. I think it is also dangerous to have a barrage of wise men around dancers; they should be much more responsible for themselves.

I am very curious that the word integrity has not been mentioned. What really annoys me is that we are talking about excellence. I am not an English speaking person naturally, so I looked it up in the Oxford dictionary. Excellence means "ex something" or out of something, better than anybody. This puts enormous stress on students and sometimes pushes them into unhealthy competition which should not be encouraged. My friends know that I will never jury a dance competition. I think it is always measuring apples against pears. Dance is not a sport; it is an intellectual or spiritual exercise. I think teachers should not build excellence and perfection in dancers; their number one focus should be to encourage dancers' integrity as human beings.

IVETTE FORSTER: But what makes the difference between a so-so performance and a great performance?

JIRÍ KYLIÁN: The dancer with integrity will give you a fantastic performance. If you are able, as a choreographer, to bring that dancer to the state where he believes in what he is doing and you equip him with everything he needs to perform at his best, then you are doing the right thing. But we are all insecure people. We don't know whether we are doing the right thing at the right time. It is very difficult to dig into your own insecurities and find the formula to work with a potentially excellent dancer. Unfortunately, this is not something that can be taught.

BENJAMIN HARKARVY: I agree absolutely with Jirí. Integrity is an enormously important thing.

MICHAEL CRABB: Ben, what is your experience with health problems in both modern and ballet dancers at Juilliard? Are there differences between the modern dance and ballet dance worlds?

BENJAMIN HARKARVY: At the Juilliard School, we have wonderful physiotherapists—we have our marvelous Irene Dowd, who is up here in Canada teaching anatomy and kinesiology—and we teach classic modern. Dance students learn the Alexander technique, which is also taught to drama and music students, as well as the techniques of Graham, Limon and Taylor. I usually bring in someone else for a long enough time to make an impression in another technique, too. In their last years, dancers are exposed to various other techniques. Much of what I see being called modern training is training style—each choreographer or teacher doing his own thing. I think this is immensely valuable for choreographic development; it also extends the dance vocabulary and I support that.

There are two things that concern me: the first is that I haven't heard the word love today, except I know that Jirí loves Sorella. The second is that training for dancers today is at least fifty years behind the peaks that were reached in the work of certain choreographers. Our teaching is still tied to the nineteenth century: there is a lot that has changed through our understanding of the body and a lot that still has to be changed.

I have been in dance for fifty-six years. I fell in love with what Nijinsky did when I read a book about him that described his effect on audiences and what he gave to them emotionally. I had never seen dancing and I thought to myself, my God, what a thing to be able to do with your life: to stand there on the stage and move people so deeply that they are aware of an inner being. When I saw dancing, I thought, this is it. I drove my parents crazy. I began to study and when I began to dance, I felt like I had found the other half of myself that I didn't know was missing. When I danced—moved to music—I started to feel things and became aware of an extended or an inner being which has pushed my whole career.

When I sit in the audience now I want to have that experience of feeling that I am being reached—perhaps in secret, indefinable places. If I don't feel active communication, I am not interested in being there. I am tired of watching dancers. I want to feel dancers.

I am now dealing with sixteen to twenty year olds who already have had a good deal of training, mostly ballet. What we insist on at Juilliard is that the classroom is a special place, a sphere you have to come into in order to work. We attempt to do everything with a freshness, a newness, as if it had never been done before. We work creatively. Dancers learn to perform the rituals—whatever they may be, in whatever technique—to be able to understand what it is to invest themselves. We don't let students dance the first few days because we feel they need an orientation in the work of the choreographer who is being represented by their teacher. Classical dancing is a fabulous basis for dancing—period. Because it has a three-hundred-year history, we do not look at it as a style.

I say to all successful auditioners at Juilliard, if you want to dance the romantic repertoire, or the classic, or the Balanchine, do not come to Juilliard. We want our students to know that they are the future: when they stand behind a choreographer, we want a kind of osmosis to happen because their bodies are so highly sensitive. I think dancers must keep studying. The wonderful thing about working for different choreographers is it expands your vocabulary of possibilities. I think something has to be done about mediocre teachers who have no vision of the art, never go to see performances and bore their students. We know that we fail often and we forgive ourselves constantly. But there has to be a better perception of the art. There are only a few choreographers who I think are producing "art" work. We are descended from seventeenth century theatrical dancing, where dancers were a glorious entertainment. What has happened in this century is the most extraordinary explosion of creativity and, of course, the movement vocabulary that is constantly growing is fabulous. We must train dancers for that future.

MICHAEL CRABB: Ben said that one of the problems is that dance training—ballet training—is not in sync with the demands that are being made by the best choreographers today. Any comments?

RICHARD ALSTON: Although I don't rely on classical training for the preparation of my dancers, I think that in the field of modern dance, the variety of work that is going on requires a variety of knowledge which should be part of the choreographer's responsibility to nourish. The choreographer should actually take responsibility for his or her company and his or her work. Dance is humanity in action: we have to be humane to the people who work for us.

The dancer who influenced me my whole life, more than any other, was Fonteyn who I saw when I first got involved in dance. I have never forgotten that she didn't show me what she could do, she showed me what she understood about the musicality and proportion of dancing. Young dancers often look at film of Fonteyn and wonder why her leg is so low. I think low legs can be extremely expressive. I am very interested in all sorts of choreographers showing me what their deepest sense of physicality is. I think that's where the really interesting relationships between training and performance come in.

JIRÍ KYLIÁN: I think any dance is good if it is good. But any teacher, whatever technique they're teaching, should make the dancer aware that we are a system of hinges: we not only have main hinges like the neck and the elbows, but there are also two hundred and seventy-five or so other hinges. All the wonderful physiotherapists and doctors who are around us should teach us how to use our hinges in order to learn about freedom of movement. When I was in Australia looking at the dance of the Aboriginals, they supplied me with this incredible freedom, making me actually forget (sometimes) my good education. Freedom is very important: every teacher should awaken a desire to be free and a desire to create. Creation basically is freedom, I think. And freedom is spiritual. If you don't have spiritual freedom, you cannot create.

IVETTE FORSTER: Moira, do you think it is the responsibility of the medical professionals associated with the dance company to watch over the well-being and health of the students?

MOIRA MCCORMACK: Yes. There has to be respect and trust and confidence among the teachers, the directors, the management and the dancers themselves as well as the medical people looking after the dancers. Then you can start really looking after the dancers and preventing injuries. It is the responsibility of every therapist allied with a company to watch, bring research back to the company, show, discuss, educate and altogether look after the dancers to make a success of that company.

JIRÍ KYLIÁN: You know I was thrown into this job when I was twenty-eight. I had no idea what I was doing. I think most artistic directors are basically amateurs although they should have a lot of knowledge. But there is no time. We cannot deal with dancers' problems because we are much too young and have thousands of problems of our own. Where do they teach artistic directors to be artistic directors? Nowhere. You start learning the job by making mistake after mistake, and by the time you have learned the job—like I did—you stop.

IVETTE FORSTER: Jirí, maybe you should be the director of a school to teach artistic directors.

JIRÍ KYLIÁN: No thank you.

MICHAEL CRABB: Peggy, you teach in a ballet school and you come from a modern dance background. From a health perspective, are there different issues now in the training of ballet dancers and modern dancers? Surely the thinness issue is not as much of an issue in modern dance?

PEGGY BAKER: I think thinness is pervasive in our culture: the current ideal of a grown woman's body is actually that of an adolescent, presenting a very smooth image. I equate it with sexuality but not fertility. I address it with my students by talking about the shapes of their bodies—that they curve: their butts curve, their thighs curve, their calves curve and their shoulders are rounded. A lot of my students have been dancing at the ballet school since they were little children when they were like little stick people. As they got older, their bodies began to literally bulge out into space: that's what bodies do and that's what a grown body looks like. To try to move into the contour of that body is scary and really exciting. I hope the work I am doing with my students allows for that. My classes happen on the stage. Students don't see themselves in the mirror. The stage is a big place of imagination. They all know that, I don't even have to tell them. They talk about the stage space all the time. Initial classes all happen in the centre. This has nothing to do with the megaphone shape of a proscenium stage. I want students to get used to facing different directions and seeing different levels. All the class works are studies–etudes–not exercises. We engage in these little dances and, as they get more advanced, we start distilling into more of what we recognize as dance exercise. The whole idea is to give students a movement world they get hungry to explore in more and more detail, as opposed to starting with little exercises and trying to force them into any kind of excitement about those things.

MICHAEL CRABB: Classical ballet repertory companies are now competing in an entertainment environment, where so much of the emphasis is put on the biggest, the greatest, the loudest or the most number of channels. It's like everything is pushing toward some higher quantitative level. In classical ballet, there has always been that element of boastfulness about a dancer who can do more pirouettes or jump higher. For example, in American Ballet Theatre, you see it in the way they publicize what they are doing–it's almost as if dance was an athletic event, or a spectacle that is going to be as good as *The Lion King* or *Ragtime* or whatever. Surely that percolates down through the system. How do you get back to the point where dancing is not only athletically and kinesthetically exciting, but also safe for dancers and imbued with artistic integrity? Frankly, I don't want to see a dancer jump as high as a dancer can possibly jump, I want to see a dancer jump to a height that has some motive behind it and has, in Jirí's words, integrity. How do we get that into the educational process?

PEGGY BAKER: In my class, things aren't valuable simply because they are difficult. A lot of dancers want to be constantly challenged to do the most they could ever do. They aren't really interested unless it is a huge exertion requiring a huge amount of physical ability. I want my students to focus in on the more subtle elements. I try to nurture in them a value for the rightness of things.

QUESTION: Jirí, Eastern philosophy proposes meditation to activate one's inner life before work. Today some dancers use such techniques. Do you think dance and art schools should propose such possibilities for their students, so they can deal daily with issues on a different level? Where do you see yourself communicating this in your work or mission?

JIRÍ KYLIÁN: There are many movers in our circle who teach Eastern philosophies, meditation and healing techniques. Unfortunately, I don't know enough about it. But I think it is very important to investigate these teachings. If we can profit from them, I think they should be an integral part of any curriculum teaching.

MARION WOODMAN: Jirí, you said the word "integrity" had not been mentioned, and that is true. I did use the word authenticity. Where integration is the idea of bringing worlds together to make a totality, authenticity would have to do with oneness, inner authority, reality and genuineness. These are the depths that dancers have to plumb in order for their feelings to come over and reach into the audience.

QUESTION: Jirí, could you speak about the needs of the dancer who makes the transition from ballet school to professional company at a young age?

JIRÍ KYLIÁN: Join NDT2, a dance company that actually makes the bridge between education and professional dancing. In The Netherlands, we realized early on that education cannot ever be complete because the demands of choreographers are so diverse: we created NDT2 to bridge the gap between the major dance companies and dance school.

At NDT2, dances are being choreographed: they have a wonderful, wide repertoire. NDT2 is also an education in performing and in creating with choreographers. And this is what it all comes down to I think–creating and performing–making the step from the studio to the stage, a very difficult and very important step.

QUESTION: Richard Philp, I hope that you don't lump disciplined improvisation (i.e. "instant compositions" by improvisers such as Steve Paxton, Simone Forti, Lisa Nelson and Danny Lepkoff) under your instant label. Experiment does not always have to be successful in order to be worthwhile. We need to be patient in order to allow excellence and integrity to emerge, like a flower growing in compost.

RICHARD PHILP: No, I don't lump all those things together. I am in a business where occasionally I run across dance writers–some wonderful dance writers by the way and I have been very fortunate to be able to associate with them and have their work available to me—who feel it isn't necessary to know about dance in any depth before writing about it. There are those people who, I understand from company directors, are not adequately trained by the time they come to regional companies for jobs and company directors find themselves doing the work they felt should have been done elsewhere. But no, I don't lump that idea of instant with good experimentation and the ability of experimenters to fail. What I was objecting to was the time I spent twenty or thirty years ago going to an awful lot of concerts where performers weren't prepared in any significant way. There is a lot out there that is worth seeing, that is new, that is exciting, but it needs to come from somewhere, from a base of knowledge about ourselves first—and from that emerges a very viable, flexible, art form.

QUESTION: Over the last few days, we have heard directors and choreographers referred to as he and dancers as she. How do we move forward into the future, addressing these stereotypes and realities that exist within our community?

IVETTE FORSTER: We have not noticed this in The Hague. Maybe it was in the workshops in Canada?

MICHAEL CRABB: I think, to be fair, it may not go on in Europe, but there is a tendency here for that to happen. In fact, in ballet, it is quite a reality.

BENJAMIN HARKARVY: Let's not forget Isadora Duncan, Ruth St. Denis, Martha Graham, Doris Humphry, Anna Sokolo, Agnes DeMille, Twyla Tharpe: one can go on and on naming these extraordinary women who danced, probably out of a deep need for identity in many cases. We certainly don't have a dearth of extraordinary female dancers; of course Nijinska remains on the top of my list. She was unbelievable.

MICHAEL CRABB: I think the point is how easily we jump into these stereotypes which actually can have a significant effect on young people. It is the same as the process of infantilization that goes on in ballet terminology. I have been to watch rehearsals in companies where grown men and women are still called boys and girls. These things do, eventually, have a subconscious, psychological effect.

QUESTION: Jirí, can you talk more about how a choreographer can suppress insecurities and pressures in order to allow dancers to comment on the creative process in which they are involved?

JIRÍ KYLIÁN: It is very difficult and complex. You need people around you who believe in you, who you feel can transmit your feelings, your experiences, your symbols and your ideas. We choreographers have a terribly difficult task: unlike writers, composers, painters and sculptors, we have to create in public. We are watched as our handwriting moves over the paper. The fear of an empty page is great.

By the way, I just returned from a rehearsal with NDT3 dancers. For people who don't know, NDT3 is a small company for dancers between forty and death. The youngest is forty and the oldest is sixty-two. I refer to them regularly as boys and girls and they love it. No problem at all.

SORELLA ENGLUND: Dancers, teachers and especially choreographers have to feel that they are believed in, because they are so vulnerable. They are creating something that wasn't there before—a child.

BENJAMIN HARKARVY: I think every dance school that can possibly afford it should have choreographic training. At Juilliard, everyone has to take this for the first year—to learn what the choreographer does, the relationship, and the anguish that the choreographer goes through. Some students never dream, when they take their first class in choreography, they could make something; they are so thrilled by it that they follow the study all through their four years. It electrifies the school, because every six weeks or so there is a studio workshop where a new work is shown, the product of the composition process. This seems to have an effect on all the students in the school because they become used to being creative in themselves and with other people as they march forward to the future.

QUESTION: Jirí, if the artistic director is indeed thrown into the job with minimal experience and expertise as a comprehensive director, should the concept of the artistic director as autocrat, with absolute artistic control over the lives of these dancers, be revisited?

JIRÍ KYLIÁN: I think every case should be looked at individually. There are artistic directors who may be technically unequipped but they have marvelous common sense, which is a very, very important thing. The people who hired the artistic director–the board of directors and others who made the selection–are responsible for him. There should be a whole group of people who help the artistic director on his journey.

QUESTION: Benjamin, what is the most critical factor in making the transition from loving dance to loving work?

BENJAMIN HARKARVY: I have directed five companies and sometimes I would get dancers who danced beautifully at auditions but it was the last time they ever did. Jirí was describing NDT2 as a conduit to the first company. I describe Juilliard as a bridge to the stage, because we want to teach students all about their art, the craft and all of that. I think when you really get into the study of your profession it makes it possible to go in other directions at later dates. It is so difficult. It is glorious. I love it. I love dancing and I think there are many dancers so in love with dancing that it becomes a kind of addiction. But it is very hard work. If you look in the souvenir books of many companies, you see there is nobody left in five or ten years from the corps de ballet. Often the soloists are still there because they have great luck and the skill to make it, but people get bored in a company unless there is something creative happening within them.

QUESTION: Peggy, how do you teach a dancer to become responsible for listening to their inner signals for balance, health and well-being? My experience as a ballet dancer involved asking the teacher's permission to rest or stop if I was sick or injured. Can the top-down teaching style of classical dance become a more interactive, empowering experience?

PEGGY BAKER: The students at NBS are asked to let the teacher know at the beginning of class if they have any problems that day. I always remind them to stop if they feel a little odd about anything at all and not to wait till it hurts too much. We learn in class not just to follow instructions, but take in an idea and then explore it; that's what the class is for–the personal exploration of every single individual there. If students are encouraged to work in class that way, they're listening to themselves and they are getting a lot of information back.

MICHAEL CRABB: Peggy, this isn't traditionally what happens in a ballet class. Do you think your students see a huge contrast in terms of what kind of self-tuning they are supposed to do when they go from a ballet class to your class?

PEGGY BAKER: Students are developing their own inner world, their own person. The things they learn in class–every interaction with every teacher–teach them where they fit in the world, if they are healthy. If they are not healthy, not centred, they get batted around and seem to be at odds in every single place. I think it is important for students to know they are building up spheres of relationships and activities inside the dance world. The first sphere is their personal, inner, private world, where they establish their own commitment and sense of reward about their work. The next sphere is their relationship with the other students in the class, their teachers, choreographers, coaches and physiotherapists. The outer sphere includes the public, the critics, the people who come to watch them perform. These are very different relationships and if students don't have a solid core–a world they know absolutely well–they are just like a little ship getting tossed around.

MICHAEL CRABB: In conclusion, I would like to thank all the panelists on both sides of the Atlantic for their contributions. You've done a fine job of defining what the challenges are that remain for us to tackle in advancing health and well-being in dance and dancers.

IVETTE FORSTER: Yes, Michael, I think we have made some real progress here today and we need to think about the future–about solutions–about what we each have to do.

Focus on
the Future

Photograph on previous page:
Dancers: Mavis Staines instructing Iain Rowe
At: Canada's National Ballet School
Photographer: Jeannette Edissi-Collins

DEBORAH JOWITT

On reflection, there have been so many ideas and examples and statistical models and debates and information and questions here, as I am sure there have been in Toronto, that we are experiencing NJAB overload. But, as Arie Koops demonstrated in a fascinating session on productive training and injury prevention among athletes, overload is necessary to reach optimum performance. Perhaps conference overload will put us in a state to be more receptive, to feel challenged—not threatened as Richard Alston said in relation to dancers—by the developments we have heard about.

We in the dance world take pride in our specialness. But we are not that special. Other populations share some of our problems in relation to work and health. They also share our resistance to change. Remember that abused children sometimes grow up to be abusers. I think there is some serious thinking to do. I was listening this morning to Kitty Bouten talking about her research into a small, modern, ballet company—statistically a small sample but impeccably done—where she found that 61 percent of the 21 dancers were above the Rand Mental Health Inventory level of 40, which is defined as a state of clinical depression. Eighty percent of the general dance population has a high degree of sensitivity for anxiety.

Striving for excellence in creativity and performance is a given. I don't mean in the sense that Jiří Kylián was disparaging—to compete and outdo someone else—but in the sense of outdoing one's self while reaching out for some new personal level. When do those challenges that we set for ourselves and have others set for us become threats to our health and sanity? Did the New York City Ballet, to celebrate its anniversary, have to put on one hundred ballets? Do you know what that did to those dancers? Do we need to deconstruct any myths and traditions? Are more classes better? Is a day without pliés one step on the road to hell? Richard Philp invoked Martha Graham's famous father, who said, "Martha is a racehorse that runs best on a muddy track." How muddy does that track have to be before we scratch the race or have to shoot the horse? As Sorella Englund said, "Don't glorify suffering." Are we falling into that? And Peggy Baker, when speaking of her students' quite natural love of big exertion, said, "But things aren't valuable just because they are difficult." They may be difficult *and* valuable, but difficulty is not a measure of value.

I think that students love difficult dance technique—in modern dance classes as well as ballet—because it is quantifiable. It is easier to put all your attention on it: if my leg goes up this high, I have achieved something. If I can do six pirouettes, I have achieved something. It is so much harder to measure artistry. As Richard Alston said, Fonteyn didn't show him what she could do, she showed him what she understood.

I often find myself praising dancers for being fully present in the movement, when they look as if they are making it up on the spot. How do we encourage and cherish and maintain that at the level of training? On the physical side, what can the sports model teach us? This morning, Arie Koops spoke of the athlete's training as an art tailored to the individual as well as to the team and the particular sport. To what extent can we, or do we, do this? He asks, What is the least amount of physical exertion needed? Do dancers ever think that?

I think that going beyond productive overload into over-reach and over-training demands weeks and months of recovery. Is there dance training brave enough to strike the balance between promoting the intensity and volume of work statistically shown to achieve peak performance and avoiding injury? Would any company say, let's not have a ballet class every day? Would dancers dare not take a ballet class every day, and take an Alexander class or something else for variety and recovery?

I think that traditional ballet companies might look to some of the more innovative, large companies and the smaller, modern dance companies in terms of the investment that some of the dancers have. These examples are not from small companies, but I think of William Forsythe and Pina Bausch and the opportunities they give their dancers to participate in the choreographic process. Trisha Brown's dancers are given a chunk of material and teach themselves to retrograde it—to invert it—to splice it together in any way she asks at any particular time and they volunteer suggestions when appropriate.

I think there is a great deal to be learned by exchanges within the dance world. Which companies know how to foster community? How easy is it for them to make the dancer feel that he or she has some degree of productive autonomy to reduce stress, and hence, reduce injury? (Smaller companies, of course, may not have money for health care.)

Change has to come from within, as Chrétien Felser said, because it turns out to be more expensive to keep replacing injured dancers or paying for expensive medical rehabilitation than preventing the injury in the first place. Maybe then, companies will change their way of thinking and make the necessary adjustments to avoid losing their most treasured assets.

Deborah Jowitt has been principal dance critic of the Village Voice *since 1967 and published three books. She has lectured and conducted workshops at universities, festivals and museums in the U.S. and abroad, and has been on the faculty of New York University's Tisch School of the Arts since 1975.*

* * *

MARION WOODMAN

When I finished writing this last night, I went to sleep and woke up with a line from the poet Rumi: "Out there, beyond right-doing and wrong-doing there is a field. I'll meet you there." As I was pondering all the things we've been talking about at this conference, it seemed to me so important that we move beyond the right and wrong to Rumi's field. So much has happened I can't begin to cover it all. These are points that I have written down during the past two days:

It has been said here that ballet has been put on trial. Although that is true, I think it is important to recognize that it has been put on trial with love. We have to look carefully at ideas we have always taken for granted in order to bring them to consciousness. Are these still my standards, my values? Do I have a new vision? What of the old has to be sacrificed in order to move toward this new vision? NJAB has honestly faced many contemporary issues. We are going home with new seeds to plant in our own cities. We have looked at some of our previous ideas from several sides and have decided what to hold on to, perhaps with some variations. Where even a few people hold an enlarged vision, that vision can gradually seep into the unconscious of the collective and ultimately into its consciousness. That is the position we are in. There were many wonderful seminars on education in public schools, universities and the community. I found these extremely practical and exciting in terms of actually incorporating dance into the daily life of Canada.

But I am going to concentrate on the basic questions: What is health? What is art? What is excellence? How do we balance excellence with health? The reality of the art form when it is balanced by the reality of the human being comes down to common sense. I am quoting here from things that were said in the sessions: We have to know where our own edge is. We have to know where that edge is in our dancers. We have to accept the reality of who we are. We have to test our own edges and move forward or back using our own common sense.

What do we do with our deeper sense of responsibility? New information about the body has made old conventions no longer viable. Knowing what we know now fills us with new possibilities for the future. How will the vibrational body, the energy body, ignite a future audience? Emphasis was put on the fact that what is going on in the depths of the dancer is picked up kinesthetically in the perceiver. Being conscious of that, how will the relationship between dancers and audience change? This of course came also with the question, how do we develop this kind of depth in relation to a world of young people who are out for instant gratification?

It was pointed out that it takes six to nine years for a dancer to be trained and they have to recognize that there will not be instant gratification. How do we help young dancers? Repeatedly, experienced dancers told of their own sense of vocation: I had a pact, a calling, I loved dance, I learned to work hard, I came to know what transcendence was on the stage. Choices, not sacrifices, were made on that path. The stronger we are as individuals, the stronger we are as dancers. It is the responsibility of teachers to give young dancers self esteem to know themselves and whatever their ability is or is not. The totality of the individual—body, mind, soul and spirit—is involved.

We were also looking at the balance between rigorous discipline and spontaneity. All the senses have to be alive and open to every phrase of music as if it were new: creating in the moment, fed by the imagery that brings imagination and body to life—in this moment, now, here, never to be again. That concentration takes us to our authentic core and expresses our selves in our every move.

It is the responsibility of schools to give dancers practical training: how to discipline their time; how to put out neces-

sary documents for jobs; how to choose between companies and prepare for an audition, the realities that are involved in facing the world. It seemed to me, in all of the sessions I attended, the message was, we cannot accept the body hurting itself.

Most of us in Toronto will not forget the Romeo on that balcony up there calling out his protest against forced turnout and those two pounds that are still viewed as ugly. At the same time we were reminded that classical ballet has certain values that must be honoured. Do the images of the body need to be changed? What is natural, possible, for this individual body?

Having attended this conference and shared ideas, we are challenged to adjust our thinking and our actions. Benjamin Harkarvy pointed out that education in dance is behind the great choreographers of the past. We must take the best of the present and walk into the future. Issues were raised again and again around ideal versus reality such as older dancers attempting to do things they cannot achieve.

It is the teacher's responsibility to work with the students to help them to recognize and honour the beauty of who they in themselves are, not to overprotect them. In being who we are, as dancers and human beings, surely we learn from our teachers through osmosis. In reading Shakespeare and Dostoevsky, we come into contact in ourselves with the archetypes that are the basis of all great art. They are our tradition. They are the seedbed of our values. The archetypes make the difference between a two-dimensional and a three-dimensional life, opening the door that makes experience and transcendence possible.

Body is the sacred ground of being. Its clarity depends upon its connection with spiritual depth and its connection to its own physical uniqueness. The dancer's art is to connect with their own body and thus kinesthetically with the audience—to connect us to our own inner stillness. Having found that inner stillness, the inner darkness, and having found their still point, dancers communicate with the audience and the audience says, "so the darkness shall be the light and the stillness the dancing."

Not Just Any Body

Marion Woodman is a Jungian analyst and author of Addiction to Perfection: The Still Unravished Bride. *A pioneer in the study of eating disorders and compulsive behaviors, she is a renowned lecturer and workshop leader, affiliated with the University of Southern California (Berkeley).*

* * *

PHILIPPE BRAUNSCHWEIG

Finding solutions for the health problems of dancers today depends on how important we feel dancers are in our vision of society. Understandably, the main focus of the young professional dancer during his/her relatively short career lies in dancing, not bargaining for better social conditions. As a consequence, the social and economic standards of professional dancers are among the lowest in the performing arts. Musicians and singers have created a more secure situation for themselves in our society. Various studies that the International Organization for the Transition of Professional Dancers (IOTPD) has made over the past seven years document how high risks, low salaries, short careers and little social recognition are factors affecting the number of people who choose dance as a career. Parents generally don't encourage their children to become dancers.

The IOTPD feels that the solution to the problem of transition can be found in the way our society recognizes the [cultural] importance of dance as part of our cultural heritage. The concept of transition for dancers is in evolution. In general, a professional dancer's career lasts approximately one-third of that person's life. and the number of dancers looking for new professions outside of dance is growing.

Our society must become aware of the importance of dance in our culture and of the necessity to find and stimulate new talent. This challenging profession must be clearly defined and analyzed. The transition of the professional dancer is a focal point in the relationship between society and dance. Three basic requirements need to be met in order to succeed with that transition. First, education: schools for the professional dancer must face the challenge of educating people for the twenty-first century. They not only have an obligation to produce excellent dancers, but must also be committed to providing students with a rigorous modern academic education, enabling them to cope with the inevitable transition at the end of their dancing careers. Nothing should stand in the way of university studies or higher professional education. Second, professional counseling: professional dancers must be able to contact a transition centre in their own country to get advice from specialized dance career consultants. As in any professional career, the dancer's psychological profile and skills need to be defined in order to create the best scenario for the dancer's future. Third, financing the transition: in the future, the salary of a dancer must be adapted to finance the reality and consequences of a short career followed by a period of transition. Each country needs to develop a scheme to secure this transition.

Currently, a debate is surfacing concerning the retirement of the dancer. What is the best solution–a steady but modest salary paid over a long period that will cover basic needs, or a larger amount paid over a shorter period that will bridge the years of the dancer's transition?

In June 1997, a delegation of the IOTPD convinced delegates of the UNESCO World Congress to implement recommendations concerning the status of the artist and to accept Article 32 which reads, "It is the responsibility of governments to finance on a permanent basis the training of artists to promote their development and to support the transition of certain categories of artists such as professional dancers." In 1998, the IOTPD and the School of Law at New York University began to organize a global conference on the status of the professional dancer, thanks to one of its brightest students, a former soloist of the New York City Ballet. This conference will bring representatives from governments, foundations and dance organizations together in June 2002 to implement the principles embodied in the UNESCO resolution through the following actions: first, international comparisons of the status of the professional dancer, their transition opportunities and their lifetime contribution to society; second, international comparisons of government and private sector strategies for enhancing the status and the opportunities of professional dancers as they retire from performing; and third, strategic planning based on research findings and conference discussion to maximize the lifetime productivity of professional dancers.

Key to the success of this conference is a research project contracted and monitored by the New York University Center for Labour and Employment Law. This research project has three basic goals: to develop data regarding dancers' career transitions; to identify workable solutions; and to convince interested parties to support and facilitate the implementation of these solutions. A management team will closely supervise each planning stage of the conference in collaboration with NYU, the Career Transition for Dancers in New York and IOTPD members from more than twenty countries. Last month, a professor of labour law was hired to prepare a book prior to the conference, which will become—we hope—a reference for study about the global legal, social and economic situation of the dancer.

The dance community is actively reviewing its situation in society today. We are convinced we will succeed in finding solutions to make dance a leading art form of the twenty-first century.

Philippe Braunschweig is founder of the International Organization for the Transition of Dancers which he established in 1992. Following an extensive career in business, he has been a prominent member of the Swiss Academy of Technical Services since 1981. He is currently Honorary Chairman of the Bejart Ballet Lausanne Foundation.

★　★　★

RACHEL-ANNE RIST

Dance U.K., formed in 1982, was set up for and by the dance community to listen to its concerns and take action on its behalf; it is an independent organization representing most forms of the dance profession, which lobbies and advocates on its behalf. This is a classic example of a community talking to itself.

In 1986, the first Medical Advisory Panel was set up to review problems that existed within the world of dance for dance artists. Professor Ann Bowling did a survey to study how many injuries dancers suffered within a year—the first time a study of this kind had been done within the United Kingdom. In 1990, the first Healthier Dancer conference took place at the Royal Opera House. Issues that had been around for many years were publicly discussed at this landmark conference. Out of that, the organizers put together "The Dancers' Charter," a collection of some of the information that had been discussed in the conference. There were further conferences in 1993 and 1995. The conference papers are still requested and used in research papers.

The Medical Advisory Panel also reviewed what might be needed in a dancer's first aid box—including comments and instructions on how to give yourself instant first aid in case of an injury—and got a commercial sponsor to put them in places where they could be most easily accessed by dancers. Then followed the formation of the Practitioners' Register: any dancer performing anywhere within the U.K. who suffers an injury or a problem can phone Dance U.K. and get details of a local health practitioner with dance experience. As we all know, correct early diagnosis is crucial to the management of dance injuries.

In 1996, there was a landmark inquiry of national health and injury, chaired by Doctor Peter Brinson. The results of this two-year research study involving many dance schools, companies and independent dancers were published as a book called *Fit to Dance*, which is now vital reading for everyone involved with dance and dancers.

Although obvious to all of us working in dance medicine, this was the first time these recommendations were written down and published for everyone to see. Here is a brief summary from *Fit to Dance*:

Dancers should warm up and cool down.

Dancers should eat and drink properly.

Dancers should not smoke.

Dancers should never have to work in unsuitable environments.

Dancers and teachers should know more about how the body works.

Dancers should get immediate treatment for injury.

Special consideration should be given for the menstrual cycle of female dancers.

Dancers should know how to relax, pace themselves and combat staleness.

Dancers should be physically fit.

A dancer's psychological needs should always be considered alongside their physical ones.

The current work of the Dance U.K. program is vast. Many educational talks involving months of planning are given to dance schools, large and small professional dance companies, teaching organizations, commercial companies and independent dancers. Dance U.K. matches the professional speakers and topics (over fifty are available) to the needs of participants. Formerly called the Dance U.K. Road Shows, Dance U.K. provided over sixty Healthier Dancer lectures and two-day workshops to about fifteen hundred participants–dancers, teachers and administrators–in 1999.

The Chartered Physiotherapy Group is a program for physiotherapists working in dance medicine in vocational schools and companies to discuss ongoing concerns in dance, to update constantly changing knowledge, and to advise the Healthier Dancer Program.

Current research includes Injury Prevention Screening which helps students aged eleven to eighteen develop a personal program based on their individual physique. It is hoped that this will enable young professionals entering a company to improve techniques and, most importantly, help prevent injuries. Perceived as an investment in teaching dancers more about their bodies, it is hoped that, with the support of their teachers, these screening forms will develop as a good base knowledge of what each dancer can and should be working on.

The female athlete triad in dance is also being studied at the moment. Data is being collected from eight hundred female dance students, eighteen years and over, to be published by Dance U.K. Another research group is studying stress and conflict at work from a systematic angle involving dancers, management and artistic directors and others involved in large- and medium-sized companies.

Dance U.K. has produced many posters, videos and publications including "The Survival Guide," a wonderful tool for young students just entering the dance profession which gives information on how to find people who can help them make the transition from being a dancer and look after themselves as well as information on health, welfare, pensions and contracts. There is a series of seventeen information sheets and guides for the dance community looking at such things as warming up and cooling down, core stability, basic pensions and laws. Dance U.K. is constantly upgrading these information sheets to give dancers and teachers who request them the very best up-to-date information. They also have a look at dance floors with a publication called "Look Before You Leap." Dance U.K. publishes a quarterly newsletter with a special Healthier Dancer insert that addresses important issues for the healthy dancer as well as the dance community at large. It has a circulation of more than three thousand, which is a lot of people. As Jessica Shenton says, "Dance U.K. is not people working in an office–it is the dance community talking to the dance community."

Rachel-Anne Rist is the Director of Dance at the Art Educational School, Tring Park, U.K. She is the author of many books and articles on dance and is currently engaged in research on safe dance techniques. She presented Dance U.K.'s Healthier Dancer Programming replacing Jessica Shenton.

✱   ✱   ✱

FOCUS ON THE FUTURE

A Discussion between Michael Crabb, Christopher House, Tilman O'Donnell and Mavis Staines in Toronto And Cisca van Dijk-de Bloeme, Ivette Forster, Nanine Linning, Jean-Christophe Maillot, Naomi Perlov and Dwight Rhoden in The Hague

IVETTE FORSTER: All of our panelists are in a position of authority or influence over others with the ability to make a difference through leadership. What are you doing now that maximizes creativity and excellence and health?

JEAN-CHRISTOPHE MAILLOT: In the kind of company I am directing, an institutional company with fifty dancers, there is the possibility to change the approach–what we could call the mentality or the way of working. As a choreographer and a director, I realize the world has changed and the relations we have are definitely not what they used to be twenty or thirty years ago. There are different solutions. I am a little bit sick of hearing that we should make the dancer responsible, as if he was always irresponsible. In my company in Monte Carlo, casting is done by the dancers themselves, by the way they behave. It is the way they face the choreographer and the director that makes things happen. By not casting more than one day ahead, dancers have an urgent sense in facing the work. For a few days, as we say in French, there is a "wood tongue," la langue du bois. Everybody says, "How dare he do that to the dancers? He is a monster. They are human beings." I respect the dancers I work with a lot and I don't think I need to prove that. I think it is important for the dancers to say what they can do. In a company like mine, this kind of relationship with dancers is very rare. The pressure and the fear you give dancers is extremely dictatorial and strong. I know about it because I have danced in similar companies. Dancers must understand that it is not only the choice of the director that determines whether they are able to gain from what they do. Dancers in my company are also facing themselves.

CISCA VAN DIJK-DE BLOEME: For me, because I am the director of a school, there is something really important I give students: a suitable surrounding. For confidence, self-esteem and trust, you need a place where you have no fear and feel free and safe.

MAVIS STAINES: I have had the privilege of working with Jean-Christophe's company and speaking with the dancers. It is a stimulating environment and they all speak of how they have Jean-Christophe's support and a sense of his vision. There is a shared respect. I think it is important that his example not give a wrong impression. Before the discussion continues, I would like to say that hearing a shopping list of what we should and shouldn't do makes me feel it is important to come back to what we all share: we are here because we passionately love dancing. Look at the last twenty-five years: there has been extraordinary progress and evolution in dance. Twenty-five years ago there weren't transition centres or integrated dance medicine. Of course we are not where we want to be yet with these things, so we mustn't stop talking about working to find the most satisfying process as we create great art. I have heard people say over and over again, "I must have a life. I am a dancer, but I must have a life." I think people outside the dance field are jealous of the sense of purpose people in this profession have in their lives as a result of their attachment to their art form. Yes, we have a lot of problems but we also have a great deal to celebrate. As we look at solutions, I want to say that this is not a crisis. We are not fixing something that is broken down horribly. We are a community that cares enough to continue to be an example in society of how to live deeply satisfying lives.

DWIGHT RHODEN: I agree. For seven and a half years I was with the Ailey Company and one thing that Mr. Ailey really stressed was that the dancer must become a whole person with a life outside dance. Being passionately involved in your art form is really important. We all know that. But the first thing we used to do when we came back from vacation, was to sit down and talk about what everyone did with their time off. Mr Ailey really encouraged the concept of investigating other parts of your life, because you would bring that back to your art form and your dancing would become richer. You need to be a whole person in order to bring something to your role or to an idea. It is also important to empower dancers so they feel they have a voice and are able to say something. The environment needs to be one that allows for great expression, in order to keep taking dance to the next level and not just repeat the past.

NAOMI PERLOV: I am working in the studio with dancers in different countries within different training frameworks. Usually I work with professional dancers; when I stage ballets, I assume that, since the dancers are in those companies, they must be good. I try to create for myself a belief in those dancers. I know they will have stress because they have a performance that night and I arrive in the afternoon with some new style of choreography and we will have to re-stage the ballet. They may have had a bad class or a good class that morning. If I don't believe in them, I won't help them advance. I don't want these dancers to be excellent because I find that is too strong a word; I want them to be able to advance, not for the premiere, not for the general public, but for now and tomorrow and the next day. I am like a builder, gradually helping them build and advance. I see the results on stage, but that is less important than the process and progress in the studio. There are no rules in my process of working. One dancer is very musical, another is very pretty, one dancer has great extension of legs into the heel and another has all these qualities. What do you do? I watch. My profession is in my eyes. Then I try to help each one to be their best.

CISCA VAN DIJK-DE BLOEME: I think you are completely right. We don't have a model for choreographing—this should be the dancer coming in. If we can offer dance students different choreographers they can find out what they really like and they can grow. If they've had a variety of experiences then, instead of getting outrageous or sad when something new is required, they can say, "Oh, oh. I had that feeling before. How am I going to deal with it?" That's why the school shouldn't be focused on only one thing. It is a privilege for me that we have different choreographers and teachers in the performance department—we can share things. Our students come from all over the world—thirty different nationalities. And they go out again, all over the world. The aim of education is to give them an experience in dance where they can find their way.

Time is a difficult thing; it is always too short. I always want to do more. When I hear about the things that can be done, I wonder how can I integrate them? We have a system of modular education with a free choice for several components. But after two years, the dance students can go away, especially the men. I think to myself, what a pity. If he had stayed longer, we could have given more. Time is such a pressure for the dance students, as well for the teachers.

IVETTE FORSTER: Jean-Christophe, what would you like to do that you cannot do?

JEAN-CHRISTOPHE MAILLOT: I must say that we are fortunate to have a situation that is pretty exceptional: we can do what we want. We can take care of a dancer who has an injury during work. We can finance the study—which we are doing now—of a young girl in the company who knows her limitations. I can afford to keep her in the company and pay her schooling; at the same time she is studying at university. It is important for each of us to give dance students the ability to take their destiny into their own hands—if they want to do something, we listen. I think we don't teach children how to say "no." In my company in Monaco, there are a lot of people who tell me no. I can deal with it even though it is more dangerous for the director. It is much easier to impose a power relationship: "I am the boss, you are the dancer, so shut up. I decide." Sometimes we need this kind of basic stipulation for the simple reason that tonight we are going to put a show on the stage and an audience is going to be there to see it. Everybody needs to be pushed sometimes, but you can do it respectfully.

IVETTE FORSTER: Do you maximize creativity if you make people say "no"?

JEAN-CHRISTOPHE MAILLOT: What is creativity? Creativity is to be open to the world. It is being extremely sensitive to everything you see, hear and smell. It is having a memory. Creation, to me, is not divine. It is the capacity to assimilate everything around you, to digest it and then give it back. As much as I change, a dancer also should change.

When a dancer comes to Monte Carlo, I ask them, "Why do you come here? Do you know my work? Do you know the work we do?" If they answer no, I say, "When you know the answers to those questions, come back." That is a way of letting them be responsible. I don't have to educate the dancer; I have to respect the person with whom I am working. I open my door, if there is a problem, we talk about it. If you do something wrong, I tell you because I believe deeply that what you have done is wrong.

MICHAEL CRABB: Christopher, you are an artistic director. Would you like to have gone on a management course before you became a director? How do you learn to be a director?

CHRISTOPHER HOUSE: I grew up in the company I am directing now. I have been part of it for twenty years and the director for the last six years. This is the first year I feel I have developed enough skills to do my job properly.

From a Canadian perspective–from a North American perspective–I am quite envious about the level of resources that people are working with overseas. To me, one of our big challenges in terms of developing healthy creativity is to establish the strongest sort of force–whether it is a group of dancers or a large company–where everybody can feel a sense of ownership in the organization and believe strongly enough that, in a continent where the arts and dance in particular are really under siege right now, they can move forward with a strong collective energy. I think the fact that this conference is happening right now is a testament to the fact that tremendous progress has been made in terms of how people are trained and how dancers are empowered. I think one of our great strengths in Canada is that we have an unbelievably wonderful force of dancers to work with. It is very inspiring to be working here at this time. I think that one of the things that we have to examine more deeply is how to generate an ongoing sense of energy and excitement.

Ann-Marie Holmes spoke wonderfully about a project company where you come together to do a particular show. Everybody signs on and there is great excitement and you do it and it is over. You have the freedom of knowing that once it is finished, you will move on to the next thing. With a company or a long-term commitment, it is much more difficult to do that. When the world is collapsing around you, you can get quite depressed. But if everybody were able to find a way to create that sense of immediacy all the time, it would make us all much stronger.

MAVIS STAINES: In the past ten years, in my role of artistic director, I have been privileged to have the authority to encourage communication and sharing a vision–of giving and getting regular feedback. I am exhilarated by the power of communication. It is true that this gets more difficult in larger organizations where there are more clearly defined hierarchical structures. I think, in fact, the larger an organization, the more hierarchical its nature and the more important the communication.

Regarding Cisca's comments about time, when I am able to force myself and my colleagues, in periods of great pressure, to stop and say, "Wait a minute. Why do we all feel this pressure?" That taking forty-five minutes to settle down is much more valuable than just going back into the studio and pretending there is no problem. It is in the most difficult moments when you need to leave a part of yourself free to say, "Is this truly the best use of time and do the dancers have a sense of ownership about where we are going?"

DWIGHT RHODEN: From the perspective of starting a project-based company from the ground up, a lot of times I try to make the dancers feel that this is their vehicle, because collaboration is everything for me, as a creative person. I think it is relatively new for dancers: they look at me as if I am crazy most of the time. They are beginning to run with it a little more, but I think it is still relatively new. To get people to change the way things are done and make the dancers a part of the process is more difficult in the bigger situations, but I also think communication is key. At the eleventh hour, a decision has to be made, definitely, but I do think that dancers today are more aware, or are being allowed the opportunity to voice their opinion a little bit more. And they are getting more comfortable with it, slowly but surely. I think it is necessary. I think it is exciting too.

NAOMI PERLOV: I work with many dancers all over the world, so there are no rules. I relate dancers, when I work with them, to their culture, their country, the aesthetics of their body, their practice and their training. In each country it feels very different. The way the Paris Opera dancers are trained is not the way the Israeli dancers are trained. Their bodies are different, the way they eat is different, the way they speak is different.

About four years ago I was asked to come back to Israel to work with young dancers aged eighteen to twenty-three. What could I do during those four years to advance them? I taught what I believe: they must open their minds to other things. I did projects with videos involving students of cinema, music, and choreography. After all, not all the dancers from this young company would suit the senior company. They would go abroad. I wanted to open their eyes to other things. That doesn't mean they didn't take classes or work as dancers, but I gave them their last chance to practice other things before they left to discover the world, like I did when I was nineteen. Israel is so small. As artistic directors to younger dancers, we have to introduce them to all the possibilities for their future, to help them.

JEAN-CHRISTOPHE MAILLOT: There is a way to teach an artistic director even though the term "artistic director" is so vague and doesn't mean the same thing in America as in Europe. In my case, I am as much responsible for the budget of my company as the artistic side of it—something you cannot imagine in America. What can we do to make the situation of dancers better and protect them? I think it is important to have social recognition of the individual who represents the dancer so he or she doesn't appear to be part of an extinct race in artistic fields. The dancer should be recognized, like a football player, so take the time to give them identity. Even though we are convinced dance is the most important thing in the world today, we have to take the time to convince others. If you talk to politicians about making a new house for ballet dancers, how many votes do you think that buys? None, compared to a house for children or a sports stadium. Every morning when I wake up, I realize how lucky we are—some of us—to have money to be able to do our jobs. Part of our job is to teach politicians. Who is going to do it if we don't? Who is going to convince politicians that what we do is important? I hear so many people on the artistic side saying that politicians don't know anything about art. Of course they don't. That is our

job, to understand what art and dance are about. In Monaco, I asked the government to build us a beautiful house for the dance company. When I asked to have a Jacuzzi and a sauna for the dancers, they didn't like it. I said, have you seen what they have in football? Have you seen how many saunas they have and how many kinesthesiologists, and nutritionists and other experts behind them? And I fought for the dancers.

I get what I want because I am convinced it is important and I have to talk to those people with words they understand. They will scream, but they'll get over it. I talk to the politicians about my company the way they talk about a football team. They understand that when I have a performance, I need more dancers because if somebody gets sick I have to replace them. I ask them what would happen if their football team was short a player for the European game with nobody to replace him, and they understand right away. They don't understand with a ballet company, but they understand with a football team. It works.

CISCA VAN DIJK-DE BLOEME: We are in a situation now—and it is the opposite of the Jacuzzi—where the minister wanted to build a new school to show off the arts. There was such a lot of money for this building, but it's all on paper. I think, with all this money, we could have had a beautiful Jacuzzi.

JEAN-CHRISTOPHE MAILLOT: I got the money because I believe deeply that we are doing good work. I convinced them, not just because I talked to them, but because Ballet de Monte Carlo is a good company. We are doing a good job, with integrity, with conviction and with eighteen nationalities fighting together for the same project with a common soul and an idea of doing something important.

NAOMI PERLOV: I think the Jacuzzi is not as important as the conviction of the artist who believes in what he is doing to achieve his aims. I am working with a young Israeli choreographer and we performed yesterday. To prepare this ballet, I worked every day from seven o'clock until midnight, without any money and in very bad conditions with dancers coming to the studio after they worked at other shows. Right now I think the Jacuzzi is not the issue. It is the conviction those dancers had during the last ten days to come to work at night, in order to perform like they performed yesterday.

MICHAEL CRABB: Can't you have conviction and the Jacuzzi?

JEAN-CHRISTOPHE MAILLOT: Of course we can have the conviction and the Jacuzzi, which I brought up because there used to be three showers for fifty dancers. You cannot talk about the physical and psychological health of the dancer separately. There are wonderful things happening in terrible situations and there are wonderful things happening in beautiful situations. But there are so many people, still, today–not only politicians, but others–who think dance is a completely unnecessary mixture of weirdos, drug addicts, homosexuals and the disturbed. I don't think we are a strong enough social group. I don't know why, and I don't know what we can do to change it, but that is the way it is. We need the Jacuzzi, recognition, education and money–all of these things will help the world of ballet get some weight. We need that. We also need the capacity to go into that little box. We don't even talk about TV–it is very difficult to have dance on TV.

CISCA VAN DIJK-DE BLOEME: What can we do now so we will be recognized?

JEAN-CHRISTOPHE MAILLOT: If I could talk to you in French I could be more subtle. English is not my language. I am saying that we are respected by people with whom we have already a connection.

CISCA VAN DIJK-DE BLOEME: I had the opportunity to speak to sixty men about the school. I told them about the students, how dedicated they were and how they loved their work. I thought I was telling a normal story about where I work. The audience was so thrilled; I opened their eyes to such a nice world. Actually, we are not communicating enough. When we do, others say, "Oh, what a world you are in and what a life. How you talk about children and what they can do. It's amazing!"

IVETTE FORSTER: Is the dance world isolating itself?

JEAN-CHRISTOPHE MAILLOT: I think so.

CISCA VAN DIJK-DE BLOEME: Perhaps a little bit. But I have a lot of students at the secondary level who, although they won't go on, now understand dance. They can do a lot of things quite well because they have learned what discipline and dedication are.

MICHAEL CRABB: However well you may educate dancers, however well you prepare their bodies for the strenuous career they will have, if they move into a psychotic society that cannot appreciate the supreme importance of the dancer, they are going to be very unhappy. It will be a very rude awakening. In a sense, what you are talking about is advocacy, something you clearly practice, Jean-Christophe, with politicians. Is that something you prepare dancers for to make them understand a society which, certainly on this side of the Atlantic, thinks that dance is something you do when you finish your day job?

CHRISTOPHER HOUSE: It has been the tradition in modern dance from the very beginning, when dancers had nothing and weren't paid and worked all day and then put the show on, that there was a sense of ownership. They danced because they believed very strongly in the importance of dance and its potential impact on the public. That passionate belief and the energy it generated made for a lot of thinking that has changed our world. We can improve the working conditions and salaries and have all the things that we talk about but at the same time we need to be able to find that same sort of energy. In Canada, if everybody isn't able to come to the table with that same sort of passion–every single person, whether it is the publicist in the company or the front dancer in the performance–we are going to just dissolve. Live performance is something that people are prepared for less and less. We meet young people and we see their experience and the way their minds are trained–the way they are thinking is changing. We need to make an unbelievably strong case for the importance of live performance in our lives and all the glorious things that that can bring to us. Coming back to the idea of enhancing creativity and health within a company, I think that if you can establish a flow–that sense of comfort and power, of being in the moment–in creating the work within the organization as a whole, then you are unbelievably potent as a creative force.

MAVIS STAINES: I think each of us has a really important role to play as an advocate. Over and over I am really uplifted–sometimes exhilarated–by the power of communication. In all my travels, whenever I have a chance to speak with artistic directors, we talk about the conundrum of the auditioning process; I am now seeing shifts in auditioning processes and the creation of more apprenticeship programs. I don't think it is ever a waste of time to share your dreams. Whenever we are traveling, whenever there is a festival or a gathering of colleagues, set aside some time to brainstorm and remind ourselves that we are not stuck in the status quo or isolated from society as a whole. I think it is really important that we hang onto that element of respectfulness, because it is so easy to polarize—even in our own community—and as educators to say, "Well, if only the companies did it better," and for the companies to say, "If only these people were better educated." There are no villains and there shouldn't be any victims.

MICHAEL CRABB: Today we have Tilman O'Donnell, a young dancer originally from Boston who is a recent graduate of the National Ballet School of Canada, to ask questions.

TILMAN O'DONNELL: I have a question from a group of young dancers in Salzburg, Austria: What message would you give to young people intending to make a career of dance in times when art and culture are seen as a luxuries?

MAVIS STAINES: There has never been a more important time to stay connected to your sense of purpose. If it is your dream to explore your potential and see if you can have a career as a professional dancer, then I would say, do that with your heart and soul and see how far it takes you and what you learn along the way.

IVETTE FORSTER: Asking questions here in Holland, is a young Dutch choreographer, Nanine Linning.

NANINE LINNING: The first question is from Jane Lord from the Dutch National Ballet: Do we need to train artistic directors to manage and communicate with their staff and dancers?

NAOMI PERLOV: I think many of us have progressed through various jobs, and now, as Jirí Kylián said, have all the skills. It is good for everyone to keep learning. So why not artistic directors? I learn every day and sometimes take a course.

JEAN-CHRISTOPHE MAILLOT: Of course you have to learn. I have directed a company for sixteen years and every day the dancers teach me something. What is so special about artistic directors? Don't you as a human being learn every day from life?

IVETTE FORSTER: But should there be a special course for artistic directors?

JEAN-CHRISTOPHE MAILLOT: The artistic director is someone with a huge responsibility. When I hire a dancer—when I see a dancer come in front of me and I decide to give him a contract—it is going to radically change his life. How are you going to teach an artistic director to be a good human being?

Artistic directors are different in America. We are so lucky here in Europe. I don't have to spend days and nights having dinner with rich people because without them the company would not exist. I don't have to do Nutcracker five hundred times every Christmas to make my company survive the year. We are so lucky to be able to concentrate our energy and knowledge on the work we are supposed to do, which is opening the minds and the creativity of the people in the company.

CHRISTOPHER HOUSE: I actually think it is a good time to have a conference for artistic directors. I think some really interesting issues would come up. It would be wonderful to have a face off against a panel of dancers and dancers' representatives. It takes unbelievable reserves of energy and ability to broaden your perspective in ways that a choreographer and a dancer might be quite critical of. I think it would have been handy for me to have had a little more formalized advice, in terms of people skills, how to prioritize and when to change your perspective on things.

TILMAN O'DONNELL: This question comes from a dance teacher in Ottawa: Does the lack of communication between dancers and teachers start in the classroom, where only the teacher may speak and only the teacher has a voice? Are there ways to include the students' voices in the classroom?

MAVIS STAINES: I like to think the education we are providing in school for developing communication skills will serve students well in every role they play in the dance continuum. Every single person has a responsibility to be clear and make their point in a way that is looking for solutions.

NANINE LINNING: Why are doctors seen as a threat instead of

essential partners in the communication about and the promotion of future health, well-being and excellence in dance and dancers?

NAOMI PERLOV: Doctors can say nasty things like, "You have to stop dancing for three weeks." But a good doctor is someone who understands the dancer.

JEAN-CHRISTOPHE MAILLOT: There are two kinds of doctors: one who might be able to prevent what could happen and the other who is going to repair what happened. I broke my knee when I was twenty-one and I went to see one of the most famous doctors in the city who was supposed to know a lot; he was the official dance doctor. His idea was to operate on me on the second day. We contacted another specialist who saw my knee and took me out of the hospital right away. The two doctors were both competent but they had different views about my knee. What I learned was to listen to myself and that is what I try to teach to my dancers. Very often dancers, when they have a pain somewhere, will go see a doctor who will use their elaborate new machine to discover fractural fatigue, which didn't even exist ten years ago because we couldn't see it. Probably many of us danced with fractural fatigue but we didn't know it. So the dancer has pain and he shows me the thing from the doctor saying he has to stop for fifteen days, although he may want to work over that pain because it is not that severe. I think we should stop deciding for people what they should and shouldn't do. I always tell them, "Feel. He told you to stop for fifteen days, do you know why? Because it is his responsibility if anything happens to you before these fifteen days—actually in America he would be sued right away, in France it wouldn't happen that way—he is in danger. Listen to yourself. If, after four days you feel able to move, you may want to see another doctor who will give you another opinion." The relation with doctors is not that rational. There is also the other case, which is dangerous: "Oh. No problem."

IVETTE FORSTER: So is it your responsibility to pinpoint that?

JEAN-CHRISTOPHE MAILLOT: If the doctor gives a piece of paper saying the dancer can't dance for fifteen days, then he is out of the studio for fifteen days. I am not going to tell him something else. But, if the dancer has the feeling before the fifteen days is over that he needs to come in the studio to work alone on what he feels like because he needs to move his body, I am going to open the door, of course. I respect much more what the dancer feels at that moment. I have also seen a dancer in pain so serious that she can't go on. And she goes to see a doctor and he says, "No problem." I tell her to stop. I send her home.

NAOMI PERLOV: Personally, I am very afraid of doctors. When I go to see a doctor, I think I will be sick for all my life. He will tell me, you feel bad here, and suddenly I do feel it in my back, my ears will ache. You will discover that you are sick here, sick there and maybe also in the mind. I wish for everybody to be in full health. I think professional dancers know very well when they have to push and when they have to go backwards. Young dancers, on the other hand, want to work to prove that they can do it for themselves; they don't have the experience of more mature dancers–professional dancers–who have to rely on their self-opinion 100 percent.

TILMAN O'DONNELL: This question comes from a sports physician here in Toronto: Do the panelists believe that dance training needs to be modified? If yes, how? If no, why not?

DWIGHT RHODEN: I think dancers and teachers need to be smart. We now know more than ever about the body. When I am teaching, I always tell the dancers to key in to sensation–in a plié, in a tendu–to learn their bodies really well and to listen to their bodies really well. I think mature dancers have a sense of their instrument in order to articulate it clearly. You don't always know when something is going wrong or what it is that is wrong when you are hurting. Dancers need to be a little bit more in tune with how the body moves, when it's breaking down, when it's tired, when it is good to rest, what to do with diet, and how to cross-train to keep body strength and alignment.

MAVIS STAINES: I am really proud of how the classical ballet world is evolving and how the dance world is evolving. I don't think classical ballet classes here, or at Pacific Northwest Ballet where I saw so many parallel initiatives when I was there in June, are the same today as they were ten years ago. There is an integration with sports medicine. We are all aware that today's classical ballet dancer has to be more versatile than they have ever been before. It is important to emphasize the move away from the word "modify" (because it suggests shrinking) to "evolve." I love dance. I love classical ballet. And I think there has to be ongoing evolution.

NANINE LINNING: How do we integrate information brought up in the workshops as it applies to the future of dance?

CISCA VAN DIJK-DE BLOEME: I think we do some of the things already, for instance the mental shift when talking about responsibility. I would like to talk more with teachers about making a team where we can talk things over and think together about what can we do. You can't say, as a director of a school, "I have been to dance workshops and now I am going to change." You have to feel that everyone is with you and you must communicate on which items you can integrate into your program.

NAOMI PERLOV: As I am moving all over, I cannot go to one country and say I want XYZ, because when they do X, I will be gone. If I believe in something, I would like it to influence others. To tell you the truth, my head is buzzing with so much information from this conference—international information from so many countries and so many cultures—I cannot say, "Oh, I will do that." I have to think about it.

IVETTE FORSTER: There is not one thing that came out of a workshop that struck you so much you have to implement it in your daily life?

NAOMI PERLOV: I don't know if I will go back to my country and say, "I think this company must have psychologists," but I am thinking about having therapists close to the dancers all the time. I just keep learning, listening, nothing very concrete yet.

JEAN-CHRISTOPHE MAILLOT: From now on, I am casting two weeks in advance! [laughter] Seriously though, I never want to have a ballet master who is also the teacher in the company. I think a dancer has enough challenge seeing a teacher every morning in a relationship that is very strong and difficult; to have to face him later as a ballet master in the rehearsal is really too much. So I always have a guest teacher in the company to divide the relationships permanently. I am thinking about

the diversity of teaching. I might push forward the Pilates work. But how do you make a dancer in a company like mine understand that it is important to do something else and make him do it? The only thing we can do—and it's a lot—is propose. We give. We offer. But nobody here will ever force somebody to do something he doesn't want to do.

I heard a lot of talk about the responsibility teachers have in the education of dancers. I always felt that education was the responsibility of parents and we all know how much influence parents can have. How do you learn how to deal with the parents?

MAVIS STAINES: This question comes up over and over again whenever teachers get together. It has to do with communication and partnering with parents to draw them in to a point of view. You have to build a relationship of trust. Once you have drawn the parents in, the process is more satisfying for everyone.

TILMAN O'DONNELL: We focused almost exclusively on the training of interpreters and creators at this conference. Yet in modern dance, anyway, dance artists are taking on new roles as educators, animators, cultural development workers, etc. If we want to develop a public appreciation of dance, these are important new skills for dance professionals to acquire. Do we need to think about training not only the whole person, but also the whole artist?

DWIGHT RHODEN: Being a whole artist is, I think, synonymous with being a whole person, at least as whole a person as we get to be in this life.

MICHAEL CRABB: What about the larger question, though, about how people in the modern dance world are broadening out beyond the specific practice of their art to being artists at large [in terms of] infiltrating the community?

CHRISTOPHER HOUSE: For most modern dancers, that is their experience from the beginning of their training. They are not just focusing on the dancing; they are also trying to develop skills which will allow them to perform and produce their own work. They are extremely broad and curious in the way they apply their learning.

IVETTE FORSTER: Nanine, you have just started your career as a choreographer. Were these three days inspiring for you?

NANINE LINNING: Yes they were; they were also confusing at times: once you start questioning one specific subject, your house of cards slowly falls down and you feel that we should change the whole system which we have now. Maybe this is possible, maybe not. I got confused about what you can do and what you can't do.

One of the things that struck me is that some people, whether they are dancers or artistic directors, see dancers as artists rather than as artists/athletes. I can think of doing really nice things, but as long as my body isn't able to realize them for me, I am not a dancer. I cannot, as a choreographer, ask other dancers to do something inspiring to me if they cannot achieve it physically.

I am a person who likes to learn, so when Jirí Kylián says that he has all the experience he needs now as an artistic director, I am going to phone him up and ask if I can learn from him. I don't need to invent the wheel again. I want to step in on a higher scale to produce a higher or a better or a more interesting result.

IVETTE FORSTER: Was there anything you were missing when you were in the dance school that should be taught?

NANINE LINNING: Yes, a lot. But I don't see school as a four-year thing which is over. I started learning about myself and life and dance before school and I will continue until I am dead. School is a moment where lots of information is compressed into a few years and I absorbed as much as I could from everybody around me.

IVETTE FORSTER: Do you think ballet is on trial?

NANINE LINNING: No. I think we are just trying to evaluate and reconsider a healthy way of practicing ballet in the 21st century. I don't think people should be offended by new ways.

MICHAEL CRABB: Tilman, what are your own personal responses to all this stuff you've been exposed to during the past three days? And you don't have to hold back.

TILMAN O'DONNELL: There were a few things that, for me, kept sifting out of everything that was being said. The first and foremost is the word I've heard the most over the last few days: responsibility. It has been applied to sports medicine,

choreographers and artistic directors. I would like now to apply it to dancers and to young people: take on a sense of responsibility and understand what it is you are doing. Young people are the caretakers of this art form that transcends so many things and we can learn from it, we can integrate and we can transform.

The idea that has come up again and again is, how do we educate and develop a personal vision in a dancer? I think we talked too much about dancers and psychology. The real issue is that dancers learn from experience–they learn from a model, by watching and absorbing what's happening around them.

In terms of a dancer having a vision, I have been really lucky at NBS to have tested my vision, my developing vision, with choreographers from the outside. That is such an important key in the development process. Most students cultivate a vision but have no place to plug it in.

MICHAEL CRABB: Tilman, how much of what you've heard in the past few days is relevant and inspiring?

TILMAN O'DONNELL: I have heard a lot of things and I am so inspired and awestruck and thankful that there are experienced people in important positions who are willing to change. The stereotype is that older people don't want to change. It is time for us young people to let go of our traditionalist values and start questioning the way things have been done. There is a certain amount of comfort in tradition. If I am told what to do every single day, it is really easy: I just go floating through life and I get a sense of instant gratification. A lot of young people like being told what to do all the time, because it is easy and they feel great in the moment. Four years from now when they get out of school and have to go to a company, they are going to flounder and feel terrible.

Things are not going to change immediately after this conference. We have to develop an awareness and a responsibility for the fact that something will happen. It's fate. Perhaps it's blind, but it is something you just need to be involved in. That's what I've got. That's my personal thing and I hope some of it has rubbed off on the young people who have been watching this as well.

The Dancer's
Career

Photograph on previous page:
Company: Les Ballets de Monte Carlo
At: Holland Dance Festival
Photographer: Laurent Philippe

TEACHING CREATIVITY

ELIZABETH CHITTY: I believe that creative process training positively impacts a dancer's well-being. I regret I cannot prove this statement and I invite scientists to conduct the research to do so. Notions of the benefits of empowerment abound in many fields such as drama, education, feminist theory and conflict resolution. My own experience is that most dance students are healthy and I surmise the joy of dancing and empowerment of technical and artistic achievements contribute to that. However, much in dance education involves the young dancer's fulfillment of standards designed by others. Teachers and choreographers demand certain traditions: the leg must achieve a certain height, the arm must outline a certain shape and ideals about body type have great influence. The rigour and the physical discipline require a codified type of learning and conforming behaviours. Aspects of dance training have, at the very least, the potential for disempowering effects. I wonder if that powerlessness is not connected to some of the eating and other disorders which are being addressed in the dance world these days?

I believe that creative process training provides the opportunity for a holistic experience, which I see as a balance among the physical, the intellectual, the spiritual and the emotional. I have sometimes encountered anti-intellectualism amongst dancers and dance students; there seems to be a fear that talking about dance might somehow injure the magic.

I believe in the value of a holistic approach to any education, as I believe in its value in my own art practice. Writer and teacher bell hooks speaks of an engaged pedagogy, which she describes as holistic in her book, *Teaching to Transgress: Education as the Practice of Freedom*. She writes, "To teach in a manner that respects and cares for the souls of our students is essential if we are to provide the necessary conditions where learning can most deeply and intimately begin." The context of her comment is a learning environment in which the imbalance is the over-intellectual. But I think that a holistic balance is the same regardless of the nature of the discipline's own tendency to imbalance.

Creative process training is sometimes seen as valuable time taken from the technical training that more directly and effectively impacts on the dancer's developing artistry. Its function and value is questioned for dancers with no choreographic interest or evident ability. Consider that time spent creating might offer a beneficial balance to the rigours of dance training.

In the early years of my teaching career, there was fairly widespread student resistance to creative process classes. While this resistance had multiple sources, I felt these included an element of fear which I understood as vulnerability. I remember very well that, as a young artist, the act of creation involved a sense of exposing myself. In fact, in 1977, a work called "Lean Cuts" addressed that very notion. The removal, or at least the tempering, of these vulnerabilities seemed to me to be a pre-requisite for an environment fostering the free exploration so important to creation. The risks of exposure needed to be minimized.

I found guidance as a teacher in my training as a mediator and facilitator. Conflict resolution and group decision-making may seem irrelevant to dance education; however, consider this statement in the classic text of negotiation: "Nothing is so harmful to inventing as a critical censor waiting to pounce on the drawbacks of any new idea. Judgment hinders imagination." I know from experience that not only does judgment hinder imagination and creative problem-solving, it also hinders art making.

It is difficult, especially for a beginner, to undertake creative exploration when one is at risk of censure. Students in my classes give feedback to those showing work by using the "say what you see" rule which also encourages the development of perceptual and analytical skills and verbal articulation. It is a very simple idea. When introducing the rule, I ask each student for just one comment that is a literal physical description. I also ask that they not assess whether the student has met the requirement of the assignment. Although this violates conventional evaluation, I consider it more important that the assignment act as catalyst and structure, serving the goal of creative exploration, rather than a skill-learning task.

"Say what you see" is a simple tool to focus students' attention on what is actually in front of them when they are observing peer work. When I first began to teach, I observed that comments on peer work were often based on something other than the work—usually subjective projections. It reminded me of my learning about communication blockers and the role poor listening plays in conflict. I was observing poor seeing in the studio. I was worried that students would regard saying what they saw as restrictive, but I received positive reinforcement when, soon after its introduction, a student who had been absent from class began to tell us what he would have done had he been present for the assignment. He had watched the study without seeing any of it—being preoccupied

with self. There is a place and time for criticism, but I sense that a creative process class at the beginner level is neither the place nor the time.

Facilitators are taught that premature criticism, "is often inaccurate and stifling. When ideas are criticized before they are fully formed, many people feel discouraged and stop trying." In the studio, response to work was predictably based, not on observation, but on opinion, because discriminating judgment is highly valued in art. Whether in dance or other art forms, schools of practice are based on beliefs of what is good, valued, relevant to the time, or any other specific set of criteria. My point is not whether this should or should not be, but that a specificity of values can be limiting when applied to the teaching of creative exploration. The opinionated environment can silence those who are timid and fearful of voicing an opinion, or those who have not yet developed an awareness of their opinion, or those who are the recipients of unfavourable opinion. "Say what you see" focuses student discourse away from opinion towards observation and teaches the difference between the two.

Does suspending judgment squash critical thinking? No, judgment is not abandoned. The process of observing and describing is a method of learning to see more—to open eyes, heart and mind. This is an essential life lesson and if I have imparted this ideal to any student to whom it was foreign, I truly believe my work has been worthwhile.

Critical thinking is an essential skill I wish to encourage, but it is not an adversarial tool to discredit others or to exclude what does not bolster one's own opinion. The notion of critical thinking as necessarily confrontational is part of our adversarial culture. Dance practices and education do not escape this cultural condition and in many cases are key supporters of it. As a highly opinionated person, I have experienced how specificity of taste can degenerate into poisonous negativity. There are traditions in the dance world, as in other fields, which encourage a kind of taking of sides and lining up behind loyalties and beliefs that seriously impair the ability to see and appreciate. Surely critical thinking rests on a foundation of observation and analysis based on the collection of sufficient information to provide a view broad enough from which to discriminate? The development of critical thinking is benefited by the deliberate attempt to suspend judgment in the learning environment of young pre-professionals. It is valuable for students to hear what others see in their work. I believe this data, coming from multiple sources, offers greater opportunity for discovery and growth than a directive, how-to approach from me as teacher.

The second focus in my implementation of facilitation principles in the studio is in the definition of my role. Any teacher addresses her role in relationship with students, even if we unconsciously follow models from our own experience. I do not see myself primarily as an instructor of skills; I am a facilitator to creative exploration. The word "facilitate" comes from the Latin root, "to enable or to make easy." The work and words of the students are a starting point for a facilitative teacher to elicit information about their assumptions, beliefs and values, and how they affect their creative process and the social context of their creative work.

It is important to know the boundaries in the classroom. A safe environment establishes boundaries based on sensitivity and respect for others. One of the emotional hazards of art making is the need to push boundaries and take risks. Creativity is highly personal. The notion of self-expression screams of how personal art making is. Safe emotional boundaries are certainly violated in art making; dancers and actors have been exploited for choreographers' and directors' artistic purposes. I do not equate the choices made by professionals with those available to my students. Teachers need to monitor their assumptions and beliefs about their role vis-à-vis students' personal content and expression. I believe it is irresponsible for me to behave as an amateur psychologist. I oppose intrusive teacher behaviour in which pronouncements about the students' nature, character or personal issues are made following a presentation of choreographic work.

There is, however, an important place for emotion in the holistic and empowering class. I take my cue this time from meditation, not mediation. When emotions arise in meditation, Buddhists are taught to simply label them as "thoughts" as opposed to engaging in the drama. I tell my students we all have personal stuff and what we do with it is part of the creative process. When it arises, be aware, look at it and choose to work with it or not. This approach to awareness applies also to matters not necessarily emotionally loaded. For example, recently a student asked me a question about an assignment that included the word "simple" in the directions. The question provided an opportunity to point out that implicit to her question was the assumption that "creative" and "simple" are mutually exclusive.

A key part of the method of principle negotiation is to separate the people from the problem, a concept I modified to separate the student from the work. I find it useful to point out to students at the outset that they are not their work. They are complex, multi-layered beings and their success in exploring their creativity depends in part on their willingness to explore that complexity. To label or identify a student with a single aspect of their complexity is to limit the palette at that student's disposal. To have anger or sadness identified in their choreography during feedback should not be given the weight of a therapy session. We need to monitor the limits of our ability to be neutral. For example, I have recognized my own ego investment in my self-image as open and flexible and I can feel threatened by students refusing to accept my role as I define it. It is difficult for me to maintain enthusiasm for my work and I may unintentionally communicate disapproval when the students' aesthetics are defined by something I strongly dislike such as competitive show dancing or if they display personalities or habits persistently resistant to exploration and engagement. Then my neutrality is compromised. The notion of neutrality requires a balancing act between, on the one hand, the value of applying one's own aesthetic and experience in communicating with students and, on the other hand, the understanding that it may be stifling and limiting in the context of someone else's aesthetic and experience.

Do we violate our values when we strive for equanimity towards all students instead of identifying those who might be promising choreographers and/or support our own values? The answer lies in the goal of one's teaching. If it is linked to dancer well-being, or to facilitating the individual's exploration of his own creativity, then the answer is a clear "no." Key prerequisites for facilitative teaching are respect for others and self-awareness. In support of holistic goals, the teacher must be able to leave her artistic ego at the studio door.

MULTIPLE EMBODIMENT IN CLASSICAL BALLET: ENHANCING CREATIVITY IN BALLET EDUCATION

PAULA SOLASSAARI: My research into the processes of creativity in ballet was motivated by my own frustration after lifelong studies and many years as a ballet teacher. Constant repetition of the same movements and the lack of creative possibilities left me with no room for creative dance-making. Concerns about ballet education in the present choreographic climate led to questions about the future of ballet and the needs of present-day choreographers. Ballet has been experienced as artificial and pretentious which hurts its image as a contemporary art form. Artists have turned against it as mere display of virtuosity without meaningful content. With ballet, the vocabulary is mostly form, although some people think the content in dance is in the story.

Ballet teaching has been criticized for its education methods. As part of my research, I conducted workshops in which I introduced and explored using structural images focusing on the qualitative elements inherent in dance and ballet–such as actions, body coordination, movement dynamics (flow, timing, force, etc.) and spatial and relational aspects of movement–as tools to dance making. The dancers were surprised by the information they got when dancing with an image in mind. They became aware of significant, unpredictable changes in technique and artistry.

In the experience of embodying the dance, a new way of performing was found which created tension with the traditional. Following rules is implicit in ballet although, for some reason, I was allowed to promote breaking them. As a teacher in my workshops, I aimed at open interpretation where the

dancer is an active agent making decisions of what her dance is. Mixing vocabularies is important to bridge the gap between individual movement and the traditional ballet vocabulary that had been a problem for me. Characteristic to this experience is its indeterminacy and spontaneity. By introducing structural images in an open-ended way, the teacher is neither pointing to specific sensations and feelings in the body nor leaving the dancer to his own devices altogether, but is giving the dancer tools and leaving him freedom to discover his own perception of the dance.

Ballet teaching has often been referred to as forwarding a tradition. I think, based on my research, that furthering a tradition in ballet is not about transferring fixed forms from one generation to another, but rather it is offering the traditional conventions to new persons to experience and live in them, and thereby transcend them. No two performances of ballet are the same. Multiple embodiment of ballet is individually created in variation and ballet lives in the experience of its makers. When we use multiple embodiment in teaching, it enhances the creativity of dance. We do not have to wait until a dancer has an impeccable technique before creative dance can be introduced. Tradition lives in the experiences of its users, getting new life and fresh outlooks on the way.

GENDER-BASED AND RELATIONSHIP ISSUES
Darcy McGehee, Clyde Smith and Claire Wootten
CLAIRE WOOTTEN: My master's thesis involved research around feminist pedagogy and the training of ballet dancers. Issues of power, authority, race, gender, sexual orientation and social standing intersect and affect one another in an unrelenting and often unpredictable way. In the traditional world of classical ballet, autocratic training techniques focus on students' attempts to meet the demands of the art form as interpreted by the teacher–a top down approach. The teacher is entrusted to decode the established aesthetic and artistic requisites of the dance form, making the students' success possible. In this environment, the learner is viewed as a docile body–a term coined by French philosopher, Michel Foucault, whose observations of the effects of institutionalized power on

the body have provided feminist scholars with rich material with which to theorize and effect change in the social arena. In the more specific area of education, it is the critical pedagogy of Paolo Friere that lends itself to the image of an empowered learner. In theory and practice, Friere emphasizes education as a liberatory or emancipatory act in which the empowered learner can overcome oppressive social conditions.

My training as a classical dancer and later experiences in professional company life taught me implicit lessons of power, gender, sexual identity, ethnicity and social standing. Within the ballet world itself, the lessons were confusing and contradictory. In a global context, the lessons spoke to another time and place. Society struggled to reconcile issues raised by the civil rights and women's movements when I was training and ballet culture somehow remained impervious to those forces. Few residents in my ballet sphere made the slightest effort to acknowledge the existence of these social tensions. I sensed discord very much on the physical level. I was drawn to the powerful marriage of music and movement and somehow found myself confined to weightlessness and pointe shoes. I know now that I am really just a frustrated modern dancer.

The inequity of gender-specific movement and characterization remains unresolved in classical ballet culture. Ethereal, unattainable women continue to be pursued by athletic, poised men in the heterosexual narrative. In reality, ballet dancers, regardless of gender or sexual orientation, must be athletic, powerful, poised, expressive and capable of fighting gravity. Women train as hard as men, and in most cases for more years. Yet their strength is minimized—even denied. The gender construct perpetuated by traditional training techniques and repertoire belongs to another century and is in desperate need of renovation.

I am now better equipped to name the issues of tension and also make an effort to make some changes. This is where the feminist meets the ballet teacher—that would be me. The docile body in the studio is pitted against the empowered learner and the fictional self comes face to face with the real woman. The real women in my study were five senior students at the National Ballet School. I was very lucky to be able to do my research here and was very grateful to Mavis Staines for opening the doors. I interviewed five female students as well as five academic teachers and five ballet teachers. The teacher interviews contextualized my research, but I was really focusing on the students—not only what they were in at the moment, but also how they could perceive changes being made. My analytical framework was based on Ann Manicom's work where she identified and subsequently problematized three elements in feminist pedagogical theory: experience, collaboration and authority.

Collaboration is the element where I have found the most positive experience. Ballet culture promotes collaborative and shared learning. It is integral to the transfer of skill, yet its significance is woefully under-recognized. Teachers foster collaboration—perhaps unintentionally—when using demonstrators in class. Students use other students in order to clarify steps and get nuance and phrasing. They work out troublesome steps together after class. Intimate peer tutoring reinforces camaraderie in dancers' quest for a shared goal. It also places the peer tutor in a special relationship with the material that is being taught—nothing will teach you better than actually having to teach. Interestingly, some of the ballet teachers denied using collaborative techniques. My suspicion is that, although they were identifying and sometimes demonstrating specific collaborative techniques in class, it was just never identified as such.

Shared learning at the ballet school is not perceived as specifically "girl friendly" in either academic or studio sessions. Support and encouragement are derived from shared involvement in group projects and peer tutoring in the classroom and studio, producing a work ethic that really parallels the dance world. There were obstacles that the students presented to me. Not surprisingly, in a culture that promotes adherence to accepted gender constructs, the difficulties arose around gender. One of the things that came up was competition and perfectionism. Girls were more commonly identified as perfectionists and boys were more commonly identified as physically competitive. A lot of that has to do with socialization, as well as expectations in the dance world. The gender dictate of bravado for men and lyricism for women sets up a no-win condition for dancers. It perpetuates essentialism, limits physical and artistic potential and poses a distinct threat to collaboration. One female dancer expressed her frustration at this paradoxical message of the desire to be physical and yet supposedly ethereal at the same time. She said, "I have a constant pull to be more physical–to go for it. At other times I am told, 'don't be spastic, breathe with your arms, get your leg up.' I find the word femininity a hard word–it is sort of 18th century–girls in petticoats, cameos, delicate hands. Then, I think of the word, woman and it's like, ughhh–this gut feeling. You have to be a sylph." When I asked Mavis, she acknowledged the difficulty, saying they are trying to reconcile it in the studio. There is definite movement in that area.

A further obstacle to collaborative learning lies in the perception among respondents that the school affords boys greater liberties. Some of the justifications offered for this inequity were developmental and academic differences between the genders as well as the fact that the boys are in the minority. Tardiness, unfinished homework and casual rehearsal garb were instances identified by female students where boys and girls were treated unequally: "If I want to wear a pair of shorts in rehearsal, I should be able to. The guys can." I know that had I interviewed the senior boys, I'd have gotten another perspective. We have to remember that this is contextualized within the women's class. The truth or fiction of the statement is not the issue: students are perceiving inequity and that creates a real problem with them working together collaboratively.

Another challenge to the collaborative process was the power differential between students and teachers. As representatives of the institution and society, teachers–despite their best intentions–embody a racial, sexual, gendered and classed stereotype that is called the hidden curriculum. The situation sets the teacher apart from the student in a power differential that subsequently silences the student. Ann Manicom goes on to identify various conditions of silence. One of them is not being present. Another is being present but not heard. A third condition of silence, that it is not safe to speak, seems to dominate the protocol of dance training: the good student is mute. Student respondents are sensitized to the belief that they will disrupt ballet class by speaking out. Personal experience informs me that discussion in ballet class takes place under very tightly teacher-controlled circumstances. Debate is highly unlikely. Maintaining the privilege of the ballet teacher is of great importance to these young dancers because world-class ballet training attracts them to this school–so their teachers are elevated to extraordinary positions of power. One dancer explains, "The difference between the academic and the ballet class is that in the academic you can sit there and listen to the class and take your notes and you don't have to say anything. You will lose a couple of marks for participation, but if you complete the homework, you will finish the course. In ballet class, your teacher decides so much of your fate. You don't want to piss off your ballet teacher."

Collaboration exists in several forms and often with really unpredictable results. You can have partnerships between students where you have peer tutoring, or between teacher and student. Who enjoys the emancipation and empowerment and at whose expense? Power differentials among individuals will render some silent while giving others voice.

I feel there is rich potential for collaborative learning in the training of ballet dancers, but it continues to be marginalized by an ongoing subscription to gender constructs and gender-linked behaviours, including perfectionism, competition, physicality, expressiveness and favouritism. Dismantling essentialist thinking would pave the way for students to discover their own individual strengths and weaknesses, independent–at least momentarily–of gender. Physicality and expression are no more gendered, bi-polar opposites than are competition and perfectionism. They therefore should not be placed as antagonists. Finally, the shoring up of power differentials in the studio promotes silence and limits learning. Lessons are absorbed through the hidden curriculum, which subscribes to a gendered, racial and classed environment and teachers need to be aware of these in order to overcome them.
CLYDE SMITH: My background is primarily in modern dance and the work I talk about here is with modern dancers. My

research project began in 1994 as a pilot study at the University of North Carolina at Greensborough where I work with dance educator Susan Stinson. My first impulses were to expose abusive behaviour at the major dance training centre I call "The Conservatory." Initially more journalistic than scholarly, my interest in exposing scandalous behaviour soon shifted, as I began to wonder why students put up with, and often justified or even desired, abusive treatment. As my research focus emerged, I turned to self-reflection on issues of authoritarianism in dance in order to clarify where I stood in this investigation. I was interested in forefronting my own prejudices and in developing what Sandra Harding calls, "strong objectivity," which "require[s] methods for systematically examining all the social values shaping a particular research process." I also wanted to draw from my own rich background of dance activities as both student and teacher.

I started trying to find some theory to help me out. One obvious source was Michel Foucault's, *Discipline and Punish*. Foucault drew on historical accounts of prison, military and education settings to articulate a vision of docile bodies arranged in space for easy surveillance. The appropriateness of this material was quickly brought home when I took a dance appreciation class in the studio and arranged the students in space, let them know they were watched and enjoyed the activities of those who internalized the appropriate behaviour. Foucault's work was important to me because it gave me some distance from my experiences, while also connecting the dance classroom to other social settings. A similar effect occurred with Arthur Deikman's, *The Wrong Way Home: Uncovering the Patterns of Cult Behaviour in American Society*. My interest in cults and dance training was originally spurred by a dance student's observation that, "First they break your ego down, then they build it back up in their own image." Deikman identified multiple elements of cult behaviour–including a sense of elite status among cult members and extreme focus and dependence upon a leader. While this theoretical match does not indicate that the dance classroom is a prison or cult, the striking similarities spurred me to re-examine my own teaching process and raised questions

which continue to be productive.

I brought these thoughts into my first interview with a woman I call Catherine–an extremely successful professional dancer–who attended high school at the conservatory over fifteen years before our talk. Catherine described the conservatory as a place where verbally abusive treatment of students was commonplace, where students lived emotionally and physically troubled lives, where daily life was often a struggle. Her discussion of her experiences not only corroborated the usefulness of Foucault and Deikman's work, but also complicated things by not immediately fitting into my emerging theoretical perspective.

Another student, Mo, explained a bit about the general environment and her experience of being in the modern department at the conservatory: "People are all very good but they come in at different points in their training. And what [the faculty] do is they break you down to nothing. I mean, after my first semester I felt like I had lost all the technique that I had ever had. I felt like I could not dance at all. And they break you down mentally and then build you back up to the way that they think a professional dancer should be."

I asked them why students would choose to stay in such a setting. Taylor gave a variety of reasons: "They sort of make you think that school is the be-all, end-all, first of all. And if you want to be anybody...this is the place to be...[The conservatory] felt like kind of a security blanket." Mo and Taylor described a training routine that took everything they had to give in a setting which isolated them from the larger world. Such comments resonated with Lewis Coser's (1974) concept of the "greedy institution" which "makes total claims on their members and attempts to encompass within their circle the whole personality" as well as Irving Goffman's "total institution" defined as "a place of residence and work where a large number of like-situated individuals, cut off from the wider society for an appreciable period of time, together lead an enclosed, formally administered round of life."

Catherine's comments suggest that this all-consuming enclosed world, or greedy total institution, characterizes not just professional dance training, but much of the professional dancer's life as well. "I still remember that little room that I took class in every day in high school and think of it as an incubator. Or a greenhouse. Or a prison. And somehow that never left me. That intense room I've been living in for seventeen years. Seventeen years I've put into working my butt off to be as good as I can be and that took all of my stuff. I didn't have any really successful relationships with other people...traveling all around the world wasn't really conducive for me to be in a relationship. There's a lot I feel I missed out on." This is from someone who has lived the dreams of so many of us. Such insights into dance training and dancers' lives more generally caused me to become less interested in rendering a faithful portrait of the conservatory and more in understanding it as an "extreme case" sample (Patton, 1990, pp. 169-170) which highlighted issues worth considering in dance training beyond this particular setting.

DARCY MCGEHEE: I have had the wonderful opportunity to teach both ballet and contemporary dance, and the applications of anatomy, kinesiology and somatic practices. In *The Potent Self*, Feldenkrais states, "...everybody who has ever done anything worthwhile always had to learn to paint, think and compose–but not in the way they were taught. They had to learn and work until they knew themselves sufficiently to bring themselves to the state of spontaneity in which their deepest inner self could be brought up and out." I find with the students I teach that what I would call embodiment–bringing the inside, suggestive, kinesthetic voice up and out–has not been part of their studio training experience and that is the most difficult thing I can ask of them. Students have actually told me, "No, my insides are yucky and I don't want to go there." The shaming of interiority is very real in our culture.

I have three boys. My youngest son was diagnosed on the autistic spectrum with PDD. I have done a lot of very hard and fast "mother tiger" research into somatic practices and developmental disabilities in children. I was immersing myself in those practices originally to better myself as a dancer–to better myself as a choreographer–to find a more subjective kinesthetic voice in my work. Body/mind centering is an experiential journey in just those things. I was subjected to developmental movement. I was subjected to reflective movement. I was subjected to exploring all the systems of my body and I went, "huh?" But it did allow me to feel my body. When my son was diagnosed, I went back to a lot of those people. I wanted to understand human development and I wanted to understand the relationship between how we move and how we learn and behave. Something began to happen when I was looking at research and looking at autistic children–these were mostly preschoolers–I was coming home every night from teaching and scratching my head because many of the movement problems I saw in my research into autistic children were showing up in my studio-trained or conservatory-trained students. I began to cross reference this research more academically.

One of the ways they use to landmark developmental delays in children is idiopathic toe walking–the sense of being elevated out of one's body or lifting up. Most of the students I was seeing had been trained in very strict formation of the feet. Some feel their joint was pronated. To correct that, some well-meaning teacher told them to lift the medial border of their foot, creating a great torque into suppination that brought them into parallel. So their weight is on the lateral border of the foot and they are stuck in plantar flexion–not connected to the earth, not dropping into their bodies. The other thing I saw a great deal of was very little rotational axis in the spine and an inability to flex–an inability to release–an inability to breathe. Most of the dancers I have tried to do voice work with–and I have gone through this debriefing myself in acting training–speak in very disconnected falsetto voices. They find it very difficult to breathe. They find it very difficult to move their ribs when they breathe. This ability to flex is primary to us all. I don't know what it did to my sense of what relationship was and what intelligence was to have a child who was so defensive he couldn't do that. And yet that very doe-like fragility is what I see in the ballet dancers who are in my classroom: that sense of being here and being light with an inability to access flesh and an inability to hold on or grasp.

My son's journey was very much a parallel with my

debriefing from dance. I started dancing when I was three–fortunately or unfortunately–but when I was about thirteen, I became anorexic. I didn't talk to anyone. I was in a bubble. I had very little ability to make eye contact or to shift gaze or attention. There are many who believe that autism is a movement disorder–that autistic people have trouble stopping, starting, transitioning or changing direction. They have trouble changing weight. This is also what I see in my dancers. They don't have the ability to make a change of direction from the senses; their doe-like heads just don't turn. It doesn't move. They don't have the ability to say, "no." They have problems with artistic transitions in terms of qualitative transitions. They have problems moving from one effort level. They have trouble executing and initiating from within.

Science has come a long way. Researchers have been doing somatic work for a long time–muscular repatterning, body/mind centering work, Alexander work, Feldenkreis work–with occupational therapists and sensory motor integration people. They have written volumes on human development and how physical development affects human behaviour and how if we skip developmental stages, what that does to us. Science knows now that the lower brain stem and the medulla are essential to all of our higher cognitive planning–to all of our independence as human beings. If those things aren't nurtured and we don't allow students to go through natural movement patterns in their early training, we promote them to higher grade movements at age three or four or eight or twelve, without the foundation of those lower level patterns. Science is now talking about how the endocrine system and the neural systems come together linking human emotion, human reason and human movement in a way that we can measure. We can no longer hold emotional development at bay by infantalizing movement. We must incorporate information from many disciplines to map and understand the complexity of our humanity in the aesthetic of concert dance in the future.
QUESTION: Why do women not feel they are powerful and strong physically in ballet? To me it seems they should feel that strength of moving through space in a very strong and precise way. Also, is there more of a feeling of strength in modern dance?

CLAIRE WOOTTEN: Female dancers feel restricted because this definition of femininity doesn't lend itself to being physical. Also I think there is a terrific constriction with pointe shoes: there isn't the same kind of force against the floor that you can use with bare feet or soft shoes. There is also the issue of denial of creativity or expression–particularly sexual identity–because of the kinds of roles dancers are being trained for. One of my colleagues did some research with ballet dancers doing Flamenco and feeling so empowered because they got to express their sexual side.

DANCERS BECOMING MOTHERS
Gail Lee Abrams and Marianne Schultz

GAIL LEE ABRAMS: After giving birth, I wanted to research and talk to other women–other movement practitioners and dancers–to find out whether they felt their experiences in movement training helped them through their pregnancies. What issues arose during their pregnancies–things like body image, shape and weight, and dance centering? What impact did dance have on post-partum recovery?

The 30 women I interviewed have a total of 61 children, from 14 months to 38 years old. My subjects' ages when interviewed ranged from 36 to 77; their ages at the time of births ranged from seventeen to 47. With 28 of the births occurring at age 35 and older, it is clear that many dancers wait longer to have children, making conscious decisions to do so in order to allow more time to develop performing careers.

All of the women I interviewed have or have had teaching careers, primarily in dance but also yoga, fitness and conditioning (including Alexander and Pilates) and movement analysis. Two have active practices in dance therapy and all but six were performing on some level when they became pregnant. Fifteen choreographed during their pregnancies. Most danced late into their pregnancies, with 25 teaching and 4 others taking classes. Only one or two stopped dancing within the first trimester and only one was not dancing at all immediately before, during or after her pregnancies.

Although most experienced at least some of the common

discomforts of pregnancy, such as tiredness, headaches, morning sickness and swelling, only 6 experienced the low back pain that is often associated with pregnancy. Many attributed the lack of back pain to the strength and support of their abdominals, which they believed counteracted the additional weight in front, as well as to alignment training and the use of imagery to release the lower back.

Weight gain varied greatly with about half gaining 22 to 35 pounds. Only 2 gained more than 60 pounds; one gained 80 pounds in her fourth pregnancy and another's second pregnancy with twins resulted in a 90-pound weight gain (on a normally 110-pound body!). Losing weight and getting back into shape averaged 6 months to 9 months, with some losing the weight within 7 days and some taking a year or more. However, most dancers went back to some form of dancing, exercising and teaching within 2 weeks to 4 or 5 months.

The overwhelming consensus was that movement and dance training have many positive effects on pregnancy. Coping with centering weight as the body mass changed was an important issue for nearly everyone. Training in Pilates was also felt to be beneficial by those who engaged in it. Diane Diefenderfer was able to continue her Pilates workout throughout her pregnancy by varying the order of her exercises in order not to remain on her back for too long and adjusting the intensity as she grew larger. She also commented that several of her Pilates clients who continued through their pregnancies found that it alleviated back problems as they began to occur. Many felt their abdominal strength remained intact and may in fact have been a detriment to actually delivering their babies, because they couldn't let go of the tightness or holding that had been ingrained for so many years.

Movement also has enormous power for the mind; it can reveal, enrich, communicate and heal emotional and psychological conditions. I would like to share the difficult and emotional journey of one of my subjects as her body presented her with distressing physical symptoms during pregnancy which ultimately revealed a painful trauma from her own childhood. "The beginning of my first pregnancy was very difficult because I was getting a number of boils under my arms, on my buttocks, between my legs. I was extremely nauseous and the boils were in vulnerable, sensitive areas; the pain was excruciating. I was thrilled I was pregnant...and yet I had this very sick, deep feeling inside me that there was something terribly wrong. I saw a homeopathic doctor who did some imaging with me and I had this clear sense that something terrible had happened in my childhood. I had absolutely no idea what it was, nor did I have any desire to go into it; I just wanted to acknowledge and heal from that place. The boils and morning sickness stopped when I was around three months pregnant and I felt radiantly wonderful. Obviously there was this huge relief from physical discomfort. But it was clear there was some kind of message that I had to dispel from my body before my child was born. If I wasn't so in touch with my body as a dancer and a movement person, I'm not sure I would have gotten that message. My second pregnancy was very different. I got a few boils, but not to the same extent. I seemed to have a much better understanding that the cleaning out process that began during my first pregnancy was going to continue. It was not as intense, not as painful, but it certainly was there." An important aspect of this woman's story is how she recognized that her body was communicating something vital to her. For a long time, she didn't understand what that was, but said, "The body level was the thing I was in touch with and that was the thing that was so heavy. I continued therapy, I continued working with an energy person. Although I didn't have a lot of answers, I continued to work through healing images and eventually the cloud lifted."

A recurring theme throughout my discussions with these women was that control was seen as a positive factor; almost everyone felt they had control over their bodies' fitness, discipline, strength and stamina, which served them well throughout pregnancy, delivery and recovery. However, the question of control over one's body when it came to weight gain produced varying responses. Most dancers had an extremely positive body image while pregnant. Nearly all of them loved their pregnant bodies and very few minded the weight gain. Many said that pregnancy provided an excuse to be larger, without the need to justify it. Many felt more feminine, sexy, voluptuous and proud of their bodies; several mentioned they enjoyed having fuller breasts, a new experience for many dancers.

Suchi Branfman, co-founder of Crowsfeet Dance Collective in New York and now a choreographer and teacher in the Los Angeles area, shared an interesting perspective: "I really loved my body being pregnant, after I got accustomed to the concept that I was so huge. I had expected breasts and belly, but it was hips, butt and thighs that took me by surprise. I got into the idea of being big. People treat you differently when it's obvious you're pregnant, but how you can or can't manoeuvre your body when it's big is a physical reality I knew nothing about. You can't move fast or through small spaces and you have to wait for other people to pass on crowded streets. I kept projecting this into what happens if you're an overweight person."

Negative body image seemed more common among ballet dancers than modern dancers. They expressed more concern about weight gain and tried to camouflage themselves as they grew larger. There seemed to be greater emphasis on conformity in terms of body type. Ballet dancers were not as accepting of their changing shape and mass as modern dancers.

While there was not unanimous agreement that being a dancer makes labour and delivery easier, all subjects agreed that being a dancer is an advantage in pregnancy and postpartum recovery. Nearly everyone, with the exception of the two oldest subjects (ages fifty-nine and seventy-seven) felt their labours would have been more difficult to manage had they not had training as dancers, body workers, movement analysts or yoga practitioners.

There was widespread belief that dancers' bodies are more highly trained, in better condition, more connected and more integrated with mind and spirit than the average, non-dancing person's. We have greater muscle strength, flexibility and stamina and we are accustomed to dealing with physical discomforts and pain. We are more kinesthetically tuned in and are sensitive to changes occurring in our bodies as well as the psychological ramifications of physical events. We are accustomed to using breath in support of movement, as an aid to releasing tension, and as a calming, centering agent. We often use visual imagery to facilitate movement, changes in alignment and psychological well-being. We are highly disciplined, accustomed to long periods of strenuous physical activity and have the endurance to persevere through whatever is necessary in order to accomplish a goal. As creative people, we welcome opportunities to improvise and explore various solutions to a problem, and are more willing to travel the less traditional path to our destination.

The profound ways in which dance and movement training can benefit pregnancy and childbirth experiences exist on many levels–physical, mental and spiritual. It is my hope that not only will other dancers benefit from hearing about the experiences of their colleagues, but also that this awareness, knowledge and wisdom can be used to help non-dancers as well. To me, what is so special about these stories is their universality, their uniqueness, and their affirmation of the wondrous power of dance, body knowledge and movement in our lives.

MARIANNE SCHULTZ: The American poet Alicia Ostriker said, "For women as artists, the most obvious truth is that the decision to have children is irrevocable." For all people, men and women alike, the decision to have children is irrevocable and life changing. "Your life will never be the same again," is a common cliché heard after the birth of one's first child, but what of, "Your art will never be the same again" or, "Your creativity will never be the same again" or even, "Your technique will never be the same again"? Where have women artists and particularly dance artists seen or heard these words after childbirth? If, as Ostriker says, "[t]he advantage of motherhood for a woman artist is that it puts her in immediate and inescapable contact with the sources of life, death, beauty, growth, corruption," then motherhood provides new ground for creativity and inspiration. Motherhood also provides new obstacles, challenges and perspectives for performing and dance artists. As Susan Lee comments in her essay included in *Dancing Females: Lives and Issues of Women in Contemporary Dance*, "Clearly the issue of child-bearing is an especially complicated one in dance, where body image is central." It can be argued that it is not only body image that makes childbearing complicated in dance but the embodiment of the art itself.

The impetus for this study of the impact and effect of motherhood on contemporary dance artists, performers, choreographers and teachers comes from my personal experiences following two miscarriages, two pregnancies and subsequent births of my two children.

Given that, as Susan Lee explains, the dance world is "a social system," all dance artists must assume a position or role within that system. Since the majority of women start their dance training earlier than men, they are exposed to the restrictions and constraints of a traditional dance class as young girls. More than likely these agendas are set and maintained by women. The authoritarian approach to the learning of a creative, expressive, embodied art form must have conflicting effects upon the dancer.

As a dancer matures and climbs the hierarchy of the dance world, adherence to this system moulds her notion of who she is and what place she occupies within this world. Susan Lee mentions the "fine line between self, identity and career" in dance. Notions of identity connected to perceptions of the physical body as well as the lived experiences of the body are shaped by the transition from dancer to dancer as mother. Within the social system that is the world of dance, these altered notions can have a marked impact on many aspects of a dancer's career. Alongside the physical changes of motherhood, the development of hitherto unknown emotional states heralds a shift in the notion of who she is.

If a dancer's body is her art, then what happens to that art when another body, the child's, invades and dominates it? Art critic Rosemary Betterton has written, "...the pregnant body signifies the state in which boundaries of inside and outside, self and other, dissolve." The self-absorption that is deemed necessary for a dancer is put aside, possibly forever, when she becomes a mother. Some see this as a positive change but, for other dancers, the author included, being denied time of solitude, time for technique class, or even just time to "play" in the studio is a deep loss. My sense of, "This is who I am" has only

ever been found through dance.

Of course there are times when all mothers assume the cultural role of "mother." Dancers might have a more romantic notion of what this role is since their lives have been dominated by what has been described above as the authoritarian hierarchy of the dance world. Motherhood may seem like an escape to the "normal world:" the world of "normal" womanhood. But in assuming a new identity–socially, physically and emotionally–the dancer may struggle for her place within these two worlds. As Adrienne Rich states in her groundbreaking book on motherhood, *Of Woman Born*, "Motherhood...is one part of female process; it is not an identity for all time...it is not enough to let our children go; we need selves of our own to return to."

Issues surrounding the body, including the body as site of art and the perception of the body in art, are relevant here: the body represented and the body as flesh. The perception of the body is linked to the notion of identity. The dualistic notion of dancer as mother contributes to a polarity of conceptual ideas of one's body. For all women the transformation from a "woman's" body to a "maternal" body is a major life-changing event. The body, which up until this point has been hers alone, becomes the unborn child's source of nourishment, housing and protection. After birth, the body is altered and continues as a source of food and comfort for the child. Paradoxically, dance artists may not be prepared for this transformation in spite of their constant monitoring, regulating and preoccupation with their own bodies.

In *Competing with the Sylph*, L.M. Vincent discusses the "notion of asexuality" that surfaced in his interviews with young female dancers. He goes on to say, "Those who aspire to and achieve an asexual body configuration cannot help but de-sexualize and de-feminize themselves as well." Of course his area of study deals primarily with ballet dancers but there are parallels in the contemporary dance world. The athleticism of contemporary dance in many choreographies demands a neutral body.

There are many unknowns for a dancer, as for every woman, when she becomes pregnant. Rozann Kraus has said,

"When it comes to pregnancy, there are almost no guidelines on how we are to conduct our dance lives during this time." In a study published in *Kinesiology and Medicine in Dance* in 1991, she states, "Pregnancy does not bring on an eating disorder, nor does it aggravate one in remission...but this fear of loss of control is deep seated in many dancers who think about getting pregnant."

Some choreographers have used the physical limitations of pregnancy as vocabulary for their work. Rosemary Lee choreographed and performed her solo, *Exhale* at seven months pregnant with her second child. The dance, as described by Lee, is, "Very static...done on the spot" and consisted of, "A lot of movement in the upper body and torso." Emilyn Claid also performed a solo at seven months pregnant. Her piece, *Making a Baby* examined the experience of pregnancy and used her pregnant body as the subject of the work. She incorporated both speech and movement to confront the audience's notions of pregnant women and the birth process. For both these women, the physical processes of the pregnant body are integrated into their work so that rather than disguise their maternal body, they in fact celebrate and exploit it.

As giving birth is a complete physical act, dancers may experience complex emotions associated with it. On the one hand, the loss of control during labour and birth may be frightening for dancers who are so used to being in control of their physical selves. Yet, since it is the most physically demanding endeavour they may ever undertake, some dancers respond instinctively to aspects of the birth process and anticipate the challenge. Yuriko, a choreographer, and Graham, a dancer, said in *Dance Magazine*, "...It had to do with me, but it had nothing to do with my brain telling my body what to do...and of course I said, 'If I could put this into a dance.' I was already turning that physical sensation into a dance or choreographic idea—a source."

At the end of the twentieth century—which began with Isadora Duncan proclaiming, "I was stretched and bleeding, torn and helpless, while this little being sucked and howled. Life, life, life! Give me life!"—dance artists should still be celebrating their ability to be pregnant, give birth and dance.

There are of course dance artists who are primarily performers and not choreographers. For them technique is at the very heart of what they do. Since the hormonal changes during pregnancy and lactation affect the ligaments and joints, dancers may suddenly feel wonderfully loose and flexible. Pregnancy changes a woman's centre of gravity but this displacement gradually recedes after giving birth.

Many dancers who are able to work professionally after childbirth find they are more relaxed about achieving perfect technique. Rosemary Lee mentions release technique as suitable for the type of work she now does. For her, strength is not as important as alignment and direction of movement. Speaking as a choreographer who works with dancing mothers, Siobhan Davies said of pregnant dancers in an interview in the journal *Animated*, "I think their own work is somehow released by it—the worrying about perfection is diminished; it can be quite liberating." One of those dancers she speaks of, Cathy Quinn, describes her experience, "I had always been quite an energetic dancer and I suppose that having children tempered that a little and made me more aware of what could be accomplished without all that gung ho." Anna Teresa De Keersmaeker echoes Davies' sentiments and adds her own thoughts on working with dancers as mothers: "It is never these people who are late or miss rehearsals or class. They have much more energy than the younger kids."

Though gender issues have come to the forefront in contemporary dance in the last decade or two, a feminist perspective on pregnancy, birth and the institution of motherhood has not seemed to filter down to the dance community. By this I mean the sharing of information and the support of other artists for dancers as mothers. Kristeva's statement, "Genuine feminine innovation...will not be possible until we have elucidated motherhood and feminine creation, and the relationship between them," resonates clearly here.

The possibility exists that the competitive nature of the professional dance world combined with the self-disciplined attitude of dancers themselves may contribute to this lack of information and support. Emilyn Claid explained her experience in the early 1980s: "Working with X6 was a serious feminist, consciousness-raising time which meant you didn't give much time to motherhood...you just got on with your work and being a mother took second place."

Mother-guilt has a long and established history and performing artists do not escape the effects of the "Patriarchal institution of motherhood" as described by Adrienne Rich. Rosemary Lee said, "I'm frustrated...that perhaps I could be a better artist by doing more. But then I'm frustrated that I could be doing more as a mother as well. I had a lot of ideals or delusions about who I would be as a mother. I really thought I'd be an earth mother and I'm not."

Looking at the vocabulary and subject material of choreographers with children, it is interesting to note the range in responses when asked what effect they noticed in their work. For Rosemary Lee, not only had the texture of her work changed but also her choice in the gender of the dancer on whom her work was presented. She said, "It got darker, I don't know why...it's not a conscious thing. I think it's to do with having a son. I'm sure that I'm dealing with masculinity or with male energy." The issues of birth and death became real experiential sources for her choreography. She continues, "...somehow it got less hopeful. But I possibly think that the work is richer because of having children. I think that the darker side had to be dealt with and probably still has to be dealt with."

Emilyn Claid, in discussing the impact of motherhood on her work, cites her son's presence: "I think the good thing was that as my son got older it kept me in touch with all the youthful, on-the-edge stuff which really affected my work in terms of music, horror films, the edge of media. Things that were in his life became very much a part of my work." Anna Teresa De Keersmaeker, when asked if she thought that her subject material had changed after becoming a mother, answered that she didn't think so, but added, "Before, there was only the work and now there is another work, another creation which is as important or even more important than the work. What is different and sometimes difficult is this divided concentration."

When one has experienced children literally "jumping for joy" or "running for their lives," conveying these actions and movements takes on new meanings in a dance class. The possible superficiality of technique becomes obvious. Patricia Rianne says of her teaching, "Because of the changes that your body has gone through by giving birth, you are differently aware of the body. This has certainly changed my teaching. But also just looking at a child's physicality and suddenly being aware of how a child moves...way back, dance was not taught like that. It was some 'technique,' some unreal thing that you learned and imposed on your body. Dealing with students, I have found it really useful to be a mother but I also found it really useful being a teacher with my own children." In describing her approach to teaching, she added, "I think that I am fearless now. I've learned how to do it and I think that being a mother made me less nervous. Once you've been a mother, God, you can survive anything!"

In the past, age and motherhood were certain deciding factors in exclusion from many aspects of professional dance. Combining these two factors a dancer may indeed feel anxious concerning her future in her career. Emilyn Claid explained her position once she became artistic director of Extemporary: "I did as much as possible to make sure that I didn't lose my place by being a mother. But it was an uphill struggle all the way." When asked, where do dancing mothers fit into the dance community? Cathy Quinn replied, "In a very small, slightly wearisome space, unless the choreographer has children. Hopefully this picture is changing as more dancers have children."

Finally, the notions of identity, creativity and work referred to in this study of dancers as mothers have been revealed to be inextricably connected. A dancer's identity is composed of her body, her spirit and her output. When that dancer is also a mother, her identity expands and includes her cultural notion of mother as well. What is shared by all dancers as mothers are the lived experiences of motherhood that inform their dance. In conclusion, echoing Susan Suleiman's statement from her essay "Writing and Motherhood," when she speaks of writing mothers (substituting "dancing" for "writing"): "We need to have more...interviews, more diaries, more memoirs, more essays, and more reminiscences by [dancing] mothers...about, or out of, their own experiences of the relationship between [dancing] and motherhood." We, as members and observers of the dance community want to see, read, hear and share more of this information.

A LIFE IN DANCE

COLEEN DAVIS: I am a principal dancer with The Dutch National Ballet. I have been a member of Het Nationale Ballet for almost twenty-three seasons. At the age of seventeen, I arrived in The Netherlands, believing I would be here for a year or two to gain some experience. I then intended to return to America and really begin my dancing life. Little did I know my dance career would take place in Holland and that I would be happy and proud to be affiliated with Het Nationale Ballet.

Reflecting back, not every period in my career has been smooth or easy or injury free, but what always kept me going was the blind love and passion I had—and still have—for my art. Love alone, however, is not always enough to give dancers the strength and stamina they need to live their art in the way they would like. Dancers must be able to show their vulnerability, relate their experiences on stage and use their physicality to move an audience.

The two basic elements I feel are necessary for longevity in a dancer are physical and emotional health, and a well-fed soul. If these two elements are nurtured then the dancer will be a whole person with the ability to perform to their optimum, enjoy their life in and out of the theatre and cope with the ups and downs they encounter.

Most ballet dancers join companies at a young age. Our bodies are young and our spirits are full of enthusiasm. We are ready to conquer the world. Youth, as we know, forgives a lot of sins but eventually age and physical limitations do creep in. The body can no longer jump up from sitting on the floor to execute a variation. And if it does, there are repercussions the next day. How does a dancer learn how and when he can push himself? Eventually experience is the teacher. But before

experiences have been created, it would be wonderful if a young dancer was taught how to preserve his body so as to ensure a long and fruitful career.

Diet is an obvious starting point. The food dancers put into their bodies not only serves their limbs but also their brains. Dance is not limited to working just the extremities. For example, we watch combinations and then execute them; we interpret rules imagining how the body should look to evoke a certain feeling from the audience; we listen to music and move accordingly. Everything we do begins with what our brain absorbs, translates and then signals to our body. If the brain is starved, then so is the dancer.

Another daily ritual for a dancer is taking class. It is the start of the day. It is also the start of building strong and supple muscles although it is not the only way to develop a young person's physique. Most competitive athletes such as runners, tennis players and football players not only practice their chosen sport, they also do cross-training. This is a fairly new concept for the dance world where, "I have taken class. That's enough. What else do I need?" is a common attitude. Stretching your muscles in a variety of ways builds an all round healthy body. Working in only one medium often strengthens only one group of muscles, leaving others untouched. The danger of this is overusing one set of muscles to the point of damaging them, leaving underused muscles too weak to support the stronger ones. Cross-training activities include swimming, riding a stationary bike or using a stair machine. I personally find doing other sorts of exercise refreshing.

Other types of body work dancers often find attractive but usually do not discover until nursing an injury include aqua aerobics, which is still not as common in The Netherlands as it is in America. It is a safe, non-weight bearing exercise in which water helps to pump swelling away from the joints. If a dancer decides to do a barre with water up to his shoulders, he is carrying only 10 percent of his body weight. This is perfect for someone who is seriously injured and frightened to begin again. Pilates, also a non-weight bearing form of workout, allows the dancer to become aware of his placement or non-placement. By developing the muscles around the spine, a centre is created around the limbs so they can move freely. Control, concentration, flow and balance are the basic elements behind Pilates. The exercises require you to be fully conscious to execute them properly.

White Cloud, another technique similar to Pilates, also develops control, concentration and flow. Again, certain muscle groups are developed with a keen awareness on breathing, an area dancers are often unconscious of. The body, fortunately, breathes automatically, but how often after a combination or variation does a dancer realize he has not taken a breath throughout the whole thing? White Cloud teaches the body to breathe consciously. I was amazed how energetic I felt after my first lesson.

No matter what alternative training dancers choose, the awareness they discover about their bodies will be advantageous to keeping them injury free and make them realize the possibilities their bodies have. While exerting for a choreographer, a dancer's muscles, unused to certain movements, will still be strong and willing.

There will, unfortunately, be times when a dancer is injured. How do you deal with this? The first approach is a practical one: use ice immediately and then evaluate the injury. Is an x-ray needed? Should a physiotherapist be called? Is rest demanded? Physiotherapists have become such an important part of dancers' lives. In Holland, we are extremely fortunate with ours—I do not know how Het Nationale Ballet ever existed without a physiotherapist. They are the company's and, more importantly, the dancers' life savers.

The physiotherapist manipulates and stretches the patient. He places ultrasound electricity currents—sound waves—on the injury. Exercises are also suggested to help rebuild the area or prevent other muscles from compensating for the injured part. Visiting the physiotherapist becomes the focal point of the dancer's day providing the vulnerable dancer with reassurance he is on the right path to recovery. Not only does the dancer's body need healing, so does his psyche.

Sometimes dancers turn to other alternative medical methods such as acupuncture. Usually an acupuncturist asks a dancer about his injury, but he also asks about sleep patterns, digestion and his thoughts. The acupuncturist's approach is that to heal a body, everything must be running properly and the mind must be clear.

Reflexology is another healing method. Not only does every organ have its function, but it also has a spiritual association. The pancreas, for example, produces insulin for the body. If it is overactive, it produces too much glucose. This could be from consuming too much sugar, but it could also be from seeking out and asking for more affection and love. Every healer knows an injury heals quicker when their patient has a positive attitude. State of mind is so important, but so often ignored.

This is an issue that is seldom talked about in a ballet company: the relationship between injuries and the emotional state of the dancer before the injury. Time and time again, I have seen angry dancers walk out of class cursing anyone and everyone, then walk back into class and injure themselves. Or they argue with direction, don't resolve the argument and, later that night, hurt themselves on stage. Or, feeling overused and underrated, they complain or cry about their situation to colleagues and then attend a rehearsal, only to leave hurt.

Of course not all injuries are dance related. Some are personal. But almost all injuries stem from an emotional state. If a young dancer can learn this, he might not always be able to prevent an injury but he can be aware of why he is injured and be able to heal himself physically and emotionally. Through experience he might learn to prevent injurious situations.

Healing oneself physically is easily accepted in society. Healing oneself emotionally is becoming more accepted. People are conscious of the power of the mind and believe in finding ways to help themselves. Dancers, on the whole, have always searched for spiritual development. Their true selves are exposed on stage. After glimpsing a part of their soul, they begin to look for another side of themselves. This leaves them vulnerable and when an accident occurs their vulnerability is bared again. Their spiritual development is stopped until their confidence is regained. This is emotional healing.

The healing process, physical and emotional, is conducted on an individual basis. People today generally want to take their careers into their own hands. So it makes sense that they would want to determine their own healing process as well. Dancers turn to their loved ones and friends for support, but often hide as much as possible from their company, which may not want to hear about the unhappiness of any of its members.

Large companies can be breeding grounds for complaining. What dancers do not realize is that their individual comments combine to create the atmosphere of the company. Every single employee in a group helps to create the pulse of that group. So if the group is unhappy and miserable, then it is not the fault of just one person, but of the collective whole.

So often today it is the end result, the performance, on which a company is judged. Lack of time, deadlines and pressure for success put stress on a group. There are two ways for a company to deal with this. Short tempers, yelling and exasperation are the most common reactions to the stress. Nerves and adrenaline usually save the production, but the aftermath is a lot of exhausted people. Another approach would be to make dancers feel they are a part of something important, compliment them, believe in them. The power of enthusiasm is unbeatable. The company is healthy, the dancers are happy and the audience benefits from their productivity. Excellence is achieved. This approach is seldom seen although it is not a difficult path to follow and the benefits are enormous. We need to teach ourselves a feeling of love that will produce healthy dancers by feeding their souls and creating performances the community is proud to have witnessed. Remember, each individual is responsible for helping to create or recreate the atmosphere they work in. Good luck.

DANCERS IN TRANSITION

SUZIE JARY: Dance is a profession that is time-limited because of its physical demands. It is a fragile career relative to other careers because of its short duration, particularly in regard to the time and training invested. To succeed, a dancer will usually encounter social, economic and physical sacrifices. With so much time, energy, heart, body and soul poured into becoming a dancer and perfecting their dreams, dancers have little time to consider their career's end. Facing transition is something we as dancers do not welcome; however, the reality is that there are many transitions throughout the dancer's life. Developing transition coping skills can be useful throughout the career of a dancer.

Career counseling can aid dancers in facing the transition process and coping with transitions throughout their careers, helping them manage and ideally embrace each new passage in their life's journey. The self-assessment phase of career counseling provides the opportunity for individuals to take stock of their abilities, qualities, talents, interests, skills, values and personality style. It is a process that utilizes quantitative and qualitative instruments or tools which provide the conscious uncovering of the information and self-knowledge dancers need about themselves in order to make career decisions. Armed with this information, they can begin to take charge of their career management and development. The tools that make this possible are various questionnaires, checklists, card sorts, writing exercises, sentence completions and interviews.

In helping dancers with transition, it is important to emphasize the transferable skills and abilities they develop from their training and profession. Pointing out to dancers that they have developed valuable and marketable skills that can be transferred to other fields is vital to their mind-set in approaching transition. The positive personal qualities and work-related traits and skills that dancers develop include:

- the ability to work independently or as a member of a team
- the ability to take direction
- the ability to concentrate and focus mentally
- intelligence, diligence and discipline
- dedication and persistence
- high motivation to achieve excellence by improving and perfecting skills
- flexibility and adaptability to change
- the ability to think quickly on one's feet and under pressure

- energy, stamina and an engaging physical presence

This added self-knowledge empowers dancers with a new way of looking at both themselves and the possibilities for their future. Dancers often are blind to their own unique abilities and take them for granted. Limited knowledge of other work environments contributes to the dancer not realizing their capabilities are marketable and transferable. Instead of the inaccurate self-appraisal, "I have no skills," dancers can claim and take ownership of their "soft" or adaptive skills which will help them feel more hopeful and increase their belief in their ability to succeed in a new arena.

At Career Transition For Dancers in the United States, as well as at the other three existing transition centres throughout the world, we consistently observe that dancers returning to school and working in a wide variety of new fields continue to be high achievers and outstanding performers. Dancers are a valuable resource in the world of work and refocusing their work-related traits and characteristics to new arenas benefits society.

My direct experience working with professional dancers for close to six years, along with my knowledge of career development and psychological and social factors, and my own personal career transition experience, have motivated me to create a framework and organizing tool to help dancers manage the transition process. This "tool for transition" is a visual model of a flower with twelve petals. The representation of a flower is a common device used in career counseling and visual representations of concepts are engaging and can be particularly so for visually oriented artists such as dancers. Key aspects of a person's life and work are labeled on each petal. These aspects or areas emerged as significant from my interaction with dancers and the particular challenges they can encounter in transition. I have entitled this model, "The Petals and Possibilities of My Life" and the areas labeled on each of the petals are:

- dance (or one's art or creative work)
- short-term income producing work
- taking charge of money

- interest, exploration and connecting
- long-term career planning
- education and retraining
- personal supports
- leisure and play
- relationships
- family
- self-nourishment and renewal
- personal growth and development

This tool for transition has aided dancers to visually and consciously identify where their life is out of balance. It can help them see where energy may need to be directed to create a sense of control in their life. Within this framework are areas on a personal level that can allow the individual to nurture and sustain themselves while in the process of change, thus lessening the impact of stress. Attention to these areas can contribute to life/work balance and allow the dancer to create a multi-faceted life. As an organizing tool it identifies what components are necessary to prepare for eventual career transition from dance. The areas represent ways that an individual can provide for their present situation and start to create possibilities for their future.

These areas can be useful to acknowledge whether the transition is one from a dance career to another career or, during a freelance career, from one project to the next. Also, these areas can be useful and significant in the case of a dance student transitioning to the professional level. They could also be applied to a dance company member looking to grow and move within the ranks of the company. Taking charge of these career and personal elements is a pro-active approach and can help to enhance artistry, create career longevity, promote a satisfying personal life and provide awareness for creating options for future opportunities.

An illustration of how the model can be useful is personified by the life of one female modern dancer, age 30, and single, who relocated to New York from France. The dancer had experienced a successful modern dance career for more than eight years. A personal relationship had precipitated her move to New York. At this point in her life, the study of acting had become her artistic passion in place of "dance." She was babysitting for "short-term, income-producing work," and had "taken charge of her money" in order to take a video-editing course to create a higher paying and more creatively challenging line of income-producing work.

The dancer's "interest and exploration and connecting" was related to her video-editing job search and to her "long-term career plan" of working with children in a health care profession such as physical therapy. She was open to speaking to people about these careers and researching educational programs. In regard to the "education and retraining" aspect, she was also committed to continued training in acting and to a desire to have acting engagements be a part of her life. Her education and retraining had already encompassed her acquiring skills in video-editing.

The "personal supports" petal represented the organizations and professionals that helped her with the practical matters in her life, including physicians and massage therapists, an attorney for her immigration issues and organizations such as Career Transition for Dancers which served as a support structure and resource for her. The dancer had established "relationships" and friendships with individuals in her acting class and the family for whom she babysat. She also had recently started dating after ending the initial relationship that brought her to New York. She had frequent contact with her "family" and spent time with her sister who had recently had a baby. Taking walks, writing in her journal, exploring spiritual beliefs and practices, and occasional dance and yoga classes, was how the dancer attended to her "self-nourishment and renewal." For "personal growth and development," this dancer was in ongoing psychotherapy to gain deeper insight into her attitudes and behavior.

As one can see from my description of this dancer's life, she is particularly industrious, focused and hard working, the common profile for most dancers. The one petal that has yet to be discussed in this dancer's life is "leisure and play." In a counseling session, as the dancer and I discussed searching for a job with her newly acquired skill in video-editing, coping

with the overwhelming stress of making changes became the topic. I introduced "The Petals and Possibilities of My Life" into our conversation. The model visually helped her to organize and focus on all the parts of her life. Seeing the model, she readily identified that she rarely included leisure and play in her life. The process pinpointed where she needed to direct some attention and energy in order to balance her life and cope optimally. Seeing the flower model with "leisure and play" included on it gave her permission to see "play" as an acceptable and even necessary component in a whole life and in managing the transition process.

The flower model also had an empowering effect on this dancer. Seeing all the different petals with their accompanying labels she could visually identify and affirm all the actions she had taken. The dancer was confronted with the realization that despite the ambiguity and slow process of transition, she was "on the path" and had accomplished much. Her sense of competence and self-esteem was enhanced from gaining this self-knowledge. At the end of the counseling session the dancer appeared in a lighter and more energetic mood. She stated that she felt more hopeful and believed she could persevere in this new job search. She had this to say about the flower model: "It helped me to become more aware of all the different areas of my life and allow each of them some room. I have a tendency to forget about leisure and play. Visualizing it made me think that I had to consciously make some time for that and that it was OK to play. The flower also somehow made concrete my accomplishments. I could look at it and think, good, now I have a little bit of everything I need in my life. I would remember things I did every week which belong to each petal. Or, I would realize that I didn't honour one or two petals this week and I would try to do it next week."

In conclusion, facing transition is an ongoing and critical part of the dancer's life. It can be manageable. Providing financial resources, support, information and tools for transition can assist dancers with the opportunity to have fulfilling careers in dance and in their lives after dance. As a global community that is interested and committed to advancing the health, well-being and excellence of dance and dancers, attention to the whole individual and to all stages of the dancer's life is vital in accomplishing those objectives.

Career Counseling Concepts for the Transitions in a Dancer's Life

These concepts can be useful for career management and career development within the transitions in a dancer's career. They are applicable when making the transition from dance student to professional, and during the professional career from one company to another or when freelancing, and also for post-performing career transition:

1. Assess or take stock of yourself: strengths, talents, traits, qualities, characteristics, abilities, knowledge, skills, values, needs, personality style and interests.

2. Explore options and gather information by reading, talking to people and getting an experiential sense of the option. (Observe, take a class, apprentice, internship, volunteer.)

3. Clarify a direction and create an action plan, setting short-term and long-term goals.

4. Engage in life long learning, continuing to upgrade and acquire new skills and knowledge.

5. Develop pro-active job search skills and create dynamic self-marketing materials.

6. Participate in a peer to peer encounter to ensure a "suitable match" and a "good fit" between yourself and the repertory/artistic director/choreographer or employer/client.

7. Engage in career management in the new position or endeavour to make adjustments as needed.

8. Perform career development to stay attuned to one's professional and personal growth by asking, "What is next for me?" and continuing to assess, make plans and set goals.

The Dancer
as Athlete

Photograph on previous page:
Dancers: Christopher Body and Greta Hodgkinson
Ballet: *One Hundred Words For Snow*
Photographer: Andrew Oxenham

SPORTS MEDICINE
Robbart van Linschoten with Arthur Kleipool

ROBBART VAN LINSCHOTEN: There are about sixty sports physicians in The Netherlands, with thirty more in training. Established as a specialty in 1980, the training takes four years after becoming a doctor. There are sports physicians with similar training in a couple of other European countries. In the U.S., sports medicine is done by orthopedic surgeons.

What do sports physicians do? Their mission statement is to cure and care for injured athletes, legitimately enhance physical performance, provide physical fitness for the chronically ill and promote physical fitness for all, because lack of physical fitness is a risk factor for developing a lot of diseases in the Western world. Sports medical centres–which are not in hospitals–are mostly financed by local or semi-public organizations to offer care and cure for athletes. In the future, more sports medicine will take place in working hospitals so doctors can work together with other specialists and have ready access to diagnostic means. Quite a few sports physicians work for national sports organizations and are financed by the government which noticed that top athletes without medical surveillance develop a lot of problems. There are also a few sports physicians in private practice. Our patients, of course, are athletes, both competitive and recreational.

Although sports physicians are trained in both chronic and acute injuries, we are confronted with mostly chronic muscular-skeletal injuries. Injury cure and care, injury prevention, sports medical screening, exercise, physiology and training for the chronically ill are the main areas in our work. In daily practice, we perform diagnosis, treatment (trying to get the provoking factors out of the injury) and secondary prevention. This seems rather logical, but what we find is that quite a few injuries are treated on a trial and error basis. People walk in to sports physicians with injuries treated months earlier by others, when healing does not occur. We have to start over at the beginning and make a clear diagnosis. We are trained by orthopedic surgeons to know how to treat chronic injuries in a non-surgical way. We know a lot about both the biomechanical processes in the body and sports movements. We try to reduce the chance of getting re-injured in the same way. About 30 percent of injuries are recidivive–the same injury at the same location–because the original injury was not cured completely.

Sports medical screening exists for athletes who are not injured to come to the sports physician so we can try to make a strength/weakness analysis based on their sport. We have to know the athlete's medical history, current health status and overall fitness as well as the specific needs of the sport. We go into the training history because a lot of injuries, especially overload injuries, occur because people are training too hard in a short time. When you know the way people train and you know their aims, you can reduce the injury risk. Checking current fitness levels involves tests for flexibility, aerobic capacity, strength, motor skills and speed. When you work as a sports physician for a highly competitive team, you do these things on a regular basis. You can talk with the trainer, talk with the coach and try to influence the training program–to advise about workload. Sports physicians also work with individual top athletes in order to prevent injuries–what we call biological overload–and thereby enhance physical performance.

In my opinion, a sports injury means time lost from performing. Under what circumstance do the injuries occur–during a class or performance? And what are the locations in the body involved? What do we know about dance injuries? I looked in the Medline (the worldwide medical and biological library) and I didn't find a lot of articles about dance. One study cited 309 injuries in 104 dancers in three years–an incidence rate of almost one per year. A study in 1989 found about half of dance injuries were acute and half were chronic injuries during half a year. This is different from sports medicine, where 90 percent of injuries are acute. There was a study done at a dance school in 1983 that found that about 85 percent of the students were injured during the school year. A study of a professional Broadway dance company found that 40 percent of the dancers were injured while performing in that company. The overall conclusion seems to be that there are a lot of injuries in the dance world and that the incidence rates are higher than in sport.

What areas are injured? There are a lot of injuries in the foot, ankle and the lower leg–especially stress fractures–and a lot of ankle sprains and joint injuries during class and performance. When we look at the similarities between athletes and dancers, we see that both are very injury prone; maybe dancers are more so. We see that overuse and acute injuries play an important role in injury rate. Dancers and other athletes are usually young. In both sports and dance there is a very high performance drive, but the artistic and physical requirements are different. Athletes have a lot of scheduled training, working to one or two peak performances a year, while dancers work on peak performances without scheduled training. I think the psy-

che of a dancer is different than the psyche of an athlete. Dancers have a different way of looking at and thinking about both their bodies and movement. In my opinion, athletes think more about biomechanics than dancers. That's why it is hard for me to explain to dancers what kind of processes are going on in their body.

COMMENT: I found it very striking when you talked about a definition of injury as time lost from performance. I wasn't at all surprised to see such a high level of chronic injury, because dancers keep going.

ROBBART VAN LINSCHOTEN: Yes, dancers keep performing. So actually, according to the sports medicine definition, they don't have an injury.

COMMENT: One way to integrate your knowledge would be to work with choreographers and dancers to bridge the gap of understanding between biomechanic movement and the movements dancers are trying to get at.

ROBBART VAN LINSCHOTEN: I think this is one of the baselines to prevent injury: the doctor must know what the dancers do from the biomechanical model to give feedback to the dancer or the choreographer. I think it is very important for dancers themselves, who work all day long with their own bodies, to really know about the basics.

ARTHUR KLEIPOOL: I think, very slowly, dance teachers are getting more into injury prevention as we get more knowledge. We have seen in certain sports that it takes awhile for sports physicians to be considered as peers able to instruct teachers. Sports physicians, not being dancers, have to instruct the dance instructor to give better instructions and some don't accept that very easily.

ROBBART VAN LINSCHOTEN: Maybe dance teachers will accept sports physicians because they know something about injury, but the physicians still know nothing about dance. In sports medicine, we have worked with athletes for years and coaches are trained by sports physicians to learn about injury prevention and exercise physiology.

COMMENT: There is also a language problem. I know when I speak with dancers, it is different than speaking with athletes. Also, athletes are not faced with the idea of how they look. I think it should be required for doctors to attend dance classes.

COMMENT: Dance is very different from soccer. We are trying to say something with our bodies—interpret a piece of music or a piece of choreography. Dance is an art form. When a dancer is dancing, they shouldn't be thinking, "Am I going to hurt my foot if I do that?" While performing, they should be thinking about the choreography and communicating to the audience.

COMMENT: I was a dance student with really bad feet, a bad turn out and a bad back. Everything was bad for me, but I have been dancing for ten years professionally. I think of all of my colleagues with bad bodies; maybe they had the mental power or the talent to overcome this too?

ROBBART VAN LINSCHOTEN: I know what you mean. I did the medical part of the Rotterdam Dance Academy auditions. Every year we checked 80 to 100 children, making a global examination to shift students with bad bodies out of the program. I could take maybe one or two children a year out of the program because I thought they were not physically fit enough for it, but most of the students are fine.

COMMENT: I truly don't understand why the dancers use art as an alibi for an unhealthy life where they can smoke and abuse their bodies.

COMMENT: I agree that change has to happen with physicians working with dancers, but physicians also need to work with the artistic directors.

ROBBART VAN LINSCHOTEN: There were times, especially when we did the auditioning for the school, when I had good discussions with the teachers.

COMMENT: I am aware that the management at Rotterdam is really taking care of the dancers. Their goal is to make the individual the best possible dancer they want to be or can be. They have a very good approach, in my opinion, to injury prevention. The same applies to the Amsterdam Academy and the National Ballet Academy.

COMMENT: I was teaching at a professional school in St. Petersburg. There are 5,000 professional dancers in Russia and more than 200,000 students. In Vienna, dancers have a very good connection with the athletes. In Germany, if you send a dance student to a doctor, he tells them they should quit danc-ing. Dancers go in with broken feet and in six weeks they no longer have jobs.

ROBBART VAN LINSCHOTEN: A sports physician knows if you put an athlete in a cast for three weeks, they are out for three months; they know there is no difference between treating a dancer and treating a soccer player or a volleyball player.

COMMENT: When I look at sports photos I am often much more excited by the physicality of the athletes than when I look at dance photos. There is an immediacy, a spontaneity and a concern with the accomplishment of a task that I do not see often in dance. I am really interested—as a dancer, choreographer and a teacher—in training that deals with body movement, rather than fitting a body into an existing form. Do sports physicians work with body therapies such as body/mind centering, craniosacral work, acupuncture and visualization? Do you look at the whole body, the whole person or do you just look at a specific part? I have students who go to a physiotherapist and they come back and say to me, he looked at my leg and that was it. Do you just give the exercise or do you really work with the dancer or athlete to find out how they do that exercise? I have students who say, well I was told to do this, and actually the way they are doing it is making their injury worse.

ROBBART VAN LINSCHOTEN: Sports physicians start with the diagnosis—the medical diagnosis—and then look for provoking factors—why the injury occurs. What we do is find functional weaknesses surrounding the injury to work on. We give advice, we give homework. And when we think things are too complex, we refer patients to the physiotherapist. The thing we do most is work on strength. In sports, a lot of injuries occur because there is such a strong difference in strength between sides. So we work to try and balance the strength on the left and right sides.

COMMENT: I have had students who have amazed physiotherapists with the speed at which they healed because they were able to bring their minds into the healing process.

ROBBART VAN LINSCHOTEN: For me this is very intangible. I try to focus on the medical, the biological—things which I can be aware of and try to influence.

COMMENT: I was very happy to hear that there is such a close link between the dance academy and the medical world. I would like to know, in your ten years in dance, which preventive measures have you implemented and have you checked on the results?

ROBBART VAN LINSCHOTEN: The most important preventive measure has been the medical auditioning for the schools and informing teachers about the strong and weak points of their dancers. When teachers are aware of the physical shortcomings of the children, they do not focus too much, for example, on improving the hamstrings of someone who has short hamstrings.

COMMENT: I was trying to get a clearer idea of what these provoking factors are. In an area such as basketball, what would you say are the provoking factors and how do you judge them?

ROBBART VAN LINSCHOTEN: We talk about the provoking factors within the person–such as flexibility, strength, former injuries–and outside the person–such as the conditions of the hall, the shoes worn and the training program.

COMMENT: What about their movement habits? Do you notice things like how they always approach the ball or the net in a certain way that might be leading to an injury or weakness?

ROBBART VAN LINSCHOTEN: We try to improve those things which are objectively not good at the moment and we try to heal the injury. The program I use also works to reduce and adjust training loads, so the body as a whole can recover.

QUESTION: Do you give this advice to the companies or the schools as well as the dancers?

ROBBART VAN LINSCHOTEN: I do. When I say to a dancer, I think it is better for you to have aqua aerobics for the next two or three weeks, they look at me strangely but they have to get used to it. Keeping up their physical condition with other kinds of movement means the injury will recover and the body will be fit at the moment they have to perform.

COMMENT: I think one of the differences between sport and dance is that sports training, most of the time, is very individual while dance training is in a group, a class where everybody does the same exercise at the same time. Can you give us ways to make more individual training to combine with class training, not outside the company, but within the company?

ROBBART VAN LINSCHOTEN: We think about this every day for athletes. In gymnastics when a girl has a knee problem and I say, don't jump for three or four weeks, she can do strength training, physiotherapy and some things in the training hall. In the Dance Academy in Amsterdam, they have a physician class especially for injured dancers and dance students with a very individual approach. There is also Pilates exercise, based on the floor barre, but unfortunately there is only one Pilates studio in The Netherlands.

COMMENT: When you work in sports you have a specific aim: there is a marathon you are going to run or there are a certain number of soccer moves you know you are going to encounter. But with dance we are constantly shifting the goalposts. How do you strengthen people when, in the course of a day, they are going to do four different styles of dancing?

ROBBART VAN LINSCHOTEN: I go back to the starting point, which is diagnosis. What is medically wrong with the structure? We try to figure out what can we do and what dancers had better not do. Then I try to find my way in the creative process. What kind of exercise can you do and what do you have to leave behind? Sometimes it is too hard. You can't expect a doctor to tell you from minute to minute what exercise or what kind of training you should do.

COMMENT: I worked as a physical therapist for eight years and I worked a lot with dancers. I noticed classical ballet, if performed well, is a very good base to get back to. I worked with people who danced in the musical *Cats* and, once they were injured, I said to them, go do classes even though they were not provided by the company. None of them wanted to do classes in the morning because they already had eight performances a week, but once they started, they were healthier.

COMMENT: This is not a medical question, it is a financial question. I just would like to know, who pays you?

ROBBART VAN LINSCHOTEN: That is a very good question because it is one of the main problems to get anything going and to keep it going. I am happy to announce that we are paid by the normal Dutch health insurance companies; all the people I know in this area understand it is important to take good care of dancers and musicians.

COMMENT: In dance companies that may not have the flexibility of second casts, there is a lot of pressure from artistic directors on doctors to get injured dancers back onstage. Where do you draw the line?

ROBBART VAN LINSCHOTEN: When we work with professional teams we have to face this regularly. For us, the bottom line is there can't be any damage to the athlete now or in the near future. Otherwise, we stand firm and say no.

ARTHUR KLEIPOOL: What works very well is to tell them that if you force the athlete to do this performance, he or she will not be able to do the next three performances.

COMMENT: One advantage an artistic director has is that there are hundreds of dancers waiting to get that job. In sports, I am sure there is a lot of competition, but the pressure on dancers is whether to heed their physician or their artistic director.

ARTHUR KLEIPOOL: I think it is very important for an artistic director to find a physician they can communicate with, preferably someone who, once in a while, comes in and does a class or at least watches, and knows the company and the teachers.

COMMENT: Coaches and athletes place a huge value on rest and recovery, whereas in dance there is no such luxury.

COMMENT: I think a lot of dancers chase after the doctors who say you can dance tomorrow.

PREVENTION OF PHYSICAL AND MENTAL OVERLOAD

Kitty Bouten and Arie Koops with Yiannis Koutedakis

ARIE KOOPS: My background is sports. I don't know anything about dance except that I like to see it. I don't want to prevent overload. Everybody knows that if you don't train because you are injured or sick, your performance will decrease. Don't start back with the same training load you had before–that doesn't work. The training today is not the same as the training tomorrow or two weeks from now because the body adapts to the training load. Dance, to me, is a really high level of sport. You have to train specifically to be a better dancer. You can't be a cyclist and then do a dance performance. It would look very bad if we got ten cyclists from the professional team and put them on stage.

When I began as a trainer, I was really glad when I could make one program, but I had ten athletes who each needed different training programs. If dancers are injured and need more muscle mass, they might do a little bit of bodybuilding training but it won't be the same program that the 110 kilo bodybuilder does. How few loads do they need to get the best performance? Nowadays we need more rest.

Training is an acute bout of intense exercise. Overload is a repeated bout of intense exercise. We need some overload but overtraining will cause the athlete to become sick or injured. But you do have to push yourself a little bit. Training is an art. What we are looking for is the optimal training load, or even a small overload.

There is an important training principle called adaptation. As we train, our performance decreases because we get tired. If I ride my bicycle for two hours at forty kilometres an hour, you can be sure that somewhere after two hours my performance will decrease. I am tired. After that I rest. If only these two happen, your performance state will be the same every time: get tired and recover. But that is not training. Our bodies are not stupid. We can adapt to anything. So, I have to train harder and harder or smarter and smarter to increase intensity and decrease volume. I can't have both for a long time. In the end, when the intensity is really high, there is your performance. But the volume is really low, because there is a lot of stress. After the performance, you can increase your volume in training again and lessen your intensity. Then you perform again. As you get used to it, you can increase the volume and the intensity.

COMMENT: This is all very nice, maybe, for sport, but it is not pertinent to dance in which we have to comply with schedules.

ARIE KOOPS: If I have a player who is injured, I immediately decrease training intensity and increase training volume. I do individual training, not team training. Everybody is not the same. It's art, not science.

COMMENT: It sounds so mechanical, as if the athlete is some kind of machine.

ARIE KOOPS: I recommend a training diary where you write down the training schedule. The dancer fills in a work scale, showing the length of time and the perceived rate of exertion. Zero is rest, lying in bed doing nothing. Ten is an extreme, intense training or a really hard performance–a lot of stress. By multiplying the two, you get your load. It is really subjective. Count your daily load for one week to establish the mean and the standard deviation. Now you can monitor your training. Watch it for a year. Then look what happens. When are dancers injured? When do they have symptoms of overtraining?

QUESTION: If sleeping is counted as zero, what about rest and recovery?

ARIE KOOPS: For me, lying in bed is zero. But if you are highly active in your head, it could be a one or a two. If I have a lot of stress in my body, even the recovery could be a high number. This is what is nice about the diary, because it records the rate of perceived exertion. Sometimes a performance could be quite easy–it could be a five. For another dancer, maybe it was a ten.

YIANNIS KOUTEDAKIS: Don't expect to learn everything about optimization now. It took the sports world about seventy years to develop it. But the message is–and I agree with the speaker here–that there is some room to incorporate these techniques into dance.

KITTY BOUTEN: If you are constantly working in front of mirrors, you are constantly confronted with your own limitations. Ultimately, I think that is what tires dancers who have very little influence on their own working situation. The training load of the dancers is determined by their number of performances. Rehearsal time is often very short. Dancing isn't just a job. It is far too hard to be just a job.

Dancers follow their work. They might change cultures every two or three years. They lack a stable social surrounding. In literature about stress, you find that being dependent on subjective norms, lack of autonomy and continual confrontation with your own limitations is very stressful. You can imagine the situation the dancer is in. When we compared the suicide and depression scale of dancers with the general population, 61 percent of the dancers scored above the general population. These mental health scores seem to be relevant to injuries. But even more important than the actual level of stress is the sensitivity to stress, measured by anxiety.

There is quite a lot of research done on the influence of stress in the workplace. The main factors are psychological job demands, such as the speed you have to work and the difficulty of your work; how much influence you have on your job; and your work support–your social support and your relationship with management. If there is low work control and low psychological demands, you get passive workers. If there is high work control and high psychological demands, then you get active workers. For example, managers work hard but they have a lot of opportunities to influence the workplace. You might be surprised, but that is a situation that doesn't give too much stress. If you have a high workload, but you feel you are in control, then you don't feel as much stress. The situation with high work control and low psychological demands also won't give you too much stress.

The last situation–the most stressful–involves low work control and high psychological demands. Where do you think dancers fit in? I think they are, for the most part, in this last situation. You probably don't want dancers who aren't sensitive to stress, because sensitivity is part of being an artist. If you chuck out your most sensitive dancers, you may be chucking out your best artists. That doesn't seem wise. The question is, how can you control the level of stress? The workload of dancers is not just physical, it is a mental workload, too. What was very clear in my research was that performing many new parts was very exhausting. So you shouldn't just look at the hours dancers are working, but also, what are they doing there physically and mentally? And that's where you can make changes in your company. There used to be a different program every night. Now companies are dancing the same program for three months, and then moving on to the next program.

Job control isn't there for dancers, but it could be. You could let a dancer decide each day whether he will follow the lesson or do another type of training. You could talk with dancers about which parts they do and how they do them in ballet. That is quite controversial in ballet companies, I think. But you shouldn't see dancers just as objects. The management of the company and the dancers should search for solutions together and create a stable environment in the company with positive group spirit to give dancers the feeling they are taken care of. Dancers who feel commitment will show commitment. If they feel less stress, there will be less injuries. I think it is worth it to put energy in that.

There is a relationship between the stages of physical overload and the stages of mental overload. In overload training, you get stronger which gives you time to recover. A real overtraining period is not just physical overload, but it is mental overload too. And that is what you see very often with dancers. I think even though they are in love with dancing they get fed up with it at the same time every now and then.

I am a physiotherapist and a manual therapist, working in private practice with two colleagues. Since 1985 I have worked with professional dancers, particularly the Introdans dancers. Recently I got my master's degree in movement science at the University of Maastricht, examining the relationship between physical activity and health. For my master's thesis I carried out research with the Introdans dancers for one season. The title of my research was The Responsiveness of the Rand Mental Health Inventory (RMHI): A pilot study to the responsiveness of the RMHI and the relationship between the RMHI score and the occurrence of injuries with professional ballet dancers.

The impression exists that mental stress plays a role in the occurrence of injuries. If this assumption is true, the phenomenon should certainly occur for dancers. Is the RMHI sensitive enough to determine changes in stress level in order to examine the relationship between mental stress and vulnerability of the movement apparatus? Does a relationship between mental stress and the occurrence of injuries exist in the research population of professional ballet dancers?

My research was conducted on a group of 21 professional dancers. To examine the sensitivity for change of the RMHI, the mean score of 0 at the start of the season was compared with the mean score on the RMHI in periods preceding a premiere (respectively 2 and 5 months later). In addition to the RMHI, the State Trait Anxiety Inventory (STAI) and the Zung Self Rating Depression Scale (SDS) were also administered. The RMHI measures mental health by means of five factors: anxiety, depression, loss of behavioural/emotional control, general positive feelings and emotional ties. The SDS measures the severity of depression. The STAI contains two parts: a "State"–part measuring the actual stress level; and the "Trait"–part measuring the sensitivity for stress. The scores on the RMHI were compared with scores on the State part of the STAI.

To examine the influence of the the scores on the RMHI on the occurrence of injuries a statistical analysis was conducted in which the next variables were concerned: the perceived physical working load, the score on the RMHI, the score on the Zung SDS and the scores on the STAI. The scores on the Zung SDS and the scores on the STAI were compared with the norm scores for these questionnaires. The RMHI turned out to be sensitive for change in mental stress. The changes on the RMHI were too large to be coincidental. Besides the changes corresponded with the expectations about the periods in which higher stress levels were to appear. To predict the chance for an injury to occur, the actual stress level as measured with the RMHI was relevant. More important to predict an injury, however, was the sensitivity for stress as measured with the Trait part of the STAI. The scores of the dancers on the questionnaires were different from what was to be expected on the basis of the norm scores for comparable populations. The examined population of dancers turned out to be more depressive, more sensitive to anxiety and to have a higher actual level of anxiety than comparable populations.

TAKING THE NEXT STEP IN BODY CONDITIONING

Roger Hobden, Sylvain Lafortune, Sarah McCutcheon, Mikko Nissinen and Betty Tate-Pineau

MIKKO NISSINEN: Physical conditioning in dance–whether it is done in training, as a hobby or as a profession–is vital. I think it is extremely important for dancers to understand what kind

83

of body they have and what their strengths and weaknesses are. Through proper ballet training, students have an opportunity to do a tremendous job of improving on their weak areas. But ballet training might stress some areas more than others and that is where the extra conditioning comes in which leads us to the harmonious, healthy body.

How do we view our bodies? How well do we really understand them? The skeletal system is moved by muscles and the nervous system makes a tremendous contribution to how we function. I learned a little bit from Eastern ways of thinking about the body–energy channels–and this opened a totally different world for me as a dancer. Of course, in professional dance, it is very sad–once you finally start to put these things together, you are too old and your body starts to give in.

If you really want to be a successful professional dancer, you have to learn how to dance, how to perform and how to take care of injuries. Injuries happen. Usually there is a reason and if you can learn from an injury, you will develop a wealth of knowledge. Everybody has to figure this out individually. There are lots of good methods that will help you such as Pilates, Gyrotonics and the White Cloud system from New York, which is built on yoga, swimming, gymnastics and ballet training. I hate to sound like a commercial, but this is the way of the future. Dancers' days are really long. It is not how much you do, but how you do it.

ROGER HOBDEN: I have never danced in my life. I am your average general practitioner with an interest in family and sports medicine, and training in osteopathic manual medicine. My comments are from a medical point of view, based on the experiences of hundreds of professional dancers and dance students from different backgrounds–both ballet and modern. Why am I seeing all these patients? Also, what about something I call the failed dancer syndrome? All of us are familiar with dancers who succeed and have magnificent careers, but how about the ones you don't hear about–the ones who struggle to make it and finally drop out? I think there are a lot of lessons to learn from these people too.

Injuries in a dance class or a choreography give us clues to correct the situation. Each case is like a puzzle that tells us if

the patient or the ballet or modern dance training is sick.

What can we do? I am finding that if there was one major change that could be brought to the dance class or the dance schedule, it would be freeing time for specific training for individual students: Is he or she very tight? Very loose? Hypermobile? Very muscular? What are his or her weaknesses? The patient should be given a very specific prescription which may be for either physical qualities such as strength, speed and flexibility or psychological needs.

SYLVAIN LAFORTUNE: I am not a scientist, I am a dancer very interested in training. I think dance training is at a crossroads right now, because we have an enormous amount of information from sports medicine, sports training and dance medicine, yet we are very attached to our traditional way of doing things. Twenty years ago it didn't matter. Now that we know more, we have a responsibility to choose to do things the way we do them. We need to state very clearly what our objective is in training–is it artistic or physical, musical interpretation or ability to meditate? I am just throwing things out, I haven't actually made a list. If strength, what kind of strength? What kind of stability? Speed? Flexibility? Cardiovascular? We need to look at everything offered to us for training and decide what will allow us to meet those objectives. I think there are things to be gained in the dance class that can be identified as part of our objective. But to me the dance class is just one tool among many including repertory, improvisation and creation. Unfortunately, I think the dance class has become the end in itself. We train in order to do nice classes. But the objective really is to dance, right? Major breakthroughs I have made as a dancer–technically and artistically–did not happen in the dance class, they came from being exposed to various choreographers.

Essentially, if we want to train more cardiovascularly, then perhaps we need to do an aerobics class twice a week. If we want to work on stretch and suppleness, we need to dedicate two hours a week specifically on that–not just five minutes at the barre. If we want to work on improvisation, then we make a specific class for that. But we can't add all these things to an already full schedule. We need to clear the table and decide what our objectives are in order to create a global training program that includes the tools that are best suited to reach those objectives.

SARAH MCCUTCHEON: Ideally one objective that we all share is optimizing performance or skill in whatever form that may take. From a physiotherapist's perspective, it is also important to consider maximizing the length of a dancer's career and trying to minimize their risk of injury as much as possible. How cardiovascularly demanding is dancers' training? What is required in their performance? It appears that training is not aerobically demanding yet performing is quite an aerobic, cardiovascularly demanding skill.

BETTY TATE-PINEAU: Fortunately, we do have a program here at the National Ballet School where we look at physical aptitudes, motor aptitudes and the dancer as athlete, trying not to compromise artistic expression. Our entire endeavour is to enhance ballet training so dancers can have that long, healthy career they have aspired to for so long. The sports sciences have been doing this for a long time and it's not rocket science. Let's not expect our dancers to dance themselves into shape. Let's condition them so they can maximize their effort in a technique class and then perform. A team of ballet staff, physiotherapy staff and body-conditioning staff all ought to be making an effort to watch and promote this athlete–this dancer–through their career.

MIKKO NISSINEN: There is a contradiction between, on the one hand, dance companies and schools who say, "OK, we want to train these dancers," and, on the other hand, people with different body types, morphologies and ways of functioning who say they want to become dancers. Have these two agendas been matched in the past? Ballet has a very strong agenda. Do all students fit? Will the school make a decision to keep a student even though we know she has terrible antiversion of the hips and outward rotation of the fibia? We have seen dancers with these problems who have had magnificent careers. At the same time, we know that this body alignment could cause an injury. There is a trade-off between how responsible the school is to accept this student, and how responsible the parents are to enter their child into this training program knowing there are risk factors that can generate problems. If we start eliminating everybody who has any potential for injury, we won't have anybody left. None of the most interesting dancers are perfect physically.

SARAH MCCUTCHEON: From a physiotherapist/medical standpoint, why are we seeing the same type of injuries year after year?

MIKKO NISSINEN: You can stand on a leg so many different ways. Sometimes with less you can achieve more, but the key is really the understanding of what the balancing activity is that this individual needs. We need awareness, knowledge and individual responsibility.

SYLVAIN LAFORTUNE: Ballet class should not become the spearhead of our training. I would like to place it equal to other tools. My mind has been blown several times in recent years. A physiotherapist told me that it is known in sports medicine that if you do the same training every day you develop chronic injury. And what are we doing? We are training the same way every day. And 60, 70, 90 percent of the dancers have chronic injuries! So, wake up! Keep the dance class, sure, but balance it out with other things, not by adding more things. I read a thesis where someone was actually trying to prove that conditioning was good for the dancer so she added more. One of the principles of cross-training is that you don't develop overuse. If you do the same class every day and add other things, you still do the same class every day–you are still overusing, plus you are getting tired doing everything. Let's be realistic. I think there is a certain amount of dance class that is necessary. How much? Some big schools are still arguing that we need two dance classes every day. We don't become dancers because of our current training system—we become dancers in spite of it. The lucky ones get through. All the others end up injured, discouraged and unmotivated. So let's talk about that success rate. We pride ourselves on the difficulty of our art. It is hard, but we wouldn't want it to be any easier.

ROGER HOBDEN: When I asked why dancers have so many injuries, I was told, "We are turning out all these famous dancers who have magnificent careers." In epidemiology, this is known as the well-work-per-effect phenomenon, meaning you have a pyramidal type of training with students coming in and leaving and coming in and leaving and what you see are the survivors who have magnificent careers. What about all the others? What happens to the dancers who can't stay in ballet? What kind of counseling should be done in ballet schools to direct drop-outs to the types of dance where they would be very proficient and would have successful careers? Failed ballet dancers don't see themselves as potentially successful modern dancers or flamenco dancers.

Betty Tate-Pineau: I am under the belief that if dancers are in shape–if they are strong enough, flexible enough and have enough power and cardio endurance–they are going to be easily able to sustain the technique training. They will be physically prepared to meet those demands. Conditioning gives you increased energy and if we increase the ability of the body, we tire it much more slowly. You don't have to be tired to be very good. You can get into shape and then perform. Class time needs to be protected so you can actually see the training's effect. If you train cardio two days a week, you are not really going to see its effect. The adaptation isn't going to be there. If you don't do strength training on a regular basis then you are not going to get stronger.

There are seasons in dance: the pre-season, the competitive season, the post-season and the recovery/transition season. We know when the hard work happens. Let's not waste our time at the beginning of the year letting students settle in. Let's get them conditioned and performing.

Sarah McCutcheon: I think one of the challenges dancers and dance educators face is that, unlike sports, dance is very complicated. A sprinter just has to run fast for a set period of time, while dancers have to gauge their physical demands. I think it is important to try and educate dancers and dance educators on the principles of training and learn from the field of sports medicine to provide dancers with the information they need to develop complementary training programs specific to their individual needs. Dancers should know how to develop a training program that best suits their needs and their demands.

Sylvain Lafortune: I think that in professional companies it is very hard to address a lot of these issues while a school has the ability to control the environment over many, many years.

It is true that dance is more complex, but it is also true that we are not trying to break records all the time. To me the whole idea of a global training program is not only to enhance performance, but also to prevent injuries and make dancers more functional. Because dance is an art form, jumping the highest you can is not necessarily going to be the statement the choreographer wants. You have music to take into consideration. You have relationships with other dancers. So the height of the jump is, at some point, adequate, and you don't need to aim at jumping higher because it is just wasted energy. Physical training needs to be taken from an injury prevention point of view. We have to stop thinking about daily training and start thinking about weekly training: we are not going to do everything every day. And maybe we can train at the end of the day?

The other thing I have learned is that pain is OK. By doing body training I have realized that you need to stress the body in order to become stronger. The body reacts to stress, and then it recuperates and gets stronger. I think it is OK for dance class to be stressful. It just shouldn't be stressful every day. In a dance class, you can work on positions to the point where the muscle aches and burns and the legs shake. But the next day, you don't even lift the leg.

Roger Hobden: I think we have to invent the physical education of dance. It doesn't exist yet.

Betty Tate-Pineau: It is curious you mentioned that because sometimes we try to sell body conditioning to our dancers here. We give them exactly that scenario of the athlete who is totally anaerobic or totally aerobic and how it is easy to train them. But in a single performance, one dancer may have to use all of those phenomena. My personal objective here at the school is to make myself redundant. The dancer can be a whole person, trained for all the demands they are facing–whether the demands are technical, physical or psychological.

Mikko Nissinen: Dancers, after their rehearsal or between rehearsals, often sit down. There is lots of damage caused by the way they sit without supporting the lower back. It is one thing to look at what we do when we are active, it is also extremely important to emphasize how to relax.

Sylvain Lafortune: It is easy to teach professionals because I am just teaching what I would like to do myself, but when it comes to training in a long-term sense, I don't know what I am doing. I think the solution is not to find one training that is going to cover everything; we need a global training program that includes a lot of different things. I don't think there is anything wrong with the dance class. This is where we learn how to dance. Training is there to maximize performance. We can rehearse without having taken a dance class. I have done it many, many times. We can dance without doing the dance class. It's possible, especially when we have very experienced dancers. The dance class becomes just a routine to get the body going.

MIKKO NISSINEN: You do pliés for twenty years as a professional dancer. If you think about them the same way in year twelve as you did in year one—my God, we are in huge trouble. You have to find new ways to explore.

ROGER HOBDEN: Ballet has two hundred years of history so there is no question it works—where do all these injuries come from?

MIKKO NISSINEN: The unfortunate thing about the learning process in ballet is that if we were to know all the things at the beginning that we know after twenty years in the profession, we would have hardly any injuries. We learn by our mistakes. We make certain errors and keep correcting them. Our knowledge is at a heightened level ten or fifteen years after we start. At day one our knowledge is very limited. It is key that we have knowledgeable teachers who hold the reins and don't do things they are not supposed to. If the foundation of the sculpture is not there and you put it up, it is going to collapse. That is why the foundation is so important. Unfortunately the way dance is learned is so complex that we are not at the advanced level immediately. We have to go very slowly.

SARAH MCCUTCHEON: I think just like any sport, ballet is obviously a very complicated skill and the ballet class is imperative. You have to practice the skill to optimize performance. Are you using the ballet class to train cardiovascular fitness as well as strength, flexibility and performance? Or, are you using the ballet class to hone your ballet skills? Also, it is a fine line between optimizing performance and injuries. Consider the principle of overload: you have to push yourself to improve,

and if you push too far you risk injury. Professional dancers are walking a tightrope.

ROGER HOBDEN: I am still confused. I see so many injured ballet and modern dancers. Is it possible the teachers are not applying properly the correct ballet principles that we are talking about? The other thing is, we are talking a lot about ballet, but what about modern dance? A lot of dancers define themselves as "ABB"–anything but ballet. They don't even want to hear the "B" word. What kind of help can we give these people? Are you saying they are lost and one day they will see the truth and come back to the fold?

SYLVAIN LAFORTUNE: Training needs have changed tremendously. The needs also change within the year. We might follow Giselle with a program where we roll on the floor and jump on our heads. But we still train the same way. Another thing, why are we still working on pliés after twenty years? I think my pliés are as good as they're going to get. Even if I could improve one tiny bit more, is that really going to change my dancing?

MIKKO NISSINEN: There is different training for different types of dance. In the ballet world every movement is based on three basic movements and one of them is the plié. We go back to those essentials every day to sharpen our knife. It is our instrument. It is not the purpose in itself. But if your knife is not really sharp, what kind of jump are you going to do?

QUESTION: Are the injuries in modern dance comparable to the injuries in ballet?

ROGER HOBDEN: One of the reasons there is much more data on ballet injuries is that dance medicine originated in ballet companies and was invented by dance teachers. Ballet, if done correctly, is one of the safest dances because everything that is dangerous and obnoxious has been discarded. You see absolutely horrific things in modern dance that result in serious injuries that are very difficult for the dancer to overcome.

SYLVAIN LAFORTUNE: In dance class, we do the hardest and most strenuous things at the end when we are the most tired and the least focused. It is the way we have been doing it for centuries. Is the structure of the class–from the pliés at the beginning to the big jump at the end–the best progression?

SARAH MCCUTCHEON: A lot of the injuries we see are because

of improper cool-downs and improper stretching. Across the board, ballet dancers do not know how to stretch properly.

MIKKO NISSINEN: There are dance schools where students receive the intellectual tools necessary to enable them to be active participants in their training. I am stunned by the statement that in ballet we have been doing this for centuries and we know what we are doing. Why does this knowledge have to be secret?

SYLVAIN LAFORTUNE: We heard how dancers are submissive. One of the first times I worked with a trainer he said, "You never give me any feedback, I never know how you are feeling about what you are doing." I thought, "I am reproducing the relationship I had with a traditional teacher who told me what to do and I did it without question. I didn't disrespect their instructions by questioning them." The danger is that we perpetuate the situation with choreographers and company directors. Essentially we do what we are told to do. It is very, very critical for us to speak up on banal subjects as well as very important ones like, "I feel tired today, maybe I will take it easy." How can we say that without disrespecting the master?

BETTY TATE-PINEAU: In gymnastics, it is a given that you do two hours of conditioning and then you go to work on your technical. In ballet, students still ask me, "Why do I need to do this? Why do I need a strong core?" That connection isn't as strong as perhaps we would like it to be. Also, all gymnasts have an incredibly strong upper body as well as lower strength and stability. Dancers, especially female dancers, often have an upper body that can't support even their own weight. When they get to partnering, it can often get precarious. There is a perception that strength and size are synonymous and they are not. You can be very, very strong without looking big.

SARAH MCCUTCHEON: I think the first quantitative studies on aerobic fitness in dancers happened in the early 1980s. Dancers were tested during training and then again during rehearsal and performance and there was a big discrepancy between their heart rates during training and performance. They also compared dancers to other athletes and found the dancers' aerobic capacity comparable to other non-endurance athletes. It is interesting to look at the fact that they weren't training aerobi-

cally, but they were demanding aerobic capacity during performance. There doesn't seem to be any literature on taking that one step further and developing a complementary program to train dancers aerobically and see if that training translates into either performance improvements or decreased injury.

One of the strengths of dancers that I see is that they are very conscious of the quality of movement and efficiency. They are not sweating just to sweat. Their artistic perspective is really helping them to address the complexity of movement they are able to bring to their training more than other athletes.

AEROBIC FITNESS FOR PROFESSIONAL DANCERS – THE CHALLENGE

EILEEN WANKE: During the long history of ballet, increasing demands for technical perfection and a physical ideal have led to maximum physical and mental demands on today's dancer. In order to preserve this work of art–the dancer–and to guarantee a long career, onstage injuries must be treated properly and, if possible, prevented. Studies have shown that dancers have muscle strength comparable to athletes in other types of sport. Their cardiopulmonary efficiency is similar to non-endurance athletes; however, increasingly demanding choreographies and higher requirements as to virtuosity and technical perfection require more aerobic endurance capability which could help avoid injuries and maintain working capability. How can dancers get a better endurance capability? Do we need additional endurance training?

To begin with, the demands of dancers have to be evaluated. The daily physical demands of dancers are:

• Active warm-up–This prepares dancers physically and mentally for training or work on stage (examples include stretching and passive warming-up).

• Daily exercise–Classical training is the basis for various forms of dance. It begins at the barre and continues in the centre. The elements are carried out with the right and left leg and are varied daily to avoid boredom. Average time is about 90 minutes. The exercise not only enhances coordination, it also helps to correct faults and prepare the body for demands in rehearsals and performances. Daily exercise should be the best protection from injuries.

• Rehearsal—Dancers acquire new and known choreographies.

• Performance—Dancers do not like to run because their muscles have changed over the years. Besides, additional sport after daily training is often avoided due to a higher risk of injury because the movements are either not what dancers are used to or they counteract dance movements. Lack of time could be another reason. And, very often a dancer's contract does not allow additional sports activities.

But dancers need specific endurance training integrated into their daily training.

When I discussed endurance training with dancers of the ballet company, they thought immediately of running, swimming, cycling and endless cinder tracks. What a torture, some remembered, and I felt guilty because I couldn't promise endurance training without torture. What I could promise was a dance specific endurance training. No cinder track, no Nike shoes. I would use their well-known studio, their training shoes and their own music. The only strange things were the methods to register the development such as blood lactate acid. Some dancers said that was the torture.

A complete ballet company consisting of twelve dancers was tested. Their daily training was changed and the effects on their physical efficiency were observed during a four-week-period. Questionnaires were completed by the dancers before and after the measuring phase to collect spontaneous and emotional statements as to the expectations and effects of the four-week modified training.

The aim of the modification was to minimize breaks between the exercises because former studies had shown during breaks (approximately 50 percent of the total training time) resting heart rates were reached. Changes included introducing new elements differently and choosing elements that were easy to remember to avoid losses in the performance, technical skills, and concentration. These modifications resulted in relatively long practice phases with shorter breaks aimed at a non-stop

training. Very dynamic and space-requiring step combinations were not executed in the centre, allowing as many dancers as possible to perform at the same time and keeping breaks at a minimum.

Field test (choreography): A 3.30-minute-long dance choreography, done by Ricardo Fernando, the leading choreographer of the Bremerhaven Ballet and the Chemnitz Ballet (both in Germany), was worked out to test the effects of the modified training. Due to the type of music and speed and dynamic of the step combinations, this choreography was within the maximum intensity range for male and female dancers. The choreography itself was danced after the regular training under comparable conditions at the beginning and end of the study; it was not danced in the middle of this study to prevent effects on the heart rates by getting accustomed to it.

Procedure of investigation: Heart rates were registered during the choreography and the modified training elements by mobile test equipment consisting of a transmitter with elastic chest belt and a receiver worn on the wrist. At the same time, the movements of the dancers were recorded in writing. Furthermore, measuring of the blood lactate acid was directly carried out by a mobile testing unit during the modified training as well as after the choreography. Care was taken to ensure that the times of the investigations were comparable. By measuring the blood lactate acid and heart rates before and at the beginning of the modified training, it was possible to determine a maximum training intensity (aerobic/anaerobic) for this dance company.

Findings: As in former studies the training intensity rose considerably with increasing length, but because of the modifications, a drop of heart rates to resting level seldom happened as a result of the shorter breaks. A decrease of the heart rate level was clearly recognized with dancers who had regularly taken part in the modified training. Under identical conditions the average maximum heart rate of the male dancers was higher before this study and dropped four weeks later. The same development was registered with the female dancers. A decrease of the heart rate level could signify an increase of the physical capacity, if physical engagement and conditions are identical. The results of measuring blood lactate acid also showed a decrease as an effect of the program.

Discussion: Classical training is the basis for various types of dance and prepares dancers for rehearsals and performances, therefore, it should give the best protection from injuries. Former studies have shown that anaerobics may lead to early exhaustion and a loss of concentration which might increase the danger of getting injured. This usually happens in phases of training with allegro and grand allegro jumps that require a high degree of physical coordination.

As the findings of this study show, it is easily possible to achieve subjective and objective improvement of the physical capability of dancers by modifying daily training without additional time or costs. Under identical conditions, that is to say motivation and time, there was a distinct drop in heart rates. Seven of ten dancers made positive comments about the modified training in the questionnaires and considered themselves physically fitter at the end of this study. They found rehearsals and performances less exhausting and less physically demanding. Although this study was carried out at the end of a season when dancers usually suffer from burn-out syndrome, they experienced a subjective increase of their capability.

It cannot be excluded that non-dance specific endurance training such as swimming, cycling or running affects muscle flexibility over the years and develops unwanted muscles, particularly in the upper thighs. Furthermore, it is difficult to add traditional endurance training to the daily demands of dance. Integrating endurance training in daily training, however, offers the possibility to enhance the physical capability in a dance-specific way.

A dancer's career involves considerable physical demands and hard work. That can also be said of endurance training; whether it is dance-specific and integrated in the daily training or carried out after daily work is not important.

The decision to improve the physical capability of dancers in order to prevent injuries is to be aware of the connection between physical capability and susceptibility to injuries. A dance-specific integrated training to enhance aerobic endurance in a well-known training location could help make the walk to the cinder track or the fitness studio redundant for dancers and thus contribute to minimizing injuries and guaranteeing a long career on stage.

GENDER DIFFERENCES

YIANNIS KOUTEDAKIS: I have a background with one foot in sports and the other in dance. Despite the fact that I've heard from dancers they are different, they have the same bodies, unfortunately, as athletes. They have the same muscles, the same heart and the same liver. Looking at a dancer and an athlete, you will see very few differences as far as the physiology is concerned. The difference is the outcome–the technique. I am not a dance teacher and I'm not going to talk about that at all.

What I do is similar to what we call the MOT in England. This is a test to ensure the engine of a car is properly running and that its safety system is working properly. I do MOT tests on dancers. Of course, it is still up to the driver–in this case, the dancer and the dance teacher–to get a good performance out of the engine. What I am looking at is the engine itself.

The other thing I've heard, of course, is that dance has a great tradition and it is difficult for it to change. I come from a sport called rowing which was described by Homer in the prehistoric ages. Rowing is still more or less the same. Talking about tradition in dance is, of course, very important. But we have to be careful, because there are other physical activities which are more traditional and much older than ballet, which started only one hundred and fifty years ago.

But having said that, I am now back in Greece after working for nineteen years in England. Originally, the Olympics included drama, dance and sports. For some reason we kept the sports and forgot the other two elements. My job is to reinstate dance into the Olympics. I don't know how successful I will be.

I am trying to see what the differences are between the two genders–the two sexes–as far as fitness and exercise. And of course, talking about fitness and exercise, we are talking about dance as well. I hope you agree dance is a physical activity, at least. What we have seen, at least in this century, is that women have shown more than twice as much progress as men. Based on this data, we can make a prediction that after sixty or seventy years, most of the world records–at least in sport–will be held by women. Fortunately I'll be dead by then, so I won't see it. Of course this is not true, because although women have had a great increase, we are now approaching a plateau. We are facing a disaster in terms of world athletics.

What does this mean? Athletes have evidence; there are world records that can be measured from year to year. And the differences between the sexes are becoming smaller. We don't have the same in dance. In dance we know you cannot measure things. And women are now back in action–that was not the case in the previous century–and that affects dance as well as other sporting activities, even rowing. We now have women performing bodybuilding events and trying to match men. Are these increases in female levels of physical performance–and I'm talking about all kinds of physical performance, including dance–the result of better training methods? Are training methods better now? At least in dance, I say, no. Is the female engine better? I say the answer is yes. The female engine adapts very quickly. Women have shown a dramatic improvement in the past century. Is that the result of changes in society? Again, I would say yes. A hundred or two hundred years ago, it was unthinkable for a woman to do things other than cooking and reading and things like that. Now that has changed, of course. But at the same time–and this is something that we need to remember–while women were sitting at home and doing all the work there–all the wonderful cooking and the housework, men were required to be heroes, fighting and chasing the animals to bring home some food. That was a form of exercise. So over the years, men became bigger and stronger, partly as a result of physical exercise that it was not possible for women to do. We find that now, as women get back into action, the differences between men and women are beginning to disappear. God knows what is going to happen.

What we are going to do, therefore, is start to answer these questions. Let's consider size and skeletal differences between the two genders. Are there any differences? What sort of dif-ferences can we see? Should we treat a male and female dancer the same, as far as physiology is concerned? I would say, yes. The difference is in the outcome. It's like rowing and swimming: although the outcome is different, the training methods–not the technique–of rowers and swimmers are very much the same. The technique of dance is something you are much better equipped to talk about.

Let's see a few of these differences that affect physical performance. It is easy to understand that size is important. You cannot have, for example, a basketball player who is one metre tall. Equally, you cannot have a gymnast who is two metres tall. So size and skeletal difference do affect physical performance. And girls actually grow faster and, I would say, earlier than boys. There are lots of reasons for that, but don't worry about them. We need to know that girls grow earlier compared to boys. This is very important. Growth means changes in the mechanics of the body, changes to the relationships between forces that apply to muscles and bones. So growth is normally related to lost or disturbed techniques. We see that in sports. Swimming is a very good example. With both boys and girls, but specifically with girls, the shape of the body changes and the dynamics of the friction of the water change dramatically–within a month or less. A girl thinks, "I used to beat this girl, now she beats me!" Of course, she thinks she must leave the sport. It is up to us–up to the teachers–to explain to these girls, "Don't worry, this is part of your natural development and things will become easier and better later on." For some reason the average man is 175 cm and the average woman is 163 cm. As far as the skeleton itself–men have broader shoulders. Now we have a practical problem. Women having smaller shoulders means they have less muscle in the upper body area. Having less muscle mass affects their final strength. So women are, perhaps at the moment, not very good for lifting heavy weights or, in a dance performance, lifting another woman or a man. But men, in theory, have this ability because they have broader shoulders and that means they have more muscle mass and therefore more strength. It is easier for them to do a lifting performance. Men also have relatively longer arms and women have broader pelvises. While it is of course very good for reproductive purposes–sometimes in dance performance this may lead to some problems.

Another aspect that is different in men and women is body fat. For a man, 6 to 10 percent body fat is excellent–for women, it is 12 to 16 percent. In fact, this is the level women should be careful not to go below. The differences begin to appear after puberty and stay there through adulthood and then begin to disappear after the age of sixty or seventy. We have two kinds of fat: essential fat, which as the name implies is essential for a number of functions including childbearing, the functioning of the brain and the nervous system in general. All cells in the body have a membrane and this membrane has a great element of essential fat. Without it we couldn't live. And, of course, we also have storage fat. If you see the storage fat in men and women, 12 percent is the average in men and 15 percent is the average in women. Not a great difference. But 3 percent of the male's body is essential fat compared to 12 percent in women. So women have more essential fat compared to men. It is essential, because as I said it plays an important role in a number of functions including childbearing. Of course this leads to a great number of problems that women may have if they try to keep their body weight very low, as dancers do. If we dramatically lose weight, we lose fat–we also lose carbohydrates, water and muscle, but not the muscle we use for exercise. Fat is related to menstruation and the strength of the skeleton. If we have two different groups–one fasting and the other training very hard–the result is the same–the women developed problems with their periods. They began to have delays and abnormalities. Sometimes their periods disappear altogether. To begin with, only 10 percent of the group has some sort of problem. At the end of the studies, almost 90 percent of the women had some sort of problem. If you put these two aspects together–both fasting and training hard–which is the case in dance, then you have a recipe for disaster.

I used to work at the British Olympic Medical Centre. We did a lot of work with osteoporosis in women–of course dancers were a very big group. Women of eighteen and twenty years of age had skeletons similar to what you would normally see in women of sixty or sixty-five years of age. These women had one thing in common–they were very thin, very lean and very hard training individuals. So while success and artistic expression are probably improved by being lean, we have problems in terms of health.

There is a direct link between body fat and energy in women because fat conserves energy. If we eat something and we don't use it, the body converts that energy into fat and saves it for future use. The reason? Two or three hundred thousand years ago, men and women were not able to eat every day. They would eat a lot when they had food and store the extra energy as fat in order to use it during periods when there was very little food. We can't change thousands and perhaps millions of years of evolution in a hundred or two hundred years. The role of this extra fat that we see in women is to make sure they are able to bring a pregnancy to a successful outcome, so there is enough energy for the unborn baby to develop and be born. When women try to be very lean, and this extra fat becomes less and less, the body knows they do not have enough energy to become pregnant. The result is a message that says, "Don't produce more eggs." Then, you don't have periods. Somebody may say, "OK. That's excellent." But the side effect is loss of bone and bone strength. As we see girls becoming more involved with energy-demanding activities, they are using more fat and there is a delay in menarche. When we tested a group of dancers in London, we saw very quickly they were very good as professional dancers, but not fit at all and of course, they had very little fat. While their height was average, their weight was not. We asked, do you have normal periods? Yes? Well, carry on. No? Well, let's talk about it.

Safety
in
Dance

Photograph on previous page:
Company: IT Dansa - Jove Companyia de l'Institut del Teatre
At: Holland Dance Festival
Photographer: Ros Ribas

HEALTH, WELL-BEING AND SAFETY IN DANCE COMPANIES

Els Frankhuijzen, Barbara Leach and Toine Schermer

TOINE SCHERMER: As a dance company doctor, I deal with injuries and illnesses that interfere with the work of dancers. It is clear to me that my duties should also include preventative health advice. When I started offering regular medical check-ups, very few dancers used this opportunity in part, I think, because they had little influence on the factors stressing their health. So in 1983, I set up an occupational health and safety service company here in Holland with a number of colleagues from other disciplines, in order to provide advice directly to dance companies rather than to individual dancers. We specialize in the performing arts including dance companies, orchestras, musical productions, theatres and so on.

Since 1996 in The Netherlands, as a result of European legislation, the Working Conditions Act requires all employers to pursue a policy that aims to provide a healthy and safe work environment and promotes the welfare of employees who must not sustain damage to their health as a result of carrying out their work. Every organization in The Netherlands is obliged to draw up an activity plan aimed at preventing conditions that can lead to health damage. It must be clarified who in the organization is responsible for doing what. In order to chart all the factors that can affect the health of dancers, we have developed a risk inventory of working conditions and specific health risks for dancers in companies. My colleague, Els Frankhuijzen, who has been involved in drawing up the risk inventory for very different dance companies will tell you about the method for working with such an inventory and also about the kind of pressure points we have encountered in various companies.

ELS FRANKHUIJZEN: My everyday work consists of advising clients in very different types of organizations with regard to safety, health and welfare at work. I also carry out regular studies mainly to optimize conditions on the work floor. Before I start, it is very important to have commitment from staff and dancers. One of the most important instruments for optimizing working conditions is a **Risk Inventory and Assessment (RI&A)**. We develop special questionnaires in Dutch and English for the dancers, we interview dancers and staff, and we do desk research in order to inventory all the occupational risks that exist. Then we draw up an activity plan for the next year to optimize working conditions.

What do we look at? We start by checking present safety, health and absenteeism policies. What is written down? How is the organization working? We also look at how the dancers appear. What are the intentions of the company? Do they think of health and safety? Are they providing a nice company for the dancers? We look at the general facilities—the floors, the dancers' experiences with the floors, the dressing rooms, showers and other facilities such as gyms and swimming pools, the stages and the wings. We consider the noise exposure, the lighting, the climate and the complaints dancers have. Also, maybe the most important, we look at the physical stress of the dancers. We look at how they are trained to avoid unnecessary physical stress. How are their classes carried out? How much time does someone have to train and learn something new? And of course, we ask dancers about their physical stress on an individual basis, how much input every individual can have in his or her work and what the company offers as extras for employees. We also look at hours worked and agreements that exist on traveling time, etc.

By checking all these points, we get a complete overview of the working conditions and use this to determine if it is acceptable according to legislation as well as the staff and dancers. Necessary changes are itemized on activity plans. In The Netherlands, every company has to adjust their yearly activity plan based on this list of designated improvements.

There are five main conclusions we drew based on the RI&A we did on organizations which did not pursue a policy whereby the safety and health of the dancers was guaranteed, both on and off the stage. We found that the internal communication was insufficient, especially if we compared it to other companies we work for. There was a lack of individual coaching, career development and annual reviews. This needs to be improved—more like a social policy. We encountered a lot of complaints about the floors. Often they were too hard and there were also problems with sloping floors that frequently caused injuries to knees, ankles and backs. Maybe the sloping floor is nice for the audience, but for the dancer it is a disaster. Another point is safety, in particular the safety of the stages and everything that is behind in the wings where minor accidents or near accidents often happen. Finally, and I don't think this is a surprise, the physical stress for dancers is very high, leading to injuries or extreme fatigue. Pain is not something that is normal. Maybe a little, but not every day.

Optimizing working conditions is only possible if staff

and dancers cooperate in the whole process. It is their work, not mine. If there is no commitment, there is no point in starting the process.

COMMENT: We can talk about these problems as much we like, but the person who really has all the control—both from the point of view of jobs and psychological control—is the dance director.

TOINE SCHERMER: The administrative director, most often responsible for personnel, work environment, and so on, is usually our entree into the company. It is important to get his or her commitment first. But if the artistic staff is not committed to the process and remains focused on the production and not the people, then it is harder to get things done. To me, if the artistic director has dancers who are motivated and feeling that he is supporting them, then he has better material to work with.

ELS FRANKHUIJZEN: We have to get optimum—not ideal—working conditions. Is there a conflict? No? OK, that's fine. If there is a conflict, then what are we going to do? In other types of industries we work with norms. For dancers, or other performing arts, it's different. You have to make your own acceptable norms for your company.

COMMENT: You put commitment as the top priority and the commitment has to come from the relevant person. Dance U.K. and an organization called The Healthier Dancer have given advice and lectures. These have interested me because I want my dancers to be healthy and to give me a company I can maintain. What happens when you find out a company is dancing on dangerous stages? What can you actually do?

BARBARA LEACH: Just to clarify, there are very few companies that have a resident theatre in The Netherlands, so it is always a question of touring around. Inspectors are becoming stricter in theatres about safety standards.

COMMENT: It's the same in England, definitely. There are very few established, funded companies in England. And dancers will work under the most appalling conditions because they are so committed to what they do. But we all surely agree that this is not the future. For twelve years, I worked with a medium-sized, established dance repertory company. We found the risk of injuries was very high because we had such different demands from one choreographer to another. This was a really active concern. A physiotherapist said to me, "Of course your company is going to be very prone to injury because you have such different physiques." So that started me thinking about how to optimize the workload. We shortened the working day and we got just as much done. You know, we are talking about safety and we are talking about floors, but the physical language can be equally risky. Sometimes I have to tell a choreographer, "I don't think you should ask someone to do things three times on their head." There is a lot of new information about fitness training and stamina building that I find really fascinating. For me it is liberating. It allows you to know more about your craft and your job and therefore about your art.

COMMENT: I am a senior dancer with the Royal Ballet, so in some ways I'm coming from the other end of this–I'm coming from the bottom, not the top. It seems to me we have another option, which is to make the dancers make the difference. I know it is difficult: I've been there and I've done it–not wanting to say things because of my career. But in the end, if it is not going to come from the top, then the dancers have got to do it. As a group we have an enormous amount of power. We don't have to pout, we don't have to bang our little pointe shoes down, we just have to say no.

COMMENT: I have a company of ten dancers now–my own company–and they all have check-ups from the top down with an osteopath who does a medical summary when they join as part of their contract. It is a simple procedure so we don't inadvertently take someone with a real structural weakness that is going to be a problem. But it also has proven to be much more fruitful because the written report, which goes through all their weaknesses and strengths, is shared with the dancer so it actually makes them think a little bit about why I've given them a job. It tells them what is strong about their dancing as well as what it is we need to work on. I think they know that I'm not going to sack them if they complain.

BARBARA LEACH: Els, have you encountered a difference in communication problems between big and small companies?

ELS FRANKHUIJZEN: The size of the company doesn't matter, it is how staff and dancers think about these kinds of issues.

TOINE SCHERMER: There are fewer problems if staff nourish the individual capacity of dancers. This happens more in modern companies (where individual expression is given more importance) than in classical companies where you have to fit into the classical image unless you are the soloist.

COMMENT: I'm the artistic director of the Swedish Ballet School. If we start teaching children in a less abusive way, giving them more say and more responsibility, then, when they go into companies, they will have learned that they have a right to be more active. If we are going to end up with a better situation in twenty years, we must change our teaching now.

TOINE SCHERMER: I think this is very true. It takes time, but it is very productive. We'll have more success in the long run if we aim at the schools rather than aiming now at the artistic directors.

COMMENT: I think communication and commitment apathy is the strongest disease that we as teachers have to deal with. Even at an early age, a child can take responsibility for a weakness or a strength in his or her body, and of course the responsibility can be increased within the training as the student gets older. Verbal skills–ability to choose and have an opinion–can also be built into the training.

QUESTION: One of the five high risk points was physical stress. Is it possible to measure mental stress? Sometimes when I come to the National Ballet, I can feel the mental stress, it is so high.

ELS FRANKHUIJZEN: The risk inventory we talked about is a general investigation. If you want to focus on mental stress, well-being, we conduct a special investigation.

TOINE SCHERMER: If a company does not commit itself to doing something with the results, then it is better not to start an investigation of work stress. It is easier to work on physical things like floors, lighting or climate than it is to work on things which contribute to work stress such as communication, organization, the leader's role, the direction and so on.

COMMENT: The dancer wants to survive today. Tomorrow they may get an injury and won't be able to dance anymore. The artistic director wants to get the program on the stage. Maybe tomorrow there will be no funding for the company. How do we get past the stumbling block of only thinking about today and start planning for our dancers' situation ten years or twenty years from now?

TOINE SCHERMER: I think artistic directors with a broader view have companies that will flourish. Maybe that is something for the boards to take into account when they appoint their artistic directors.

COMMENT: What we need is a realistic time-scale of achievement because dancers live in the here and now. Maybe everything is a little too immediate. We are a touring company and we go to a lot of different locations and encounter conditions that we can't do anything about immediately. For example, even if there is a really archaic heating system and it's too cold, we've still got to put the show on, although we know that if we are going back to the same theatre next year, we can warn them in advance that it's too cold. In five years, the theatre finally realizes they have an archaic heating system that they have to improve. If we set ourselves a time-scale that says in five years, I expect all these theatres to be upgraded, the present conditions in those theatres won't depress us so much.

COMMENT: In Britain, the dancers' union spokesman has said, "We are not performing tonight unless you put the bloody heating on." You can do something about it. If you haven't got a company stage manager who knows that the stage has to be warm for class, they're not going to apply the right sort of pressure until it's too late.

TOINE SCHERMER: The dancer has such a short career and he has to do everything in a very short time. But staff and others in the company must have a broader view.

ELS FRANKHUIJZEN: Here in Holland, the theatres are checked by labour inspectors as well as their own people. We have started to work with standard contracts based not only on money, but also on circumstances. The theatre has a responsibility and I know that the legislation for theatres has become stricter in recent years.

QUESTION: If a company had on its staff a guidance counselor who would not reveal or betray any specific information but might make general recommendations to management, would the dancers speak with the counselor?

COMMENT: We do have that and yes, the dancers do confide in the counselor. The counselor also helps dancers deal with stage fright and recovering from injuries.

QUESTION: How do you interest a doctor in dance? The doctors in Germany don't know anything about dance.

COMMENT: There is an organization in Germany made up of doctors who used to be dancers which just started a couple of years ago. They would love to hear from dancers and dance companies. I think it is a very important thing, especially in central Europe where we are a little bit behind in a lot of these things.

BARBARA LEACH: To paraphrase a comment made earlier, the health of the dancers is more interesting to see on stage than some kind of strange pyrotechnics in the set.

COMMENT: We are talking about the future when we are talking about the health of the dance company. Dancers must think beyond the here and now. Choreographers have to think the same way–for their work and for their workers.

SUCCESSFUL IMPLEMENTATION OF PREVENTION

CHRÉTIEN FELSER: I am a generalist working as a designer of post-graduate education for consultants of all kinds, but especially those in occupational health services. I have never done anything for dancers or dance companies, so I know very little about your working conditions. What I do know a lot about is how changes in working conditions at companies and branch organizations occur.

I don't think about my work as a job. I think about it as a profession. Dancers also don't think about their work as a nine-to-five job. It is a profession done out of a passion and dancers have a special relationship with the organization they work with. For instance, my organization is a small foundation that provides education for consultants. For me, it is a stage on which to perform. I think the organization is as much dependent on me as I am on it. I think that also might be the case for professional dancers who set their own goals in life, in their career. They need an organization–a dance company–to provide the stage, but dance companies are also dependent on dancers for results. Like me, dancers think of their work in terms of quality of product and the satisfaction of customers or the public. It is never enough. When I think about my work, I can always think of improvements. When I was a manager of professionals, I had a different point of view: the quality of product was still important, but it was also important to facilitate professionals to perform with excellence. Also, I had an organization to run with other performance standards. The manager of a dance company also has to watch financial results, time resources and a limited number of personnel. Good health is an asset for a professional dancer. You can't do without it. But for the finance manager, good health has an economic value, because health and safety influence time resources. When dancers get sick, you have to hire replacements and change choreography, which costs a lot of money, time and energy. Also, due to changes in legislation around health and safety, the costs of absenteeism, disability and sick leave are now the responsibility of the organization. How much does this loss of health, time and personnel cost? Is it worthwhile to invest in prevention to gain back this kind of loss?

I think it is necessary to look for a win-win relationship between finances and quality-capital management and professionalism in a dance company. In Holland we have a working population of six million people with an average absenteeism of almost 6 percent. Every day, 350,000 people are at home–absent, sick or otherwise. Eighty percent of them are back at work within a week, the rest pinball first to occupational health, then to commercial health care or public health care and then maybe to Reintegration Service, where caseworkers try to shorten the time that people are off. After nine months, they are eligible for social security and, after one year, they are either back at work or in a disability scheme. There are over 900,000 people on disability in Holland, which is 15 percent of the whole working population. Every year, 1.5 per-

cent of the absentees, or forty to fifty thousand workers, come into disability schemes; fewer are coming out again. The total cost of this to society is almost six billion Euros, some of which might be gained back by investing in prevention.

Most absenteeism and disability is caused either by physical or psycho-social factors; they are almost in balance. Does this apply to dance companies as well? Is there an average of 6 percent absenteeism, 1.5 percent disability and a balance between physical and psycho-social disability? There are no figures for dance companies in Holland, which is a pity, because this means you can't calculate the costs, making it difficult to decide about investments to reduce those costs.

When we talk about prevention, what do we mean? There is usually a distinction between prevention that is directed towards individuals or groups of individuals and prevention that is directed toward the work environment and the organization. The other distinction is between primary prevention (when we try to eliminate or modify the source of the risk), secondary prevention (when we can't do anything about the source but we try to eliminate or reduce the effects on health and safety) and tertiary prevention (which occurs when the damage is already done–people are sick, absent or whatever–but we try to prevent it from getting worse through treatment, coaching, reintegration and control).

In my opinion, education and health promotion is primary prevention. We spend a lot of money, expertise and personnel trying to make things better but more time, money and expertise is spent on control, treatment and reintegration after the damage is done. Doctors, physiotherapists and counselors are all dealing with tertiary prevention because to prevent dancers from getting sick and injured, you have to do things within the company.

COMMENT: I think we all agree that when dancers are injured, they often feel completely abandoned by their employer.

CHRÉTIEN FELSER: This is not specific to dance companies, but I can imagine it is more of a fear, because dance contracts are not very long. If dancers had more permanent contracts, the dance companies would feel more responsible for reintegration of dancers who get sick or injured.

COMMENT: My experience is that dancers are often blamed for the injuries they incur.

COMMENT: Sometimes you get punished when you come back.

CHRÉTIEN FELSER: Don't be afraid if the main reason for change is financial or labour scarcity or quality of results. Look for prevention from within the company, not outside.

COMMENT: I think it comes back to how big the company is and how much money it has. I worked for a company where if you were injured, they kicked you out. They didn't care.

CHRÉTIEN FELSER: But when the costs go back to the companies–which is happening in Holland now because companies have to pay for one year's sickness and possibly ongoing disability–those in charge of financial management start thinking, hey, let's look at prevention. All these people in Holland who get sick for psycho-social reasons–burnout and depression–go to the company doctor who sends them to public health care or commercial health care for very effective cognitive behaviour therapy with very good results. People get back to work faster. But what happens when I put one person on the right track and I shove them under the curtain and the same thing happens again? Sometimes the first person gets stronger, but another one of his colleagues gets ill. There has to be some connection between the tertiary prevention, the treatment and the internal prevention. We know a lot about health and safety problems and we know a lot about solutions. We know that we want to change things, but it is difficult.

There are three questions to ask before you start on a prevention program: Where am I doing it? (i.e., what are the conditions of the "physical plant") Why am I doing it? What are my standards and values? You have to have an idea of what you are going to do. Most change is directed towards one of these four circles: people; interaction; products and process; and organization and control.

I read a questionnaire that was done three years ago with artistic and financial managers of dance companies about preventing injuries. Most of the responses were directed towards people: warming up, awareness, education. There was not much about organization and control, style of management or system functionality. There was nothing about product or process and I could find only one or two references to interaction. Again, it is not a judgment, but when you direct your prevention programs towards individual people, remember that they are not stand-alone units. People interact with each other and work within the organization. In my past career, I often gave health promotion talks to groups of workers who said, "Well it is very good to know, but I am the wrong person–my boss should have been here. Tomorrow, I have work to do that doesn't match with the information you have just given me. I know I should work differently, but there is no way I can change because when I talk with my bosses about things like this, they laugh at me or doubt my motivation."

The road to change is a three-lane highway: Who, What, How. Who refers to the actors involved in the prevention program. It is like a dance production in which you need someone who takes the initiative, as well supporters: a sponsor (someone with power) and a producer to arrange everything. Everybody has to know their role and think about the roles others are playing. Otherwise, you start your performance and suddenly someone enters the stage playing a role that isn't in the script. What are you going to change? You need a proper diagnosis: what's wrong and what's right? All companies in Holland now have to get a risk inventory which most of the time is rubbish. I am sorry, but it is. It only looks at small health and safety problems and not at the organization as a whole, with its own goals and problems. A proper diagnosis should look at more things than just health and safety; it should look at the labour market, customer satisfaction and finances. How are you going to make change? You have to have a strategy, a lever for change and you have to communicate with everybody. Often, communication is the medium of change. Now, what needs to be changed in the dance world?

AUDIENCE: Overload, bad training techniques, direct physical working conditions (heating, ventilation, air quality, floors...), stage effects (dry ice, strobe lights), the way people are treated, the attitude of management, lack of knowledge about physical possibilities.

CHRÉTIEN FELSER: You have mentioned problems in all four circles–interaction, personnel, work process and organization, and control. That is remarkable. What are the obstacles to change?

AUDIENCE: Companies are very short-term oriented, management is completely unconcerned, change is frightening, there is a lack of money and lack of resources, ignorance of the necessary strategies, mistrust between dancers and management, product orientation rather than process orientation.

CHRÉTIEN FELSER: I have some too: denial of the problem, conflicting interests among dancers, dance companies and venue managers. How can we change?

AUDIENCE: Provide more information, create a central clearinghouse for resources, have cooperation between companies, provide education, improve communication.

LIMITS TO RESPONSIBILITIES

LUCIA VAN WESTERLAAK: Artistic leaders and choreographers have to deal with the limits of dancers. These panelists from the artistic and creative side include dancers (who know all about limits of their own bodies), dance teachers and a physiotherapist.

COMMENT: The question of responsibility can be diverse depending on the context. What is the framework for the dancer? In the Paris Opera, there is always a second cast waiting, in full makeup, in tutu, everything, in the wings. But in a small company where you don't have two casts, dancers know there is nobody to replace them. This affects the way they take care of themselves, the way they warm-up before the show and the way they dance during the show. Think about it. When I began to work, we were ten dancers. Nobody got injured. When I was working with a big company, there were a lot of injuries. Is it because, psychologically, unconsciously, dancers knew they could be replaced?

COMMENT: Having a safety net does allow people to be injured. On the other hand, the pressure from the up-and-coming young dancers waiting in the wings on the lovely sixty-five-year-old ballerina desperate to hang on to her part is extreme. If I give in to my injury and the next girl is in, then I'm on the scrap heap.

COMMENT: It's not just that you lose your role, it's that you lose your job. In order to make changes, you have to have an artistic director who will acknowledge that the dancer's well-being is more important than replacing her. Directors need to be able to recognize when a dancer has reached their limit.

COMMENT: I think we have many clichés in classical ballet. Personally I never saw dancers waiting in the wings in the Paris Opera. In my company, most of the time, the dancer performed because there was no choice. I have seen many dance at the limit of what is acceptable, maybe putting themselves in danger, because otherwise the show would not happen. This gives the performance strength. That is the danger. Of course if you looked at it from a medical point of view, maybe it is wrong. But isn't it also part of that wonderful job–to go a little bit beyond normal limits? I have seen many dancers go beyond their limits and sometimes they give us and themselves such a wonderful experience and performance. It is true that when I get a group of fifty dancers, like in Monaco, I can see them consciously or unconsciously give themselves more of a chance to take care of their bodies because they know that it's OK to be off that night, because there is somebody else to replace them. But this can also create a situation where there is much less a sense of people working together to bring a project forward.

COMMENT: If we go out to see a movie, we pay a lot of money to see that specific movie. We sit there. The lights go down, the film starts. If somebody suddenly says, "Sorry, the movie broke and the man who fixes the camera has gone home because he doesn't feel very well. You have to leave," do you sit there with a smile and say, "Oh, poor man. It doesn't matter that it took me two hours to get into town to see this movie. I can come back next month"? I don't think so. It is the responsibility of the Paris Opera to have dancers waiting in the wings so the performance can continue.

COMMENT: Dancers and directors exist collectively in a world that has perpetuated the myth that directors are the be-all and end-all and dancers are the peons. Expecting directors to change is not enough. Perhaps the dancers, because we are the ones with the complaints, have to instigate the change?

COMMENT: I think what helps a student or a young

dancer–what gives them the ability to say no–has to do not only with their awareness of their well-developed body, but also with their awareness of the creative process and their breadth of aesthetic knowledge. Dancers know that if a choreographer tells them to do something that endangers them physically, mentally or spiritually, they can perhaps negotiate a compromise. That shouldn't stymie the ability of the choreographer to push the form forward–to innovate. The ability to say no requires maturity, education and knowledge. How do you build that into somebody who is eighteen years old?

COMMENT: Most artistic directors have been dancers, so it really begins with the education right from the beginning. We have such a small focus: education in dance schools is about producing one thing–a dancer–instead of an artist within this art form.

COMMENT: If dancers want to throw themselves out the window in the name of art, we have to ask ourselves, is this a free choice? You can't say, all of a sudden at nineteen or twenty, dancers are now supposed to know what yes and no are. Responsibility starts the day you take your first breath.

COMMENT: I have a small company with only ten dancers. If one of them gets injured, I have to change my program, which may disappoint the audience. Critics may destroy the show, suggesting it was not well thought out. I am concerned for my dancers' welfare, but I also have the dubious responsibility of having to confront politically and culturally a whole barrage of critics, audience members and stakeholders such as funding bodies who tell me I have to do a quota of performances per year which I know will kill my dancers. Are there any ideas for dealing with government? They say, we want you to do seventy performances a year, and you tell them, that's not possible with ten dancers, and then the funding is cut. How do you make them realize the pressures when all they see is the end product?

COMMENT: As a student you have to deal with a lot of teachers who each have their own information. Of course, it is good to have several points of view, but there should be one person, a mentor, who can guide you to find your talent–to find what is good for your body and to go in that direction.

COMMENT: As a psychologist I see there is really another way of thinking in the dance world. More is better. More training means better results and a higher performance. But physiologically, less is better. Not taking rest is not giving you the possibility to recuperate and have a better performance the next day.

COMMENT: We had a very interesting discussion yesterday with a top athlete and a dancer. The athlete was so well informed. He knew exactly how to pace himself. When to rest. What to eat. When to sleep. The dancer was really dealing with things as they came.

COMMENT: I think a lot of ballet training is in the Dark Ages, because it doesn't take into consideration what is known now about how an individual actually learns–there is still a great number of people who teach the way they were taught. We need to get all the teachers to look at why we do things. Is there a better way?

COMMENT: When we get children in the school, it is so important that we take care of their souls; if their souls are not healthy, they will never give out in their body language what they could. Dance is from the inside out. You can't learn a dance from the outside in. I think it is good that we learn so much from athletes, but dance is so different. The athlete has to do one leap or one run to get a gold medal. A dancer goes on evening after evening–training, choreographing new projects, doing a ballet, doing a modern piece. Of course dancers should sleep and rest too, but we shouldn't buy everything from the sports world. We have to do it our way.

COMMENT: For the last six years, I have worked in exactly the same way as that athlete: I eat at the right time, I sleep at the right time, I eat the right foods, I even make sure there is the right percentage of sugar in my fluids. It enhances me. We are all enlightened people. That's why we are here. But let's look at the people who aren't here and how influential they are. Where are the major British ballet schools? They aren't here. How do we get the message out?

COMMENT: During an audition, one of my students asked something of the artistic director who said, are you a student from Rotterdam? The dancer thought, oh, I am something special, but she discovered that there was this stigma because she had asked something.

COMMENT: In sports there is a lot of money coming from all

kinds of networks. Because of that, you have specialists to study this and study that. We dancers are the poor people in this field where we use our bodies. We can try to take advantage of what sport has done, but we have to find our own way. There is an occupational difference between sport and dance–the objectives are different. We must not become confused.

LUCIA VAN WESTERLAAK: Do artistic directors and choreographers know enough? Have they been taught enough about how dancers work?

COMMENT: They need more knowledge, people skills and observation skills. They need to remember how many sharp edges there are on the ladder they climbed up.

COMMENT: It seems to me that there is more help being given to the choreographers than to the artistic directors. I think, as Jirí Kylián has said, you become an artistic director by accident: you have no education about how group dynamics work or how to finish a project with a number of different groups of people or what you need.

COMMENT: All of a sudden you have to make decisions–somebody's got pneumonia and you need to negotiate with the venue manager to change the program–all based on your dancers' well-being.

COMMENT: We know there are some choreographers who are monsters, but sometimes they are geniuses. What are we going to do with a beautiful world where everybody respects everybody, everybody is nice with everybody? Where is the talent? Where is the craft? Where are the geniuses?

COMMENT: We haven't talked about the political context in which everyone is working. The reason there are differences is that sport has a different status than art, which is reflected in the amount of money that goes into it. The difference is also reflected in the strength of the voice that the practitioners have. A very well paid football player in England has a much stronger voice than a relatively well paid dancer. So while we have people who are tirelessly advocating in the field of dance, how often are they heard and in what kind of environment? The second thing is why can't we do something radical like saying the funding system is a service industry there to serve the needs of the artists? It doesn't create policies or artistic priorities. It should follow them. It is the artists who should be setting the agenda.

LUCIA VAN WESTERLAAK: Should we be taking this to the unions that are active in the various countries and to the E.U.?

COMMENT: No. The unions can help a little but dancers themselves have to take responsibility for this. Then maybe we decide to ask the union to come and help us.

COMMENT: I think the solution is international. Each company has done a lot of work and has information about practical things, but they are all working on their own.

COMMENT: I think if you made a central health centre, it would not be so hard to do some investigating. If you don't get the numbers and the information, you won't get the money from the government.

COMMENT: I think it is the nature of dance people to look for someone else to do it. Unless something has the support of every dancer, every director and every manager, it is possible to pass the buck and say someone else is going to fix it; that is the danger of how we were taught.

Choreography
and Dancing

Photograph on previous page:
Dancers: Sergiu Stefanschi instructing Brett Bauer and Tara Bharnani
At: Canada's National Ballet School
Photographer: Jeannette Edissi-Collins

ENCOURAGING AND DEVELOPING CHOREOGRAPHERS

Serge Bennathan, Dominique Dumais, Danny Grossman, Bengt Jörgen, James Kudelka, Claudia Moore, Penelope Reed Doob and Grant Strate

PENELOPE REED DOOB: Choreographers are used to having other people perform for them, so if anyone seems particularly nervous, don't blame them, this discussion is simply a way of getting them all back on stage again where they all started out. The session is about encouraging and developing choreographers and, when I sat down to think about it, I realized that it assumes there are "yes" answers to two questions, which is debatable. First, can we develop choreographers? If you think choreographers are entirely born and not at all made, of course you would say, "No, you can't so why are we talking about this." But I say, yes, there are things people can learn in addition to what they may be born with. Second, should we be supportive and encouraging of choreographers? Or are there too many choreographers in the world already? Should aspiring choreographers have to struggle through lack of encouragement and recognition so we can weed out the incompetent and the mediocre? I don't think so. What you weed out is often those people who, for one reason or another, are a little diffident and shy.

I assume we can develop choreography and that we should do what we can to support people who wish to choreograph. So the question is, how do we encourage them? Remember, there are going to be as many different answers as there are choreographers. If we could find one way to create choreographers, chances are they would all turn out the same and we would be bored silly. We are not looking for a formula. We are looking for a way to draw from—or broaden—the pool of possible choreographers.

There are lots of women choreographers in modern dance and very few in ballet. In my own research it has been very clear that there are some women who just don't get involved in choreography, even though they might be very good at it. Young women don't want to choreograph because they are afraid they will seem bossy. Girls are afraid they will be laughed at. They are afraid they won't finish the piece and they will let people down. Boys—who are, by definition, special in a ballet school—don't seem to have that fear. They seem to be much more confident, even if only a few are sure they are going to become the next George Balanchine. That is the kind of joking thought that a boy might have while most of the young women who are just starting off in choreography would never have. So what I have found is that there are an awful lot of potential choreographers who are probably not being encouraged at the beginning and hence are self-selecting out of the pool of choreographers. Instead of theorizing what we might do to encourage choreographers, I have a wonderful panel of choreographers and we are going to ask them what has helped them, what might help them and what advice they would give to choreographers. Serge Bennathan is the artistic director of Dance Makers, who trained in France in both classical and modern technique and came to Canada in 1985. Dominique Dumais came to the National Ballet School from Quebec and fanned out from her role as a dancer. She left the National Ballet Company a year ago to concentrate on choreography. Danny Grossman is another "crosser of boundaries." San Francisco-born, activist-bred, he danced with Paul Taylor's company for ten years. He came to Canada as a faculty member at York University. In 1975, he founded his own company and since then he has created over thirty works for his and for other companies–crossing classical and contemporary boundaries, as he did as a performer. Bengt Jörgen is a Swedish-born alumnus of the National Ballet School and a former member of the National Ballet of Canada. He has created several impressive new works for company workshops and within three years he took the risk of leaving the company to work on his own choreography. In 1987, he founded Ballet Jörgen, which is a small company of classical trained dancers with a mandate of creating and presenting new works–typically by emerging choreographers and often by women. Grant Strate is an Alberta born lawyer who saw the error of his ways and became a charter member of the National Ballet of Canada in 1951, becoming resident choreographer and assistant to the artistic director. He founded York University's dance department–the first in Canada–and then went on to Simon Fraser University where he was founding director of the Centre for the Arts. He is now president of the World Dance Alliance for the Americas and recognized as one of the most important and best-loved figures in Canadian dance.

I guess the first question I would like you to comment on is, what was an important early milestone in your career as a choreographer? What made you think that you really had a knack for this?

DANNY GROSSMAN: I didn't choreograph until 1975, but I will go back a little before that. I was a cheerleader when I was

around fifteen. We learned all the dances of the day that the kids loved. My first encouragement was that my parents did not mind the fact that I danced and improvised. The student body encouraged me too, but it is very hard to find space to teach children to dance. So I wasn't encouraged in that way, but I didn't know there was an art form anyway, so maybe I wouldn't even have enjoyed classes. But I did stop going to high school when the arts were no longer important to me. The most important thing became how to be a good soldier or get a good job. I was encouraged back then, but I could have been encouraged more.

BENGT JÖRGEN: I think the greatest support I got was from my colleagues at the National Ballet Company. Without that, I wouldn't have continued because I just didn't have enough confidence to look at my work and decide if it was good or bad. I looked for affirmation from my colleagues. So it was stumbling steps right at the beginning and gradually I built confidence as I went along. But right from the beginning and to this day I have tremendous support from my colleagues and dancers. That has been the keystone of my development.

DOMINIQUE DUMAIS: When I first heard the question, I wanted to say my parent's basement. My basement at home was a place of tremendous intimacy and creativity. I could go down there and put on any record and dance around as much as I wanted to. When I was able to come to a bigger centre and be in a creative environment, they were tremendously generous to let me go. All along it was my decision to be in this environment. From that moment on–I was twelve years old–there was this polarity between wanting to be at home with my family and at the same time knowing that I absolutely had to be here in this environment. It was very important to me to work with choreographers at a very young age. I was introduced to what the creative process was all about–how someone starts to put a piece together. The choreographic workshops with the National Ballet of Canada and fringe festivals were all tremendously important to me. Other choreographers have also been very supportive and that meant a lot to me.

GRANT STRATE: My first introduction to dance was when I was six years old. My father was selling vacuum cleaners to keep the wolf from the door–this was post-depression time–and he sold a vacuum cleaner to a tap dancing teacher who couldn't pay. So she gave free tap dancing lessons to my sister, who was my best friend, for a year and I went to the lessons with her. That was the extent of my formal education until much, much later. When I was in high school they had at least two dances a week. We danced and danced because there was nothing else to do. My sister and I were very good at the jitterbug and there was a lot of improvising. In social dancing, you have to improvise. Then I decided to become a lawyer and went to University of Alberta and while I was there, I got very involved in theatre. When I joined the National Ballet, because of the conventions of ballet at that time, I had to know the classical code of movement thoroughly before I was allowed to choreograph. For five years I really struggled in the studio–day and night–performing, rehearsing and learning ballet all at the same time. All that time I was really eager to create, but I wasn't able to because of that convention. I did a small pas de deux as my first piece. A while later I became the resident choreo-grapher and choreographed sixteen works for the company. Nobody else has done it that way, nor even should.

PENELOPE REED DOOB: In your choreography, are you aware of crossing boundaries and obstacles and overcoming them? Does one work well as an outsider?

DANNY GROSSMAN: So many decisions in life are intuitive. In the beginning I saw many great choreographers and so many classics. We lived in a golden age where you could sneak into a theatre at intermission. Now at these two-hundred-dollar theatres, there is no way for poor dancers and actors to see the goods. In a way, the seeds of all my work were planted in my parent's house and in the physicality of San Francisco, but the maturity of living my life and becoming the father of my own truth led me to leave my parents and join another family with Paul Taylor. Then I came here and formed my own family–a very odd and wonderful family. Only now can I see the rhyme, reason and importance in all these different choices. Even how you use the stage: as you mature you start to reflect those emotional and geographic boundaries.

SERGE BENNATHAN: When I started to choreograph there was,

in France, a big explosion of contemporary dance which, for me, was quite natural to embrace. So of course I would go to all the performances I could and ultimately this came into my choreographic work. I tried to liberate myself from tradition. But it was also natural to go back to choreographing for ballet companies. I love it. I can bring my choreographic voice to the dancer. There were always places I wanted to go, but I always wanted to go back to the place I had left! But it is one world. It is truly about the pleasure of working with the dancers in my company and working with independent dancers, when they ask me to choreograph for them, and working for ballet companies. It is the same track, for me–just a different exploration. I keep learning.

PENELOPE REED DOOB: I want to fit this in with risk taking–raising the bar and meeting the challenge and getting dancers to do what you need them to do.

BENGT JÖRGEN: I think for most of my youthful days, I was a rebel without a cause. Quite destructive. I took that with me into the National Ballet and for two years learned a tremendous amount. In my third year, we started to do the same rep we had done for the first two years, because at that time we were on a very strict cycle, and I didn't know what to do with my energy. I got involved with everything I possibly could and I got into a lot of trouble–I'm still paying for it, I'm sure. I should have listened to my intuition and got out a year earlier. When I started choreographing, it was the first time I ever felt at peace with myself in my art form. I used to always be pushing for something else–wanting to do it differently. Choreographing gave me the ability to become a little bit more normal. I had the best education money could buy. I grew up in an opera house. I didn't have to sneak into the theatre, I lived in the theatre. It was just a wonderful period. I really fell into running a company. I set out to do my own work and I didn't want to be bound by a company structure. I totally wanted to create independent works and I realized there were no resources out there to do it. For the first couple of years, I borrowed the National Ballet. I was able to sweet talk the dancers into doing projects. Gradually we kept getting bigger and bigger and other people came into the equation. I never really had a desire to run a company in my image–a company that would just do my work. But once the structure was there, it made perfect sense that it would be the vehicle for independent choreographers.

DOMINIQUE DUMAIS: The gender thing is not so much a boundary as it is a lack of role models. It would have been nice early on to have a woman to talk to about creating. Sometimes there is a different sensibility, a different way to go about creating–not always–but sometimes.

PENELOPE REED DOOB: One of the wonderful things is that through your work, you have become a role model to a lot of young women who are now trying to choreograph and are doing very well.

DOMINIQUE DUMAIS: When a child is ready to read, you don't say, "Wait a year until you are in school." No. You get those letters down and get started. The minute you feel that the desire is there, say to yourself, "OK."

DANNY GROSSMAN: With a child, as soon as they can walk, they are taught. Somehow in dance, all the information is held back. You are the lucky one if you get to work with this person or do that thing. Part of it is the nature of our work–the fact that we have to see it. We tend to hold back and say, "Oh, I don't want anyone to see my work," or, "What if they perform it badly after I'm dead?" Who cares? Lots of people perform Bach badly too. We need a legacy of modern work. Everyone wants to create new work and hoard it. We have all this wonderful work that the public should own. Verdi is about the Italian people, not some dead guy. It is hard to do in dance.

PENELOPE REED DOOB: The control issue is quite interesting in all the arts–perhaps dance is the worst. The dead, white choreographer rules and dancers are often told, "You can't do this."

DANNY GROSSMAN: I think it is really important for artists to see great artistry, whatever it is. Right now, unfortunately, too many artists are just imitating their own little group.

DOMINIQUE DUMAIS: If I see a really great flamenco dancer, I think, "Oh, I would love to work with that dancer." I don't really care if they can put on pointe shoes or not. A dancer is a dancer. You see the intelligence of the body, the creativity, the desire for expression. I think that is what is inspiring,

more than anything else–more than genre.

DANNY GROSSMAN: You have to see great, great work, so that when you go into the studio, you "up the ante." If you are creative, you should start right where you are. Grant, what could we be doing to make more choreographers?

GRANT STRATE: Are they born or made? When I started at the National Ballet, I never quite believed some of the things I was told as absolute truths. I was told that a good choreographer does one minute of choreography an hour. I was working with large groups and was aware of what it was costing the company every minute. I had to go and do a lot of homework. In a way, that was excellent because I learned not just to go in there and expect the inspiration to fall on me. Another axiom of my work was that music is king. Music is superior to dance and your job is to follow music. It wasn't said quite that bluntly, but everybody talked about musicality. You felt bound to stay inside the musical convention. It took me years to figure out how to create another line over the music that is complementary but not parallel. Another axiom which is still around is that you don't choreograph until after a career as a dancer–even though Ashton and Tudor were successful at that time. What that ignores is that the creative impulse doesn't happen at the end of a career. You don't just suddenly metamorphose into a choreographer. It ignores the need to have signposts pointing people in the right direction–not to discover and nurture, but to allow them opportunities to emerge. The thing is to set up the right kind of conduit. Not to say this is the way to do it–although there are elements of craft that are extremely important to know–but this is the reason for doing it which has to be nurtured from the very beginning to establish the individuality of the work. Choreography is not about creating dances, it is about revealing yourself through the dance. A corps de ballet is trained to follow and it is almost impossible to train people to lead and follow at the same time. But you must make provisions for leadership. Very early on you have to make choreographers feel that they can invent–not just obey.

COMMENT: The dancer is seen as the silent partner to the choreographer–albeit ultimately the interpreter of the work. I have never been encouraged to develop as a choreographer and there has never been a process through which I can work, so I have come by curious routes to nurture myself. Somehow there has to be a structure in place whereby voices are heard during the learning process. That dichotomy between being a follower and a leader needs to be addressed early on.

SERGE BENNATHAN: Where are the kind of places you can have the opportunity to work on the process? For me, there is nothing more important for young choreographers than to have, right away, the opportunity to create. To really have the time to explore and be challenged, without the pressure of time and finances you have in a company.

COMMENT: I think that, for the optimum development of choreographers, every school around the world that can afford it should teach choreography. Everyone should have to study it whether they like it or not. That way they would learn what it means to put movement together and gain respect for the choreographer's work. I have seen people who had no idea they had choreographic ability until they were put to the test of being in the moment. We shouldn't all be sitting around waiting for a Balanchine to appear.

PENELOPE REED DOOB: Why is choreography taught at universities in modern dance, but very seldom in ballet school?

GRANT STRATE: I think everyone should take it. It doesn't necessarily mean that everybody will become a choreographer, but they will understand the process of what's happening as they are dancing. Dancers very often don't think there is any work involved. Also, in the ballet world we are still very influenced by the 19th century, and that was about the glorification and idealization of women, but for men, the power was behind the scenes. The men on the stage were not as important as the women. This kind of perfection trapped the women but things are now changing.

COMMENT: A lot of people are emerging with some choreographic training, but without the mentorship that could really take them into a choreographic career. Can mentorship, preceding infliction of a piece on an audience, be valuable? Are we talking about mentoring or coaching?

DOMINIQUE DUMAIS: We learn to be good teachers by teaching bad classes. We learn to balance by falling down a lot. We learn to be choreographers by creating really bad pieces. So we need a safety net and some kind of instruction that allows a lot of these skills.

QUESTION: Is it more important that the choreographer be pleased with their piece than the public?

GRANT STRATE: You are really lucky if the audience liked your piece, but first you have to be true to yourself. Don't be too hard on yourself, though.

DOMINIQUE DUMAIS: I ask myself these questions every day. Is this what I meant to do? Did I do this right? Maybe I need to change the structure. What if I just turned it upside down? If you are having these conversations, it means you are alive in the work. You are wanting to find out more about yourself and about the work. It is always a struggle. Sometimes it is good to just feel like you are going to get in the sandbox and see what comes up. That's why improvisation is so useful. The minute we start using words like "create," it's like, whoa, God creates—we just kind of do our thing.

SERGE BENNATHAN: Sometimes we have to accept that there are different reasons why people create. There are no parametres. There comes a moment where I don't think you should ask yourself too many questions.

PHYSICAL AND INTELLECTUAL PREPARATION FOR PERFORMANCE
Peggy Baker, Margie Gillis, Karen Kain, Joysanne Sidimus and Veronica Tennant

VERONICA TENNANT: What comprises the optimal performer and optimal performance? How do we know when we have reached our personal best? Are there healthy ways to find the edge? Do the performing dilemmas differ for the ballet dancer and the modern dancer? I danced with the National Ballet of Canada for twenty-five years. My life began in so many ways right here at the National Ballet School. When I talk about performance, it is as a result of having formed for those twenty-five years as a ballet dancer and then continuing into an extension of other careers and realizing that performance is, in fact, a part of all of our lives. There are so many aspects of daily life that can be interpreted as performance. If I have learned anything over the span of these professional careers, I think it is that the game of life is truly a collaborative art. When I look at a ballerina's career–such as mine–there is so much shared composition, endless details from countless people who have layered their committed and creative contribution to the balletic art on its personification–the dancer. This is never so true as in the case of the principal dancer. This is where we come to our first grand paradox, because unlike solo concert musicians and singers who forge careers as freelance artists, ballet dancers spend most of their lives as members of a company. After you are established with one of the major ballet companies, a classical principal dancer might receive invitations as a celebrated guest artist on the world stage. But seldom does a good, young dancer survive in only a freelance capacity. The stringent discipline and the structure of our dance have an entrenched need for reinforcement of group endeavour. It is a support system of coaching and applied motivation. It is a pooled knowledge that works in tandem with a love of the art. And here, at the National Ballet of Canada and the National Ballet School, my education about a shared pride and a group striving started very young and very early. It began with training and standards and discipline and taste and style and collaboration. These are the infusing legacies of classical ballet that have served me so well. Though the role of Juliet in John Cranko's *Romeo and Juliet* set my professional course, it was Betty Oliphant in the school who taught me how to dance and Celia Franca, by plucking me out of the school and into the role of Juliet, who showed me why to dance. It was these pioneers of dance in Canada who placed me on the map. So that is the reality of the dancer's life. It is one of communal striving. And yet, to make that distinct mark, there is, for the individual dancer, a true dichotomy. The world of ballet bequeathed me with this abundant capacity and skills of collaboration and collage.

We know classical dancers have to achieve a certain look–a very stylized way of moving–and the body, not to for-

get the mind, is selected, chained, harnessed and re-trained through endlessly repetitious instruction. How slow and fallible is that muscular memory! It needs to be refreshed daily, even hourly. You all know this. One day off and only you know. Two days off and your colleagues know. Three days off and the audience knows. Dancers live in this ever-constant battle over will. Because, quite simply, you don't always feel like working past your maximum. Therefore the enforcers of this proscribed aesthetic are the external drivers–traditionally the artistic director, the ballet mistress, the ballet master, the choreographer–they steer you and they push you. And, in this visual and performance art, they possess power. It is an unquestioned power–because they, not you, can see what you create. They, not you, can assess accurately and critically the level of your work.

Let's begin with ballet class. That stringent discipline is rooted into our training–into the fabric of our lives as dancers. From the very first day we began to study ballet, we placed our hands on that barre and we stood in first position. We trained our body to change our axis to this turned out position from the hips to the toes and we began our pliés, which were the physical point of departure on a very, very long journey of rigorous routine. Think about it. No matter what the age or the stage or the nationality of the classical dancer, the studio, the barre, the pianist and the teacher are fixed points in this continuum. When we begin as young students, can we possibly fathom that for one hundred and fifty years before us, each and every day of a dancer's life has been done in exactly the same way? Can we comprehend that nothing in this process will deviate for as many decades as we continue to dance? This dancer's toil, this daily restoring of muscular memory is the ultimate democratizer. Dancers fall and they stumble together, in the warm-up and the training sessions and they really do falter. They can't conceal anything from their colleagues. All soloists, all principal dancers, take part in the collaboration and though the rehearsals can be held separately, your abilities are known and your weaknesses are observed and scrutinized and judged and judged and judged on a daily basis. That's why trust is instilled in our collective consciousness, because there always lurks a physical danger. We literally go to the edge in each other's arms. Every dancer faces challenges that consume, and they are physical, emotional and interpretive. Rehearsals are arduous. In the classics, our yardsticks are established ballets and the steps have to be learned and mastered; these are two completely different things. The task always looms too large and right up until opening night and all the mornings after, dancers will rehearse. There can never be enough rehearsal. Interesting, isn't it, that the French word for rehearsal is repetition. So in classical ballet, there we are continuing to strive, in unison, for unity. We are enjoined to think and to care collectively. In "Swan Lake," sweeping single movements are created by dozens of separate bodies. You may say, well the soloist emerges, the soloist is sought after, the soloist is acclaimed. And yes, the highest accolade in dance is to be proclaimed an artist. In order to achieve that endorsement from our peers we need to have something to say; we need to know how to declare that essence of individuality within that stringently prescribed format.

This is what I have tried to learn and it has translated very well into my life and careers: First, no apologies about being a leader; the strength of collaboration is actually fueled by the force of independence and there have to be both equally strong, seemingly contradictory streaks to summon, harness and then to dismiss. There is a danger in dance of becoming obsessed with your instrument–your body–of being self-absorbed to the point that your performance can actually be compromised. I have been taught by injuries, by years and by careers that it is the health of the complete self that is the tool for collaborating and succeeding and performing at optimum. You know, it took the longest time to learn the simplest of lessons–how to focus on what I am doing, not on how I am doing–and taking it beyond the result while encompassing the entire process and giving that as the performance.

PEGGY BAKER: I am a contemporary dancer and my career has spanned the last twenty-five years. In fact, this is the anniversary season of a Toronto dance company, Dancemakers, of which I was a founding member in 1974. For me, I think a great deal came forward through solo dancing, because that is

a very distilled form in which the great dilemma is to try to tell the difference between the choreographer and the dancer. What I have taken on for myself is a very expansive exploration of choreography itself. I want to get inside the choreography and allow my exploration to produce an individual performance every time in rehearsal or on stage. I am engaging in a task-oriented process with the material and allowing that to lead me to places in a kind of secondary way, so that I only think about myself in response to the journey I am on with the choreography.

I think very often the approach to learning a dance is that we learn the steps and then we work on perfecting them. That is the way I was taught and I coached that way for a very long time. But I noticed over many years of working with various people that there were certain realms of interest that emerged again and again and there were also structural components of the choreography itself. I experimented early on in my solo dancing with looking at each one of those issues separately as opposed to going step-by-step and working on each element in that step, I started looking at the dance overall. For example, I looked at the choreography in terms of simply the vocabulary and began to draw connections of kinship–like putting together families of movements inside that choreography, until I came to understand how every step related to everything else in the dance. There were kinds of groupings of material that made themselves known. I could distinguish variations and resonances from other kinds of vocabulary which presented a kind of aesthetic realm in which the dance took place. Then I would look at, in separate rehearsals, all the spatial components of the dance and I would attend to nothing else but the floor pattern, the levels, the facings, the facings of my body, the internal lines of my own body, the external lines in space. I would go through the whole thing until I understood how I could distill just one element of the dance. And then I would go and do the same thing with rhythmic ideas and be able to get through the whole thing simply as a rhythmic expression. Then I would do the same thing with imaginative thinking, attaching a metaphor or an image to every single movement and not doing anything that didn't have a very clear imaginative thought attached to it. For me this creates stratas of interest in the dance. So, instead of the steps being a kind of surface that gets burnished and perfected on top, the steps themselves are a kind of permeable membrane and the shape that those steps take is produced by the structure and the process that underlie them. As I go through a rehearsal process I have invested all these different aspects of the material and the next time I dance the piece from beginning to end without that one objective in my mind, I am spontaneously drawn by my interest and attention of the moment into any of those areas. So it starts to feel less to me like a surface and more to me like a three-dimensional realm. It is as though a thread can be drawn from any element to any other element. My idea is not to go for a kind of rigid perfectionism that addresses a superficial idea about what the steps are, but to let the choreography itself be a world I enter and explore during a performance. I keep finding new things every time I do it, because I am spontaneously offered up new images from any of these various realms I've gone into. That process of addressing a task inside the structure of the choreography itself can also lead to a very deep personal experience which I feel is a parallel experience. I can look with great objectivity at any element of the choreography and then engage in it very fully as the individual I am, which changes constantly. Veronica spoke about needing to take care of your dancing by the day, by the hour, by the moment. We are that different all of the time and our interest is going to take us somewhere else constantly. That is the way I feel about dance—I want to leave room for spontaneity, to be myself inside the work, understanding that I know very truly what the structure is. This is a process that I use through my rehearsal and performance. It is very much a spontaneous attitude that I take. I have a sense of curiosity about what is going to happen, as much as I have a sense of direction that I go into the performance to begin with.

JOYSANNE SIDIMUS: What Peggy and Veronica are talking about is very much how we were trained in New York. With Balanchine, there was no such thing as the coaching of a principal dancer. I think, unless I am much mistaken, that still exists. You learn the role—you have to learn the steps—and then

what you do with that material is up to you. When Mr. Balanchine was alive, he set the standard and the standard was to make the material live within the music and then to make the music come alive in an interesting way. The underlying premise is that internally you have to be interesting. We were trained to be curious about movement. When I came to Canada, it was the first time I had ever been coached in a role. Of course with Celia Franca that was a great honour because she was a consummate coach, but it was the kind of coaching that was very alien to me; we had been given a floor plan—a map—of how movement should be expressed and we tended to play around a lot with that as individuals. Here, the structure was far more within parametres that were very prescribed and that was an interesting challenge.

I think the greatest gift we give to dancers is the equality to empower them to come to their own interesting point of material development. We need to be endlessly curious about movement. I have always hated the title, although I am honoured by it, of "Repetiteur," because there is nothing repetitive about a Repetiteur. The only thing repetitious is that you are doing the same steps. The challenge is to make those steps different and alive. These women, I assure you, could do the same phrase of music and choreography for twenty-five years and it would never look the same in any two performances. What makes that happen? It is a collaboration, but it is also a focus on the lack of an absolute. There is no approach and no teacher that I have ever worked with, no matter how great, who had all the answers. They may have had the questions. They may have been able to provoke a metaphor for an environment of movement, but that would have been their great strength. There are stylistic and technical guideposts and certainly we all must adhere to them but within that there must be freedom. I think the search and preparation for a performance comes in laying those landscapes and allowing a dancer to develop their own interesting way of moving. It has nothing to do with personality. It has to do with where the movement takes them and because we are different physically and genetically, we tend to respond differently. And our emotional response to music is different. That, of course, to me is a seminal part of the dancer. How do dancers viscerally respond to music and how does choreography sit within them in a mutable framework? As I go around the world and stage ballets, one element that I think is absolutely inherent in performance is the element of risk. The problem is that what is risk in Canada, is not risk in the Unites States. What is risk in the United States, is not risk in Europe or in Russia. These cultural differences must be respected, because if you take with you an absolute standard and impose it, the dance loses its organic quality. If a dancer dances from something profoundly deep inside, then the organic quality of their movement has to be brought out. So with the Balanchine works, you always try to get to an element of risk, but that risk has to be respected wherever you in the world. The other element is spontaneity. There comes a point at which rehearsing is over-rehearsing, where the intellectual is over-intellectualization; only a very mature artist knows when they've thought about the role too much. When you get to that point, something different should happen, hopefully, to that response to the music, that adrenaline, that artistry, that taking the movement that much further than you ever have in rehearsal. If that spontaneity is to be acknowledged from day one, it must be brought into the process of preparation for performance. There has to be an allowance for something different happening every night. Then you've done your job. It is taking responsibility yourself for making something interesting within the landscape of movement. The human being will emerge through that. That is a huge challenge, I think, for teachers and for coaches. The last thing I would say in preparation for performance is to understand always that the technical development in a school setting is always a means to an end and not an end in itself. I think we border on the athletic and that's wonderful because it means technique has developed to places it never was and it will continue to develop. And hopefully this development is always a means to the joyful expression that we call dance.

KAREN KAIN: I was a ballerina with the National Ballet of Canada for twenty-eight years and now I am the Associate Artistic Director to James Kudelka, the Artistic Director. I am now spending a lot more time trying to pass on and help younger dancers and it is giving me quite a different viewpoint from having spent so much time just dealing with my own feelings about dancing. The one thing I know to be true for me is that over the years, I had to rediscover the reasons I started to dance in the first place, because I managed to lose them along the way a few times. We've touched on a few of them already. Certainly the passion and the joy for expressing oneself as a dancer should seem to be something that you shouldn't lose too easily, but I was the type of dancer who imposed rigid perfectionist boundaries on myself and when I didn't achieve those, I was very hard on myself. For a time, I managed to kill what it was that I loved to do. Working through that process made me all the more convinced that, in so many ways, dance is a spiritual experience–yes, a physical one too, but I learned that, for me, performing is about recapturing things that I had discovered within myself in the studio–more often feelings and emotions that brought a movement to life. Just physically recreating a movement does not say anything.

I remember one of my most powerful memories of working with Celia Franca, the woman who founded the National Ballet Company. She didn't often have time to coach us, but when she did it was quite extraordinary and she had me alone for an hour one day. We were working on the second act of *Giselle*, and all she did was talk to me about the atmosphere–about the moonlight and the beach and the wind. I never did another performance of the second act of *Giselle* without hearing her words. I could instantly take myself back to that feeling inside me and around me–the atmosphere she had helped me understand. It didn't matter anymore if I held the balance for as long as I had the night before, or whether my leg faltered, or whether my pirouette was quite as good. Suddenly my perspective became much healthier and much more realistic and I could discover the freedom that Peggy referred to that forgave me for being human.

MARGIE GILLIS: I actually teach performance arts, so I have about five hours of stuff to tell you, but that's not going to happen. I was not in a company because I was emotionally disturbed, too fat, pigeon-toed and dyslexic. I have always danced. I love dancing. I began to dance because I wanted to explore the concept of inside-out. Was it possible for love to be requited? I had ideas. The only way to translate them properly and fairly was to manifest these ideas into life. There was my patriarchal brain active with constant questions. The only way for me to calm myself and deal with that is to use the wisdom of the body. I believe infinitely in the kinetic process. What you feel, what you think, turns into electricity which runs down the system and boom, you've got motion. What your audience is experiencing when you are honest on stage is the same kinetic process as you are experiencing. Voila, love. For me, that means love. Really, absolutely, we can share experience. I am a complete bliss junky. I believe in it. It has never done anything but help me. I regain my health on stage. My fatigue levels and my injuries mostly happen through other sources like the floor and the air conditioning. Bliss has always made the molecules in my body separate so that my body is toned and ready to receive the kinetic information and translate that into motion. That motion can be architectural, musical, it can be anything. One of the things about dance is that it engages every aspect of you completely. We are immediately putting ideas into life and into gesture. The body has wisdom too and we listen to it and have a conversation back and forth, you know, before we go on stage and we've had all the rehearsal and the coaching, and the hard work and the teaching and the technique. Twenty four hours before the performance, what do I care about? What am I trying to say, as a performer? I care about dance and I believe in the intrinsic healing power of dance. Because I cherish this so much, I would not do things that injure me in the long run—in fact, this keeps me healthy, because I want to return to this place and share it and be part of it. That's when I have to start accepting. I know I've got the desire. I know that magic is possible and desirable out there on stage. So I know already, this is something I want. Next, who am I at that moment? Am I miserable? Am I happy? Am I physically bound up or injured? Am I in a psychically good place? You may have to go out and do *Giselle* when you've just fallen in love and you don't want to be sad. Then you may have this joyful, exuberant dance when you've just had the worst day of your life. You have to enter into and recreate this ritual and become a vessel. I believe all

great performance is about becoming a vessel. The only way to properly do this is to accept your flaws and walk out on stage as a total, whole human being. And then, get out of the way. Get yourself into an observer position and allow this thing to move through you. You get to watch at the same time. Some of the things that stop us from being great performers are psychological thought processes. I can't think of two things at once. I can't be beautiful if I'm fat. I can't be beautiful if my technique isn't good enough. I can't be...of course I can—I just do both at once. We feel like we can only have one thought at a time and creation is a larger, encompassing thought. I really believe in this transformation and its healing power and I give everything I can to it. I can discuss certain specific exercises and problems, but I do shy away from making sweeping statements because you don't want to tell somebody who's running around in traffic to go be free. And you don't want to tell somebody who can't come out of their front door to try a little restraint. So information is contextual and must change. It does change over the course of a career. Yes, I develop my body; I've done everything from hula to walking out cold on stage. Other times I have done extensive preparation. But what is important to me is that I focus to find out where my body is at and where I am at, and then I accept that and move forward with the faith that this thing is going to move through me. The more time you spend in this kind of bliss, the more you know about its different qualities. It creates an ongoing thought process where health and beauty and love are. It really promotes self-acceptance. If you keep apologizing for who you are on stage, your audience will sit there asking, "What are you doing up there?" If you want your performance to be about what you care about, accept your flaws and at that moment, when you walk on stage, that's it, that's all, that's you.

VERONICA TENNANT: One of the themes everyone has touched on is that of utter and extreme concentration in order to arrive at utter and extreme spontaneity. One of the things I think we need to feed and think about as a tool is imagination. That is something that isn't always asked of a dancer. But I think imagination—even to the point of visualizing—can help. I want to talk about our differences. From working at a ballet company where a dancer can be performing as a member of a corps de ballet in a group situation, how do you individually have a consummate experience and yet know you have to be part of the collective?

MARGIE GILLIS: They may seem like opposites, but they are not necessarily so. Each one of us works within the context of a structure. No matter how big or narrow that structure is, we can apply the same basic philosophy of health and love and beauty and sharing. And you can still feed yourself and your own set of beliefs. Ask yourself, who am I here onstage?

PEGGY BAKER: If you are turning yourself over to the work, it is not a matter of some ego trip that can be a collective or individual thing. You can get enormous satisfaction from moving in a group and creating something wonderful together on stage. In that way, I don't think it is so different. What is different is that we have to deal with that one little thing called pointe shoes. It isn't just our bodies that are the tools, it is also these things that go on our feet that have to be part of our physicality and as expressive as the rest of us—a whole other area to deal with. Sometimes it is more than just the body and the mind and the spirit.

VERONICA TENNANT: Erik Bruhn used to say, "I'm going out front and all I want is for you to amaze me." I'd like to ask each of you, when you've had a performance that you felt was an ultimate, consummate performance, what was it that made you know it was what you were striving for? What was it you did at the performance that was transcendent?

KAREN KAIN: At the risk of sounding hokey, there were a few performances where I felt something had taken over. I was there and I enjoyed it enormously, but I was almost coming from somewhere else. I never had a technical thought in my head. I never had to think about placement or coordination or anything difficult. I just refer to it sometimes as a flow. The few times it happened to me in twenty-eight years, when it was over, I knew something special had happened, but I didn't feel responsible for it. I felt that I was lucky enough to have been around when it happened.

MARGIE GILLIS: I agree with that. You really do have a sense of being a vessel. I try to facilitate being there for that to come in. I feel really blessed that I've had a lot of those moments. I feel, oddly enough, when I'm not there that I'm learning about it too, because I get to go from one moment to the next and go through the rough spots; the answer is given to you through the physicality and you get to go back into that.

COMMENT: I think for me, in any kind of performance, it is the element of surprise–the unexpected. Allow yourself to be so prepared that you can be open to the undiscovered. Again, if I needed to find a way to do it, it was through the music.

PEGGY BAKER: I find this hard to talk about. There is a sense of being a medium for the performance. There is also a sense that your desire is constantly met. That you want that moment and it is coming and you are in it and now you want the next thing and it is coming. It is a feeling of being consumed by it and deeply satisfied. It's got a sense of building, for me, and when it is finished, it is just kind of there–it's hanging and resonating in the space. A lot of times when I see a great performance, I don't want to clap. I don't want anyone to move. I feel like it is still there and we are still all in that moment. I don't want to break it. I think I have had more of those performances as I've gotten older.

JOYSANNE SIDIMUS: I remember coming off stage and thinking, "I don't believe what just happened." I was carried away in this haze and it was better than I had imagined all my life. It never stopped all the days I was dancing. I look back on that career as a great gift because of the joy and the challenges and the loss of oneself on the stage.

VERONICA TENNANT: When you get the great gift of the dancers you are working with taking the ballet out on stage and performing it, what is it that makes that performance for you, knowing that they've done well? Obviously it goes beyond them doing the steps and delivering it as it was structured in rehearsal.

JOYSANNE SIDIMUS: I think they haven't done well, I think they have lived well on that stage. They've brought their lives and shown them collectively on the stage. I have been very blessed to see performances like that.

VERONICA TENNANT: Let's talk a little bit about rituals.

Not Just Any Body

KAREN KAIN: I think one thing I learned was that there wasn't any kind of way I could prepare myself that would guarantee a good performance. When I was very young and I had a good performance, I would try to recreate the ritual. I know that what I needed, pre-performance, changed as I matured and maybe as I understood myself better. When I was younger I loved the adrenaline rush of just getting out there. It was all about having some kind of physical release of all my nervous energy. As I matured, I began to want to know what I was doing a little bit more and be more in control. That involved being much more prepared physically because my body required it. For me, with my particular temperament, I had to do a lot of calming myself down. I learned later that I did some techniques such as visualization and self-talk, for years without actually knowing they were techniques to help cope with performing and nerves. I did an awful lot of self-talk in order to convince myself that I had the courage to get out there in front of thousands of people and do things I wasn't sure I could manage. It worked. It helped me a lot. I think I described it as having little talks with myself and I always felt really silly doing it. Just in the last few years I've read that this really is a technique. And the visualization part, I've practiced since I was a child. As soon as music was being played, my mind was seeing dancing to that music in my head. When I needed help to find what I needed to do–even technically–I used those techniques and found them to be very helpful. Depending on the role I was playing, I would have to work myself into a mood that I could carry with me on stage. If I was going to do something that required deep, heavy movement and control, then I would have to calm myself very much. I would actually gear my warm-up to the mood and feeling I wanted to have.

MARGIE GILLIS: I was in a piece a number of years ago–a beautiful piece called *The White Goddess*. I sing those songs before I go onstage because I find if I sing I know if my body is responding because if it is tight I can't get anything through it. That's injury for me–because if the muscles aren't breathing, I am in trouble. So I sing. I run through the space. I often see things before they happen–I see certain audience responses. I do a lot of focusing in. I also do practical things like I leave a spot of white light in the centre, or a little sparkle in the middle of the stage so when I walk out it is there waiting for me and I can go to it.

PEGGY BAKER: At some point in the day I like to go and sit in the house of the theatre and just look at the stage. I really love doing that. It reminds me that people are going to be coming with expectations and excitement; it's not just me who's arriving at the theatre. I really love the view from the house. Sometimes it is a bit awesome looking from the stage into the house, but when you look from the house onto the stage, it's ready and waiting. I feel that view connects me with other people who've been in the space in the big continuum of my dancing life. I love that feeling. I like arranging my dressing table. I love putting on the makeup; for me that is a big transition–there is no turning back. I have everything I could possibly need in the theatre. I've always got a black unitard with me in case all my costumes fall apart. I've always got a needle and thread ready to go. I've always got food and water. I just don't want any little things to get in the way of my performance. I can get really thrown off by a big, sudden, shift in things. I like lying on the stage, also, just seeing it from a different point of view. I really like having a couple of places in the dance that I know if I go through them, they are going to tell me where I need to be–emotionally and physically. A lot of times I do them without any music. I am vocalizing the dynamics and singing to myself. But I love having those little entry points.

COMMENT: I remember being a young dancer and needing the support and encouragement of lots of people around me. Then, when I got to be principal dancer in mostly dramatic roles, I desperately needed isolation. The day of the performance I wanted to be alone. And because I have a very difficult body, I had to do a lot physically to get ready for the performance. I had a lot of superstitions–I had to have all my little things. I would hit the stage and hit my head so I would remember things. And I would always say a prayer, just before I went on, because I needed God with me.

The Dance of
Perfection

Photograph on previous page:
Company: Nederlands Dans Theater I
At: Holland Dance Festival
Photographer: Joris-Jan Bos

CHAPTER EIGHT
THE DANCE OF PERFECTION

THE DANCE OF PERFECTION

Sorella Englund, Lori Finklestein, Mikko Nissinen, Niva Piran, Kathleen Rea and Marion Woodman

LORI FINKLESTEIN: Dance has been used for years as a metaphor for life. I like to look at life, or dance, as a work in progress. The ballet world is actually very interesting, dealing as it does with talented individuals who start to work on their dream from a young age. They are developing both the mind and the body; this involves physicality, discipline and artistry–both psychological and spiritual.

MARION WOODMAN: What I have to say comes from my own life experience. I was basically healthy until I was about twenty. I loved university and was quite scholarly. My mind was completely split off from my body and I was happy. Then I decided I really wanted to live. I didn't want to be with the microscope all the time, or with ideas. I took a teaching job in northern Ontario. In those days, if you got into northern Ontario in October, you were there until spring because there was no way out.

They had wonderful dance floors, on springs, because dancing was the basic entertainment. I became addicted to it and with that came a desire to be thin–really thin and beautiful and sexy. I started on that path and, like so many anorexics, it took over until I found it impossible to eat.

This persisted for some years. Gradually I began to real-ize that what had driven me to anorexia was the desire for per-fection. I see it now in my anorexic patients who come into my office and say, "I've got this quarter inch of fat on my thighs." Fat is such a bad word. "And, I want it off." They obsess about fat that's not even there. And I say, "But, how are you today?" They're not interested in anything except the fat on their thigh. The tragedy of the lost soul sits in the chair opposite me, not interested in anything except a non-existent thing, which they call "fat."

There's a huge illusion involved in the yearning for what-ever this perfection is. It is a total denial of life. The soul ceas-es to exist as an entity. If you take that just one step further, I think there's a double thing that goes on here: many women, particularly those I'm working with, had mothers who were not connected to the life force. They were not happy to be women. They didn't like their sexuality. They certainly didn't like their little daughters' genitals when they were born, because their daughters were going to have to endure being women. These women have a profound lack of connection with the survival chakra and, when you combine that with the fact that they choose to live in the mind, you see the huge gap that begins to exist. From my point of view, it ends up in a death wish.

Any addiction–and certainly anorexia is an addiction–is a drive towards death. Every alcoholic knows that sooner or later their addiction is going to end in death but they go on doing it. If you think of any addict you know, unconsciously they have a drive "out" of life. Even if it's just fantasy. My work is an attempt to connect an addict with reality–the reality of their own soul and their own body, and the reality of being a human being, beautiful in their imperfection.

The way I work with addiction is through deep bodywork using the imagination and imagery. I do a lot of work with cancer patients who use deep imagery to come to a place where they honour the sweetness of the body. If you talk to the body, it sometimes gets frightened and doesn't want to do whatever you're trying to make it do. But if you say, "Now listen, it's OK, sweetheart. Shhh. Just talk to me. Tell me what's wrong," you'll get an answer. And, you may be shocked. Your body will tell you what is the matter. If you set up a conversation with your body, and really learn to listen to its wisdom, your addiction to perfection will gradually vanish because you are so interested in finding out who lives in there. And you no longer care so much about the mind: to know the mind is one thing, to know the body is quite another.

You know you're going to die. But if I told you that you have cancer and may die in two months, that's a different thing. The body all of a sudden starts to go into shock and fear. You will have to deal with it at this level and that experience is what life is all about.

I attempt to work with body and with voice, opening the body up as much as the person can deal with. I have to be very, very careful because our body carries all these repressed memories. You can only let up so much at one time; otherwise, you will blow your container to pieces. Let the memories come slowly. Then gently put the voice on that. Allow the voice to drop and gradually you come to the reality of who you are. And that beautiful human being can be present to other people who are also present.

SORELLA ENGLUND: I have suffered from anorexia since my twenties, not so much as the result of a search for perfection, but rather because of addiction. I felt that, even at a young age, the only place where I could survive was dance. It was where I was allowed to feel and be me; I felt strong and some-how untouchable when I danced. When I became plump, as teenagers do, I was told, "you can't dance until you lose so-and-so many kilos." For me, this was catastrophic. I had nowhere to go. No future. So, I stopped eating and couldn't control it. I felt very ambivalent: I had this tremendous professional success but I was nearly dying. I knew it was wrong: not being alive and still being so much alive with all the success. The thinner I got, the more people said, "Ahhh, my God. You're beautiful!" and I thought, "This will never stop." I was caught in my own trap with a strange death wish. Sure enough, I had a heart attack. My mind was quite clear when it came and I felt, "OK, I'm dying. It's fine." But my body didn't want to die; it fought with absolute desperation to stay alive. I did survive.

I think "perfection" can have so many meanings for dancers. We have the perfect body. That's scary. We have the perfect technique; the perfect look–if the nose is right, then everything is right. And then, of course, we can choose to say we have the perfect artistic direction. But I still have a hard time using the word "perfect." Is art perfect? Is the goal of art perfection? I don't think so. The goal of art is deeper and bigger. It's trying to find some answers or show the mirror of what we are doing with the life in us. And then the whole world of emotions and feelings, are they perfect? I don't think so. They're just there. You have your own mud. You have your own beauty. You have your own spirit. You have everything. But it's not "perfect," and I don't think it should be. If we see a performance that really touches us, it is because the performer is telling us how it feels from the inside–the spirit, the emotions, the senses and the sexuality. It's not the product that touches us, impressive as that might be. I think, "My God, that's beautiful." But I forget it five minutes later.

I have a hard time making friends with the perfect image of both the dancer and the inner life. I think focusing more on the inner life enhances education. Students must face the "who am I?" in all this. And the one I am, she's OK. Young dancers should not try to mirror someone else or strive for Barbie-doll perfection. They need to be encouraged to become the people they can become. This is what I'm fighting for.

MIKKO NISSINEN: First of all, I am really grateful that this universe guided me toward dance at a relatively early age because it has been a wonderful tool for learning. I was told I wasn't perfect but, being a stubborn person, I survived against all odds and danced professionally for twenty years with what some might consider a successful career. I have dedicated my life to dance–I am still learning about all the psychological aspects of which I was so unaware in the beginning.

We have millions of coordinations in our bodies and it's much healthier if we look at learning as a process of eliminating the unnecessary for whatever purpose we are working toward. You can imagine what kind of pressure it takes away from the individual student when they can relax and accept themselves and start looking at what's really inside instead of always trying to bring in something from the outside. To what extent can we really take responsibility for something remarkable on stage? Maybe we would be better served if, from the beginning, we understood that we can become instruments. You hear Bach's music. Do you think some human person was able to write that by themselves because of what they learned? Maybe they learned how to become a wonderful vehicle, an instrument between the universe and the earth.

It's a hard balance. We're dealing with very young dancers. Where do we start? Do we teach a healthy attitude toward learning? Our main job, as educators, is to get more information and evoke that little spark of curiosity toward all the different subjects, trying to stay as open-minded as possible while providing students with some kind of structure and support–a way to look at it all.

Dancers are not trying to create reality. We are training our bodies, our instruments, to translate illusions. If we really use energy, recycle energy, by sending it somewhere with the movement and then bringing it back, we aren't as depleted. The movement quality is more interesting and we're more open as an instrument.

There are so many ways of looking at this. I think we're all in a process together and it is a wonderful learning experience for everybody. I really believe we're heading in the right direction. We face different obstacles today in this electronic age with the average attention span hovering around five seconds. Our product is very different from the products the mass media and television are preaching about day in and day out. But I believe dance is like a fire and it is contagious.

KATHLEEN REA: Perfectionism, for me, is the drive towards becoming the perfect form through the removal or suppression of undesired qualities or traits. And this perfect form is often dictated by the culture we live in.

I have been involved in society's pursuit of perfectionism since I can remember. I think it is not just an element of dance but an element of our society. I don't remember when this concept became clear for me. It was like a reflex to try and find out what the perfect form was for whomever I was with and then try to mold myself to become it. I knew from a very young age that there were parts of myself that just weren't acceptable. By the time I began my ballet training, I was already used to this way of being. And the ballet training seemed like the perfect place to act this out because it was a world with very strict and clear relatively unchanging views on what desired forms should be. I could know what to be and put all my effort into being it.

At the same time, this world also provided me with a place to express my soul, which had two sides to it–the perfectionistic side and the side where I could find release and a place to be. Those two sides battled in me for many years. And there still is a struggle between them.

One of the repercussions of this struggle was a ten-year battle with bulimia. I tried to balance the desire to nurture myself physically and spiritually with the desire not to feed myself physically and spiritually in order to be small enough to be allowed in my chosen world. I had chosen a profession where big girls weren't allowed. It was as if I was trying to be a stewardess when my body was too wide to fit between the rows of passenger seats. It was my own stupidity to stake my life on trying to fit into a world I was too big for, but I was only fourteen and, when you're young and have a dream, it's hard to have a clear perspective on your life choices.

The level of training I got, in terms of the push to achieve a certain technique, gave me so many skills that have

123

enhanced my dancing immensely. Is it necessary to reach for such strict ideals of form and abilities? And when have we gone too far in this pursuit? And who is there to guide a dancer when this pursuit becomes a battle for spiritual and physical life? What would happen to the profession of classical dance if we loosened our hold on what we thought a dancer should be? What would happen to *Swan Lake* if dancing became an expression of who we each actually are? I don't know the answers to these questions. All I know is my own journey.

Being a woman who has been pretty much ten pounds over the ideal weight of a ballet dancer for my whole dance career, my life, especially when I was younger, was an endless pursuit to lessen this gap at whatever cost to ensure my success. It was a battle that left me empty and in chronic emotional pain. To heal my wounds, I had to leave the classical ballet world and create my own internal world of acceptance. I then took this new frame of mind and searched to create and find places that allowed me to fulfill the role of dancer with this new way of thinking about myself.

My journey of the soul was to find a way where I could be and express myself without a censor. It is a process of letting go, of falling into the murky sea of imperfection. What gifts I have found in these places of unwanted flesh! I have found my artist, not the artist who is trying to be, but the artist who is. And now my work as choreographer and teacher demonstrates the delights of different shapes of people with different abilities. I embraced a new view of things—what was ugly becomes, when displayed with bravery and honour, a thing of radiant beauty.

When I go to see ballet, I am still so terribly drawn to the sublime, ethereal way that dancers effortlessly float across the stage, demonstrating the perfect essence of our desire to escape from the ground we stand on. I find this escape from humanness incredibly appealing, but it's just not my way anymore because I can't be healthy if I'm trying to do that. I'm also terribly drawn now to full, rounded bodies, vessels of expression, living in their flesh on earth. And, I do know this is a place where I have found acceptance that has enabled me

to find my own health as a dancer.

I know that every creative move I do now depends on maintaining an honesty of soul: I need a mind, body and spirit that actively act as channels for my creativity. Any deviation from this leads to a lack of soul in my dancing and choreography. I have found a new meaning of perfection in which I embrace all of me—every last imperfection—as a means to find the true, most honest expression of myself.

My version of healthy dance is to search out or create a form of expression, through dance, whose ideals match, as closely as possible, one's natural way, thus lessening the gap between what one is and what one feels one should be. This means there is less risk of symptoms, of self-abusive behaviour, that might occur in the driven pursuit to be the ideal. Dancers come in different sizes and different abilities; it requires an incredible strength of character to find a place where you fit in the dance world. There are often others telling you where you should be or what you should change. I hope that teachers, choreographers and coaches encourage their dancers to explore how they fit into the dance world without judgement.

In the fifteen years I've been struggling with perfection, I think I have found a simple formula: find out who you are and then find or create a place where you can be. Acceptance and letting go of perfectionism, as we know it, makes room for the beauty of what really is there.

NIVA PIRAN: I've been quite involved with the National Ballet School for almost fifteen years. First, in relation to treatment but much longer in the area of prevention—a program that has proven to be quite effective. In describing what I have learned here at this school, I would like to honour also the whole National Ballet School community—teachers, administrators and particularly students—because I learned a lot from the students with whom I dialogued in the process of preventing eating disorders.

The concept that resonates most strongly here is that of connection versus disconnection or alienation from the body. A few years ago, I overheard a new student chatting with some veteran NBS students. The new student talked about managing the body quite harshly, probably reflecting what she had learned from another training environment. She talked about fat and women's bodies in a deprecating way, pushing for thinness. She expected and accepted an injurious way of training. For her, the body was an imperfect, deficient domain that needed control–harsh management, starvation or self-denial–in the process of managing and addressing its deficiencies.

For veteran students, the body was natural and expressive, a strong, powerful domain within which one resides. I contend that the greater one's connection with her or his body, the less likely it is for the body to become a territory of harsh management for the sake of repairing and improving it towards the goal of perfection. I believe that the challenges that exist in our society become accentuated in dance.

My work has taught me that experiences that disrupt the sense of ownership of the body work to create a sense of alienation from it. Dancers, for example, are exposed to ongoing objectified gaze; they are externally monitored or controlled. Being harassed, being teased about the body, being treated in a harsh physical way or experiencing abuse can create rifts in one's sense of ownership of the body and increase the need to mend and perfect it.

In our consumer society, the body has become a much more powerful symbol. We are encouraged to over-consume but, at the same time, we get another message that we should exercise internal strength to resist the excess. The result is a kind of bulimia syndrome where thinness symbolizes the moral superiority of self-control and discipline.

Another body image, the plastic body, denies materiality and the fact that we have biological bodies. The right amount of repair, through starvation, self-denial, cosmetic surgery, confining clothes, makeup, vitamins, etc. can transform us into whatever image or shape we can be. The disempowered body of a dancer has to perform demanding physical tasks without being given the freedom to be as strong, muscular or as powerful as it can be. The silent body suppresses and restricts its wisdom, knowledge, appetite, emotions and joy or pain through self-denial and self-constraint.

I believe we need to examine these and other multiple embodied symbols in order to reinhabit the body in ballet in joyful, respectful and expressive ways.

QUESTION: I feel we live in a society where "young and thin" is in and "old and other than thin" is out. In the dance world, we're all in agreement that the body should not be the deciding factor of whether a person dances as a life-long pursuit. But, then you have artistic directors and choreographers who seem to still demand it. How do we convince choreographers and artistic directors about the healthy body? How do we instill this idea in the dance world?

SORELLA ENGLUND: I think the change is going to happen quite slowly because it's so messy. Not only in the dance world, but also in our whole society, the image of women and men is this really unnatural look. We're all running to fitness centres and having facelifts and corrections and changes. I think we are running away from life. The more focused you are on this body, the more you run away from who you are.

MIKKO NISSINEN: I think we're going in the right direction but there are lots of different kinds of artistic directors out there. Some tell professional dancers to stay skinny; their timetables are set by doctors who try to control these issues. And, if the dancer cannot stay within this timetable, they are sent home; their contract is not renewed. I'm dealing with a company with twenty-four professional dancers. Somebody else might have eighty. It's a question of what kind of supporting team you have and how you talk about these issues. We have dancers in major North American companies that, twenty years ago, would not have been principal ballerinas. Today, it's more accepted. Overall, I'm really quite optimistic.

KATHLEEN REA: I have been told to lose weight at least five hundred times throughout my career. I just have this faith in me. I really don't know how much better it is getting out there but I think the public is starting to see the loss of soul that's happening in the dance world from this total attention on the body. I'm hoping that audiences are going to get bored or saddened by it. At a grass-roots level, audiences are starting to be interested in seeing real people on stage and that's where my faith is.

MARION WOODMAN: I'd like to speak to this from the point of view of the unconscious. I work with dreams; from my point of view, healing can take place from following a dream pattern. What you see in the dreams of an anorexic is a nasty officer attempting to kill the feminine. Since the characters in our dreams are all us, I would suggest to you that, in our culture, there is an undercurrent of rejection of the feminine. However much we have made strides with the feminine, there's a backlash. When I use the word feminine, I mean being able to be present in the body, being able to hold paradox, love process, and being able to surrender. If we can help people who are anorexic, particularly young people, and say: "Let's look at what's going on in the unconscious," maybe then we could bring them to a place where they can love themselves and their femininity.

In physics, they're discovering that fear is matter. If you think about that, you understand why so many people are carrying so much weight: the body is constricted. Dancers get so frightened; their body constricts and holds water. You can force the weight down with discipline but it will come back because the thermostat is set in fear. Their body is always cold. The food they eat does not turn into energy. So, the question is not how much are they eating, but why does the matter not turn into energy? We're talking about vibrational bodies and so one has to examine the block that stops the matter from moving into energy. I really think that if the dancer's body is going to glow, you have to really look at the energy that is moving.

NIVA PIRAN: One thing that I think is important to do is give people the opportunity to examine how their ideas are related to issues of femininity or power or flight. I think those are the symbols that are not examined often. And I think those symbols are so important because they really guide the whole experience of training.

In order to create change, people have to become activists. Dancers are saying, "No, this is not acceptable." Everyone should get involved in educating others and demanding change.

QUESTION: Everybody's describing the split between mind and body. How do we make the bridge so we can make the body whole?

MARION WOODMAN: The way I work with it is through dreams. People can do a lot with their dreams without an analyst. The bridge between soul and body is the metaphor, the metaphorical body. The dream is a picture of our soul condition, so it carries both the physical and the psychic. If you want to know your spiritual condition, you look at the picture in the dream. A child who is talking in dark images–"I'm too fat, I'm just a slob"–imagine what that's doing to their body in terms of fear. If I'm working with these young ones in my office, I try to get them into the images that are coming out of their dreams. And I talk to them, I paint them, dance them. What those images are is energy. A lion is not a cat in the dream. A little pussycat is one kind of energy, a lion is another. So, get down on the floor and be the lion and the energy comes up. They start to ask, "Who am I?" For me, the connectors are to find out your own imagery and be able to talk to your own muscles, your own bones; listen to your own body and your own symptoms, because that's where your individuality is.

MIKKO NISSINEN: It's up to the individual to really ask, "Who am I as a dancer?" You can have very unsuccessful working relationships if you work for a company that views dance differently than you do. Your responsibility as a teacher is to try to guide students to the kind of companies where they have a chance to be happy and really accepted. We are saying, "Yes, this dancer is an artist, but maybe he or she is an impressionistic painter who doesn't fit into the museum of modern arts."

COMMENT: If a director says, "You're ten pounds too heavy," it's crazy. But they can say, "You are not for my company." We have to find ways, as teachers and choreographers, to really be careful of how we speak because the same thing can be negative or positive: one will destroy and one will nurture.

SORELLA ENGLUND: The biggest problem is seeing dancers as tools or instruments, not with respect but as something to be used. And, very easily, a dancer becomes a victim in her or his own life.

QUESTION: I think a lot of the problems we're talking about

come from men imposing their values and vision on women in ballet. Do you think that women have let themselves fall into that trap? The reality for female dancers is that if you stand up for yourself, there are a hundred to replace you at the drop of a hat.

LORI FINKLESTEIN: What we should be doing is educating the people who buy the tickets or read the dance magazines or listen to what the critics have to say. Because if somebody isn't buying a ticket, then a company's not going to be successful and there will have to be some changes.

QUESTION: Most dancers, I believe, are compulsive and obsessive before they even begin training as dancers. We have to step back and ask, "Why do you want to control your physical environment?" What happens is that the dancer's body becomes the victim of the attempt to control or restrain or restrict or discipline. Dance can be either a wonderful way of being a worse compulsive-obsessive or a wonderful form of therapy.

COMMENT: I think we need to have a balance. I was a very happy dancer. I loved music, I loved the discipline of ballet. I think there's a difference between perfection and being constructive or trying to fulfill a potential. I think the dignity of each dancer has to be kept intact. Otherwise, you cannot create an artist.

COMMENT: I was a dancer for many years and I was very happy. There is one basic thing I know: movement is something natural. When children are born, they move. I think when we teach and work with very young dancers, we should remember that somewhere they have in them this natural sense of movement that we should nurture and take care of. We should really make sure we develop it.

QUESTION: How do you apply your spirit and like who you are when you're on stage trying to be someone else?

SORELLA ENGLUND: Well it's quite impossible. But you can learn what the work is about. You start reading or studying it and you react to what you read. How did your character grow up? How was her relationship to her mother? Her father? Her sisters? Was she lonely? Was she outgoing? Was she introspective? The truth is somewhere and the dancer will start

responding to it.

QUESTION: Have you found people are changing their attitudes?

SORELLA ENGLUND: I think NBS, on the whole, has changed a lot. Students are heavier. They're now women in women's bodies. Some visitors to the school say, "My God, the students have breasts." They are really shocked. Actually, they say it in a way that's maybe not the most respectful, but students now have permission to actually go through puberty.

LORI FINKLESTEIN: As a consultant with NBS for twelve years, I see a marked change. When I first started, students asked, "Am I thin enough?" "Do I have the balletic body?" You don't hear that as much anymore. Students now seem to be talking more about real life issues, about themselves, their relationships, their hopes and their dreams. I think students are also learning how to speak for themselves and talk to their ballet and academic teachers. They're not so afraid of mistakes.

COMMENT: I think it's important that we remember that this weight problem is an extended obsession. It's not just about ballet. I have a little five-year-old girl who came home and said, "Mommy, am I fat? Look at my tummy." I was horrified.

MARION WOODMAN: I work with eating disorders. That is my specialty. And there's no doubt the yearning for perfection is profound in almost every woman who comes into my office. It is a fundamental yearning, but with it goes a terribly dark side–a dark voice keeps killing the spontaneity of the soul. I think it's rampant in our culture.

KATHLEEN REA: In my family, my grandmother is bulimic, my sister is bulimic and then I was bulimic. I probably chose dancing because it seemed like a perfect forum to act out this scenario.

MARION WOODMAN: I think it's so important that we stay with the idea of excellence as contrasted with perfection. You know, when I'm in the hot heat of writing–I'm not a dancer but I do write–I want it to be the best possible. Nothing else will do. What I've learned is that for certain periods of my year, I go into that phase where I work as hard as I can to make my writing as articulate as I can. And then I stop acting like that and just become an ordinary human being. During the hot fire, I'm in love with the spirit and I wouldn't take that away. Life wouldn't be worth living without it.

SORELLA ENGLUND: I think we all know that feeling. I can't go halfway and say, "It's OK." It's not OK and something in me knows it.

MARION WOODMAN: But you don't have to be there all the time.

SORELLA ENGLUND: No, you come down. Someone suggested earlier that something was boring as housework and I thought, "but I love housework." That's my way of being very normal, making something clean and nice and neat.

BODY POLITICS

ANNA AALTEN: Twenty-one years ago in September, 1978, a young Dutch dancer died as a consequence of her profession. Olga de Haas was young, beautiful and extremely gifted. She was considered one of the great talents of the Dutch ballet.

Olga's professional career started in 1960 when she was only sixteen years old. She danced with Het Nederlands Ballet (which later became Het Nationale Ballet), where she soon became one of the principal soloists, dancing all the major roles. When she was in her twenties, Olga discovered there was more to life than dancing and she started partying. This affected her dancing and caused her to lose roles.

But Olga was ambitious. She worked hard to get her roles back, taking medicine to ease the pain of the heavy training and hard physical labour. And she stopped eating so she could be as light as possible. In 1978, her body gave up on her. She died, only thirty-three years old. Maybe I am simplifying things when I say her death was caused by the physical and emotional demands of her profession. But they certainly were related.

Ever since I came across this story, I have been wondering what exactly happened to Olga de Haas? Is her story a typical one? Are the bodily practices that led to her death part and parcel of the dance profession? Or should we regard Olga's story as tragic, but exceptional?

What I want to do is draw your attention to what this story can tell us, regardless of the answer to the question of whether Olga is typical or an exception in the dance world. What does the story tell us about the specific demands of a dancer's career? What does the story tell us about the ways in which the dancer's body is viewed and how it is treated in the dance world?

A Dancer's Career. Maybe Olga de Haas's story is exceptional. But Olga undermined her own health by practices that are definitely not exceptional in the dance world. She worked too hard, trained too much and pushed her body to the limit and beyond. She did this because she had had a prominent position in a ballet company, which she had lost and now wanted back.

People always say a dancer's career is short. And it is. In February, 1998, during the Holland Dance Festival in The Hague, we talked about the shortness of dancers' careers. Our main focus then was on what comes after the dancing career. Will most dancers have a second career after their dancing years?

I now want to draw your attention to another matter. When we say that a dancer's career is short, what does that mean for the career itself? What does it mean for the young dancers and the not-so-young dancers and the almost-retired dancers to know they will have only a short career? Doesn't it mean they need to make the most of it? And what does that mean? What does it mean to "make the most of" your health and well-being? It means working harder than you should sometimes, or maybe even most of the time. It means over-training. And it means being tired very often, because there is no time to recover from a strenuous rehearsal or a performance. It means being constantly aware of the fact that you will soon be replaced by younger dancers. It also means grief and misery because you were not given a role you desperately wanted and maybe this was your only chance to dance this particular role, because next time you might be too old. It means having a constant sense of urgency, of having to make things happen now, and all the stress that comes with that. It means working with pain and injuries. It means taking painkillers to prevent feeling something you know you should not ignore, because pain can be your body's way of telling you to stop or to change your working habits. It means discovering an injury that has gone too far because you ignored it. And maybe that injury will be the reason you have to stop dancing altogether. Or suffering from an injury that is the result of forcing your body to do things it simply is not capable of doing, because you never take the time to sit down and analyze what exactly you are doing and how you could do it differently. It means teachers who know they don't give their young students enough time to rest, to relax and to give their bodies the recuperation time they need, because time is too short and they have so much to learn. And it means company dancers trying to maintain rehearsal schedules that do not permit them time to recover. Although they complain to me and to one another, the dancers do not complain to their ballet masters or choreographers because their careers are too short and they do not want to run the risk of losing out on roles.

I want to stress that I am not saying here that it is the school, the company management or the choreographers who are all being too demanding on the dancers. Dancers are intelligent enough to make their own choices, but they make them within a situation that they themselves cannot control, a situation where this "shortness of the dancer's career" looms over them as a constant warning and threat.

Body Politics. And now my second theme: the ways in which the body is viewed and treated in the dance world. What about the body politics of dance? Some time after Olga's death, Rudi van Dantzig, choreographer, writer and artistic director of Het Nationale Ballet in Olga's days, published a small booklet as a memory to her. He wrote about her talent, her ambition and her career, which was short but striking. When I first read the book, there was one particular phrase that caught my eye and got stuck in my mind. It is in the part where van Dantzig writes about Olga's first years with the company: "Her line pattern was somewhat disturbed by her upper legs that were a little too heavy, and which disturbed the harmony in her, apart from that, so fragile build... She worked a lot, almost too much, and made tremendous

progress. Not only her technique became increasingly better and more balanced, her build also changed. The heaviness disappeared from her legs. It was as if she had demanded of herself: I must look like this. Through sheer willpower and persistence, her build indeed changed. The proportions of her body became increasingly harmonious."

Van Dantzig's words clearly demonstrate a belief in the mastery of the mind over the body that is, I think, very telling for the way the body is viewed in the dance world. In this, the dance world is not alone: our Western ways of thinking about the body can be traced back to the heritage of Christianity and to the ideas of the Enlightenment. As a result of that heritage we regard the mind and body as separate and we believe the body to be inferior to the mind. Our belief in the superiority of the mind over the body has severe consequences for the ways we view our bodies and the ways in which we treat them.

In general, one could say that, in our eyes, bodies are seen as malleable. Bodies are seen as material, like clay in the hands of the artist, to be molded and formed. We work on our bodies with exercises, makeup, diets, body building and, as an ultimate form, with plastic surgery. We change our bodies according to our own will.

This is what Rudi van Dantzig was saying when he wrote about Olga de Haas, in the phrase that caught my eye: Olga's thighs were too heavy (at least for a ballet dancer), but through sheer willpower and determination she succeeded in making the surplus disappear. She moulded her body into the right form through her mind.

Bodies become objects, instruments, machines. We shape them into the right form and when something is wrong, we fix it. We are expected to do so. In our society the idea that bodies are malleable goes hand in hand with an idea about individual responsibility. We are responsible for our own bodies, for their looks and their function. If something is wrong, if some body part does not fit into the prevailing beauty ideals, or if some body part does not function well, we are supposed to work on it.

This view of the body as malleable, inferior, subject to a superior mind and the responsibility of the individual, is common to many different sectors of our society. The dance world is no exception. But who decides what is the right form when it comes to a dancer's body? And who is responsible for it?

People often say that the technical demands made on dancers' bodies have increased. Nowadays dancers can do, and are expected to do, so much more than before. Schools that train young dancers are very aware of this. They try to prepare their students as well as possible by offering them a full curriculum of widely different dancing styles. Company directors expect their dancers to excel in different styles. If one looks at theatre programs one sees companies giving performances of both a Martha Graham and a Balanchine ballet in the same evening. Imagine raising yourself on pointe to dance a Balanchine classic immediately after finishing a Graham piece! And imagine the training and the rehearsals that would have to come before the performance!

A dancer needs different "bodies" to dance a Balanchine or a Graham. The technical demands differ, as does what is seen as the right body by the choreographer. But the dancers of today frequently perform these different bodies with the one body they have.

Speaking about form, Olga became ill also as a consequence of her eating habits. She suffered from a serious eating disorder that was the result of her desperate desire to lose weight. She wanted to lose weight because when she first came into the company she was one of the lightest girls of the group. She was also one of the youngest, only sixteen, so her lightness was not surprising. But Olga was very aware of this and of the fact that she was chosen to dance the role that made her a star precisely because she was so light and easy to lift. Later, when she tried to make her comeback, she did so by the only way she knew: by trying to regain the body she had when she was sixteen.

Bodily ideals are present everywhere in the dance world. Dancers are in a difficult position because they are usually not the ones who define the ideals, but at the same time they have to embody them. They are expected to mould their bodies into whatever form the teacher, the artistic director or the choreo-

grapher prefers. And they do!

They work on their bodies, taking responsibility for creating and performing what is asked of them. But, as in the case of their career choices, they do so in an environment that is beyond their control. Because of the body politics of the dance world, with its ideals and its dependencies, they are at risk of going too far in the moulding of their bodies and in adapting to what is expected from them.

Olga de Haas's story is a tragic one. To be honest, I don't know whether she is typical or exceptional. What interests me is how her story makes us look more closely at how the dance world treats the health and well-being of its main participants: the dancers.

THE DANCER AS MYSTIC

JANET ROSEMAN: The subjects of dance and mysticism are enormous in scope. To present any definitive analysis in a short paper, when I know this is my life's work, would be rather brazen of me; however, I am interested in forging a union between them. Artist and mystic Robert Henri believed as I do that, "[t]he object which is in back of every true work of art is the attainment of a state of being; a state of high functioning, a more than ordinary moment of existence." It is this "more than ordinary moment of existence" that is revelatory and compelling to us both as artists and human beings. These states out of the ordinary consciousness, I believe, are available to both artists and mystics. Let me also say that the subject of mysticism—even the subject of the muse or divine inspiration—is baffling and individual. Words often do not serve the experience. However, it is my wish to discuss the similarities between the mystic state and the realm of creativity in dance and address their compatibility. In fact, this creative process is a mystery for all the arts and it is unique and personal. The notion of the godhead or the divine or the muse has always been present in the works of great artists. Although everyone chooses to call it something different, I believe it is the same sacred energy that is required in the artistic process. I don't use the word "sacred" in any particularly religious manner. To me, it embodies a different experience that is on a different plane than the ordinary. I also believe that some presence, other than the individual alone, is being acted upon and invoked. What is key is that there is a potent recognition in that process–the recognition of the not-so-ordinary experience and the receivership of the gifts that are used during that process.

I am not suggesting that a great work of artistry appears only through metaphysical or transcendental means. All artists work to acquire and perfect the tools of their art and dance is no exception. However, the enormous impact that this other dimension has on the creative spirit cannot be ignored. Its presence emerges in the literature of the mystics over and over again.

Before I identify the parallels specifically between dance and mysticism, I'd like to present a brief introduction to how I became enamoured of the two subjects. I am a dance critic, and I have always been drawn to dance performances in which the dancers illustrate much more than technical acumen. By this "dancing from the inside," I am referring to that state I happily experience when I watch the choreography of Alonzo King, the artistic director for LINES. His works pry open the heart–there is something so ancient and primitive in them–and that perhaps explains why I am drawn to them. His choreography turns the theatre into a sanctuary, echoing dance's earliest intention. One cannot dismiss the sacred elements of his dances and his devotion to a ceaseless exploration of the divine. Throughout time, in every culture from the Turkish whirling dervishes, African ceremonial dances and Native American ceremonies to American Jewish weddings and ancestral dances to the deities, dance has been part of the tradition honouring the sacredness of life, reclaiming both the body as divine vessel and the interconnectedness of all things. Dance has played an important role in every culture for healing, ritual, celebration, performance and personal transformation. All cultures dance. There are dances for the gods to bring on the rain, religious dances to experience exalted states, dance as performance and dance as a form of worship. In fact, the Bible has eleven verb forms to describe dancing. The link

between sacred dance and mysticism is profound. In many cultures the sacred dance is considered prayer–a form of communication between the gods and the dancer whereby god-like energies can actually enter the dancer, propelling them into an ecstatic state. Anyone who has ever watched the magnificent piece by Doris Humphrey, "Air for the G String," can witness her clear embodiment of the ecstatic state. Just watching her luminous face reminds me of what mystics must look like when they gaze upon the divine. It is a look of longing, of grace, of ecstasy, of serenity, of magnificence. Her dance is a sacred ritual in which the dancers express their intimate relationship with the divine. It is a language that is spoken by too few in our jaded culture, although it is universal in many other cultures.

We need only pay attention to the effect that dance has upon us to understand the parallel between body and spirit. When we dance, we feel good. We feel connected to our spirit and open to a greater energetic presence. In order to achieve this state, contemplation is required by both the mystic and the dancer to achieve stillness and surrender to the moment for either artistic inspiration or for prayer. During this surrender, the mystic or artist does not act, but receives. Over the years as a journalist, I have had the chance to speak with many famous dancers and choreographers. Certain subjects seem to appear again and again including: the sense of the divine when making or performing dance; the "heightened state" one may experience when performing; and the mysteries surrounding the creative process. When I thought about the similarities between dancer/choreographer and mystic, I recognized underlying unifying patterns:

Both the dancer and mystic are privy to ecstatic representations. Both can experience a mystical, transcendental state. A sense of the divine can occur, although it may not occur simply by will; it is a gift–both onstage as well as in religious settings. This changed state of consciousness intrigues me and I can honestly say that I have only witnessed a handful of dance performances where I felt the dancers had experienced that dimension. I imagine that in religious/ceremonial dances held in private and not for performance, these states occur again and again.

Both prayer (for the mystic) and dancing (for the dancer) are forms of prayer. Although these experiences are intensely personal, I am proposing that when the dancer dances from the inside, from deep within, they are praying. Dance is an activity that demands absolute attention and presence. No matter what, regardless of the merits of the dance form or technique, if it is done with all your heart and soul and attention, dance is a form of prayer which can lift you up to the heavens.

Mystics serve God or the Divine; dancers serve the art form. By serving the art form, dancers serve a higher dimension, or the divine. Over and over again, if one examines the literature, we find the theme of God or the Divine in the presentation of dance. Often, mystics prepare texts, diaries or even write poetry in praise of the Divine. Dancers serve as well, however their form of serving is the dance itself.

Both dancers and mystics experience what I call a "sacred consciousness" whereby they enter a sacred domain. Many dancers I have interviewed have told me of their own rituals before they enter the studio and often refer to the studio as "sacred ground." Dancers experience this often in the incubating and creative phase of the work through daydreams, night dreams, meditation or forms of ritual they may use for inspiration and idea play. Mystics also go into this state of consciousness to contact the Divine. Every artist and mystic can point to an occasion when this blurring of the Self with Other occurred. Whether this Other is God or the Divine or the muse is purely subjective.

The mystical experience and the creative process often involve a suspension of time, which I call "stop time," that is, no awareness of time as it really exists. During these experiences, both dancer and the mystic merge with another dimension. Entrance to this dimension can take a variety of forms; often the artist/mystic feels "possessed" in the sense that there is an absence of awareness or interest in "real time." It can be a world of reverie, or what Dr. Jane Piirto calls entrance into "beMUSED silence."

Faith in their vocation sustains dancers and mystics. The experience of being filled with one's art and being able to realize one's vision is often ecstatic and the feeling of completion that all artists experience when their work is "done" is very satisfying. Perhaps that is why we make art to begin with. However, it is the emptying, the nothingness, the void that artists experience that tests our true faith in ourselves as artists and in the Divine. This faith is essential to the capability for creating art and it is also essential for the mystic; however, it is the moment when the Divine is removed or the Divine inspiration is gone that truly tests one's confidence. Faith that reveals itself during moments of crisis, or what St. John of the Cross called, "the dark night of the soul" is key.

Both mystics and choreographers are privy to visions. Mystics often see visions of God, or angels, or even hell, when they are in a mystical state. I suggest that these visions are often healing. Choreographers often see visions as well, visions of their work embodying gestures, forms for dance and even actual dancing bodies. These visions may occur in dreamtime, or in a half-dream state, which is similar to the visionary experiences that mystics seek and experience. Both of them use these visions in their work—the mystics in their writings and teachings and the choreographer on stage. The use of dreams for inspiration and healing is not a new model.

In conclusion, no one chooses to become a mystic, and no one really chooses to become an artist. It chooses you. And, until you personally have an experience of that "other dimension" as mystic or artist, it really doesn't matter what this paper says or what you read; it is only through one's authentic lived experience of the Divine that one can truly know that this "other realm" truly exists.

DANCING IN COMMUNITY IN MEXICO
Creating "New" Performances out of "Old" Materials to Communicate Contemporary Messages; Reaching out Towards Creativity, Health, Well-being and Excellence

ANADEL LYNTON SNYDER: Although I was born in the U.S., I have lived and worked within the Mexican dance community for the past forty years. Issues of creativity, heath, well-being and excellence are important to us. Local non-professional dance standards can be seen as equally creative and important in promoting creativity, health, well-being and the excellence of optimal performance within local communities. I will describe the work my students, colleagues and I have carried out in Mexican urban and rural communities, helping to facilitate dance creation by ordinary people through what I call "Dancing in Community." I will speak of some of the social and cultural implications of these concepts in Mexican dance practices.

Performance events have taken place in the Lacandon Forest, the Highlands and the city of San Cristobal in Chiapas where dance-dramas were created by Mayan and mestizo sympathizers of the Zapatista movement. In one community, an Easter Passion Play was performed for the first time by settlers who combined their memories of similar traditional enactments in their villages of origin with some new ideas on the roles of women. In another, an original drama based on the life of Zapata and a collection of Mexican academic-style folk dances of the type propagated in public school festivals were recreated for new circumstances. One series of events took place during an Indian-Chicano Cultural Encounter where poetry, songs, murals, theatre pieces and dances were created every afternoon on social themes that had been discussed in the morning, then presented along with other local and Chicano performances, before a large audience from many Highlands towns. Creative movement experiences were offered to children from refugee families who fled from the Acteal massacre of December 22, 1997, to San Cristobal by a group of community workers who took a Dancing in Community workshop. The costumes and movements repre-senting "peace birds" for a massive peace march and the script or score for a participative dance for the Acteal children were created in this workshop.

The circumstances, participants, processes and results of these Dancing in Community processes were all quite different. However, what they shared was that dances were created by participants motivated to communicate with members of their communities, as defined by ethnicity, geography, shared experiences and religious and political ideals. In other words, they had something to say.

Dancing in Community is a philosophy of creativity which is designed to help overcome the limitations imposed by the way high art/popular art dichotomies are still often construed in Mexican dance and also, I believe, in the dance of some other countries.

Dancing in Community processes have been greatly influenced by Latin American thinkers such as Paolo Freire (liberation pedagogy), Enrique Pichon-Riviere and Ana de Quiroga (operative groups practice), Augusto Boal (liberation theatre) and the liberation theologists, among others. Their work focuses on ways to encourage people to speak out, to dialogue and listen to each other in order to communicate messages that are significant for the lived circumstances of their communities. Using art to express the need for justice, democracy, dignity and respect for all is particularly vital for those who have been colonized, dominated and oppressed due to ethnicity, gender, class, age, sexual preferences, physical and mental capacities, or culture. Traditional attitudes label what ordinary people have to say as either unimportant or dangerous for those in power. It takes effort to convince many folks that horizontal communication is just as valuable as top-down vertical communication.

When people are encouraged to realize that they have something important to say and the resources to say it, they make the effort to create in order to communicate because the positive feedback that dialogue propitiates is rewarding. When non-verbal communication through movement is involved, the process becomes even more exciting.

Dancing in Community starts out with simple movements

that are easy to follow because they are common to participants' everyday movement culture, ritual and social dance. The group can practice making and picking up on slight variations in the use of time, space, weight, flow and body parts (emphasized in Laban movement analysis) by alternating leader and follower roles. Facing each other in a circle, follow-the-leader warm-ups can be initiated and followed by everyone. Practice is offered in alternating the roles of innovator and stabilizer, using radical contrasts or small but clear and conscious variations, or by imitating movement patterns as exactly as possible. This practice is put to use when dances are created by brainstorming and trying out movement ideas to express themes structured through group discussion. Dances or parts of dances created in smaller groups are shown to the larger group for feedback. Depending on the circumstances and time frames and, of course, on the motivation and interest of the group and the community they are creating the dances for, these processes can be repeated as the dances are refined in concept and execution through practice.

Movement vocabulary, choreographic forms, non-hierarchical relations during the creation processes, exchange of roles and creation of a climate of security in order to be open and take risks, are among the more specific issues related to creativity, health and excellence which Dancing in Community practices have tried to rethink.

If we take as our premise that creativity is an essential part of what it means to be human, creativity can be seen as an essential part not only of individual health but also of the health and well-being of communities, of their ability to make creative adaptations to changing circumstances and to change the circumstances of their lives through creative practices. Thus art itself can be seen as reflecting and creating culture, and the lives of individuals and groups as determined by social and historical circumstances and determining them as well. Creativity can thus be seen as a result of the interaction between the impulse to act and the contexts within which the action must take place. Health, excellence and optimal performance are highly valued conditions that emerge through the interaction between the utopian desire for change to make

things new and perhaps better, and the propitiating conditions and real obstacles found in specific times and places, in the historical and social contexts within which people act. The only way of finding out how far positive change can be taken is with experiment, trial and error, trying and evaluating the experiences. Some changes may be found to have negative results for the values of the group, time and place, and need to be rectified while others may become incorporated into a positive practice.

Dancing in Community processes are the result of a methodology developed with the support of many of my students and colleagues over the past fifteen years. They emerge from the particular contexts of professional, ritual and social dance practices in Mexico, but the needs they seek to meet may be found more widely. Some of my colleagues and I became increasingly aware of a number of contradictions within contemporary modern, regional and traditional dance practices in which we were immersed. What we found most contradictory were the parameters that delimited and separated the traditions of different dance practices and the value systems that they implied.

In Mexico, as elsewhere, the dance practices of different social groups respond to different historical traditions. Teachers, critics, dancers, cultural administrators and audiences all interact within the field. Certain groups and individuals have the power to negotiate and judge standards of excellence in professional dance and serve as gatekeepers. Others, whose participation is usually less recognized, fulfill similar roles in popular dance practices.

Those who practice concert dance, as I did, train for many years in specialized schools and create works that are usually performed in theatres for specialized audiences who know the codes and current styles, who can "read" the dances and judge their formal innovations. In this respect, Mexican concert dance resembles that of other countries; however, particularly in Mexican contemporary dance, a populist ethos whose origins can be traced to the Mexican Revolution remains as a periodically renewed undercurrent. This ethos posits that Mexican art production should be accessible to the "people" and educate and sensitize them to their "identity." Themes relating to Mexican history and popular arts traditions are encouraged; however, arts training and public and private support for the performance and exhibition of art (the art market) demand that these themes be expressed within the canons of what is still seen as the "universal" forms represented by the succession of styles of high art practices. These canons are usually legitimated in the metropolitan centres, and followed in the peripheries or colonized countries. Mexican artists aspire to recognition by the standards of international gatekeepers. Many Mexican dancers are highly proficient in the internationally recognized movement techniques that are taught in the schools. They also try to keep informed on the latest innovations in choreographic style and genre. Creative intentions are considered the realm of professionally trained choreographers whose movement vocabularies could be clearly identified as within the parametres of international "art" dance: ballet, modern and perhaps some jazz. Thus, Mexican dancers who wish to communicate with their families and neighbours and fellow citizens may find that their real audience has become limited to their peers and the gatekeepers of the professional field. Folklore "ballets" use concert-style production values and training for their dancers and adapt semi-researched choreographies or invent others with a stereotypical Mexican flavour and a celebratory attitude. In all of these forms, innovations with certain limits are prized.

Some Mexican dance professionals, however, view innovations in traditional ritual and social dancing styles as negative or contaminating an imagined "purity." Those who adapt these dances for the stage try to "naturalize" or disguise their adaptations in order to maintain a discourse of authenticity. In traditional regional ritual and social dance practices, in contrast, any changes are often construed as negative.

On the other hand, those community members who see the need to innovate in order to use dance to communicate with their communities can find few precedents as their traditional dance forms have been viewed as ideally unchanging. When changes are identified they are usually construed as negative, as modern contaminations of the purity of ancient artistic practices.

As teachers and performers, some of my colleagues and I began to question whether a lengthy training in ballet and modern dance techniques should be required of those who seek to create dances. The culturally more accessible movement vocabularies of Mexican ritual and social dancing are idealized as handed down almost unchanged for generations. The anonymous creativity of the ancestors is recognized while that of recent generations is seen as negative and even as contaminating "true" popular culture. In reality, these attitudes reproduce colonialist social structures that posit European culture as superior and creative, and local culture as "natural" and unchanging, a survival of the past.

Actual historical processes do not correspond to this dichotomy which labels high art as creative and current, and art produced by ordinary people as an ancestral essence. The origins of most contemporary moves can be traced to Western popular culture (medieval peasant dances in ballet or the twist and other black dance forms as an antecedent for contact improv). When ballet or modern dance acclimatize in Mexico or other countries, some *mestizo* or mixed characteristics are taken on. Body types and everyday social and ritual dance movements influence movement styles. Dance embodies some national or regional elements.

As history moves on and human social groups evolve, vocabulary, movements, choreography, sound, objects, clothing and the use of physical spaces are continually semanticized and actualized in order to maintain communication. In order to dare to speak out and innovate, a climate of security for risk taking or the desperation of an emergency mobilization is needed. All cultural processes are constructed through collective cooperation as every individual contribution is more or less closely related to what is going on within the social context of the time, place and field within which the work is being carried out. In dance, the creative processes continue to take place through face-to-face contact within the oral tradition. Although in Western concert dance, the traditional hierarchy places the choreographer as more creative than the dancer, the collaboration and dialogic nature of dance construction deserve greater recognition.

Mexican contemporary dancers sometimes seek audiences among their family, friends and neighbors or others who have not been educated to form part of those knowledgeable about the professional dance field. One way has been by trying to incorporate Latin American images and movement styles into the contemporary dance genre. Another way has been to perform in public places outside the elite theaters where dance is usually presented. Most average citizens lack the cultural capital (to use the term of French sociologist Pierre Bourdieu) as well as the economic capital to access most concert dance. Even when performances are free, they do not feel at home in art theatres. Many distinguished members of the arts community work hard to ensure that arts creation and appreciation continue to remain markers of social distinction. The values of the international art market are constantly reinstated whenever they seem to be supplanted by local values. This contradicts the intentions of other Mexican cultural policies to bring art "to the people" by encouraging access to theatres, exhibitions and art classes through free or low-priced tickets and tuition.

Through a number of teaching experiences with ordinary people and university cultural extension services, I began to realize that many of my students felt an urge to dance creatively and to communicate without first dominating the movement techniques validated in New York or Paris. I began to search for ways to facilitate dance creation outside of these "professional" moulds. I realized that similar processes were beginning to take place in other creative fields. For instance, Native American writers have begun to use their own languages and images to address members of their own communities, not the outside art world.

With the help of students and colleagues, Dancing in Community methodology was developed to help find ways to overcome some of the obstacles to creativity and communication identified as: 1) specialized movement and stage codes outside the experiences of the local community of interpretation; and 2) old movement codes which are conserved as relics of social unity but whose inevitable renovations are not recognized as positive. A living movement art can never be petrified

as a stone to be kept in a museum. Dance continues to live through constant recreation.

This requires recognizing that dance creativity is not located only within European art forms that, in fact, are often used to invalidate and disempower local initiatives. Those who must learn the new and specialized movement languages in order to have their creativity legitimated may find themselves in a similar situation to those who have been told they had to learn Spanish or English in order to become "educated."

We began to ask some of the following questions: How can creativity contribute to health and well-being and lead to a richer and fuller life? Who can create? How do the gatekeepers of the field acquire and maintain their positions? How does the hegemony of particular social groups influence the processes by which art forms are recognized? Are the frontiers between high art dance and popular dance still justified? In what sense can creation be seen as collaborative or collective? Can consensus and democracy be applied to art making? Does art communicate within specific groups or is it a universal language? Could we consider that health and well-being imply that the criterion for recognizing creativity and excellence be decided within local communities and groups and not by "the new world economic order" which destines them to consume not create?

Creativity actualizes the way dance communicates with those who practice and witness it. When it is produced by and directed to a local community the recognition of this creativity should reside in this same local community. Excellence and optimal performance do not have to be judged by "world-class" values of others. Ballet traditions themselves have always incorporated some local or national characteristics.

I began to feel that health in the widest sense also implies flexibility–adaptability to circumstances within reason–for survival. Most of the colonized peoples of the world, including Mexicans, have survived through resistance. Pride in local culture has survived in spite of painful physical and symbolic violence and repression applied over centuries. A core sense of identity and dignity persists but often at the cost of simulating submission and subjection to humiliation. Today, those who are marginalized by the gods of the marketplace and high culture are slowly rebuilding alliances for survival.

The Zapatista slogan, "We seek a world where there is room for many worlds" (*Buscamos un mundo donde quepan muchos mundos*) is an ancient phrase with a contemporary meaning. Giving value to differences within the essential unity of humanness means that health, well-being, creativity and excellence should be accessible for all.

The Mexican anthropologist Guillermo Bonfil believes that the deep substrata of original culture in the Americas is submerged. In order to survive conquest, it was forced into hiding and stabilized through a very slow process of change that resisted the radical changes being forced from the outside. Bonfil sees signs of a period of flexibility and innovation currently underway, leading to a wider consciousness of the essential unity of a basic First Nations civilizing project kept alive over the generations and now flowering.

If dance is communication, I must accept as a teacher and performer that its message is polysemantic, thus always open to interpretation and reinterpretation. The speaker or mover and the listener or observer must enter into a dialogue in order to share some level of understanding between them. The speaker or mover must adapt the message to the specific context in which the communication is taking place.

In conclusion, when there is a reason to create, meaningful dances may emerge through a group process that is meaningful in and of itself. Spectators can become co-participants in the construction of meaning and even dance themselves. They can become active "witnesses" as Anna Halprin puts it, rather than passive observers. When the opportunities for critical listening and speaking become available to all, when roles are rotated and not perpetuated through rigid hierarchies, creativity may promote social, emotional and physical health. Health requires a whole being. Where a few can aspire to excellence by creating messages which the rest of society is expected to consume, the health of full humanness is compromised. Dance can occupy a central role in the construction of positive group identity. Let us help dance find that place of creativity and hope, where healthy well-being

and excellence may choose from among the myriad moves to be found in the world. We do not envision one "world-class" standard for dance but a sharing of the many ways of dancing in the world, equally valued and recognized as manifestations of human creativity.

Writing
About
Dance

Photograph on previous page:
Dancers: Irene Dowd instructing Magdalena Adamczenko
At: Canada's National Ballet School
Photographer: Jeannette Edissi-Collins

CHAPTER NINE
WRITING ABOUT DANCE

SOCIETAL IMPACT OF DANCE WRITERS AND CRITICS

John Alleyne, Paula Citron, Michael Crabb, Lindsay Fischer, William Littler, Richard Philp, Francia Russell and Gretchen Warren

RICHARD PHILP: There is a lot of tension concerning the role of dance writers. At *Dance Magazine*, we have, over the years, published more dance writing than any other publication in the world. One of our requirements is that dance writers know something about dance which is harder to come by than you might imagine. Dance writing is a specialized field, not well paid, for the most part. The requirements are tough. The one requirement to be able to write about dance, in my view, is that you would have to live with a dancer for five years. I find a lot of dance writers have a thin knowledge of the inside of dance; they spend most of their time in the audience and not as reporters of the whole event.

PAULA CITRON: I am the dance reporter for a commercial classical radio station, in fact the only one in Canada. I also am the Toronto correspondent for *Dance Magazine* and I do a lot of freelance work. My background is actually theatre, although I did take a lot of dance when I was a young person. I also have a background in dance history. Because there were so few dance writers, dance became my specialty. It was thrust upon me and it became a great love of mine.

MICHAEL CRABB: I am the host and producer of a national arts program on the Canadian broadcasting service called "The Arts Report." I started writing about dance from a point of total ignorance in about 1972 or 1973 and have improved maybe a tiny smidgen since then–partly through the efforts of people such as Deborah Jowitt. I am now the dance critic for the *National Post* and I also write for a number of international publications.

GRETCHEN WARREN: I write about dance and teach dance because I cannot dance; although it is not my whole life, dance is my consuming passion.

LINDSAY FISCHER: I am an ex-dancer presently teaching here at the National Ballet School. I oversee the Career Counseling Program, which also includes teaching about the theory of art and the relation of artists to society.

JOHN ALLEYNE: I'm currently the Artistic Director of Ballet British Columbia. I was a dancer with the National Ballet of Canada and I freelanced as a choreographer before I took over the position of Artistic Director in 1992.

FRANCIA RUSSELL: Like Lindsay and John, I was a dancer with the New York City Ballet and with Jerome Robin's company, Ballet USA. But my real obsession/passion in life is teaching young dancers and helping them realize their full potential in professional careers. My only qualification for sitting on this panel is what has been done to me by critics and the fact that I once wrote a book review for *Dance Magazine*.

WILLIAM LITTLER: I earn my daily bread as dance and music critic for the *Toronto Star*. My background is primarily in music. I think most dance writers have not been dancers or choreographers, although there is, I'm happy to say, an emerging number who are coming from that background. I was a member of the audience in terms of dance and when I decided to write about it, I went off to Connecticut College for a couple of summers and took dance classes–movement analysis and that kind of thing–and managed to feel very uncomfortable in very short order. I think I was designed for sitting. In any event, I don't think ignorance is bliss and I think we spend a lifetime trying to acquire the background. I haven't, so far, tried the Philp thesis of living five years with a dancer, but it is a thought and as rational as many. However, the field of dance criticism is a very recent one in terms of the field of criticism as a whole. I chaired the first North American dance critics conference in New York many years ago and was the founding chairman of the Dance Critics' Association.

GRETCHEN WARREN: It is my belief that the majority of people who read dance reviews are already in the field–dancers, choreographers, teachers and producers. In other words, as critics, most often we are probably preaching to the choir. I think we may be missing an important opportunity. The North American audience for dance, in comparison to the audience for music or theatre, is still relatively small. I think the dance writer has the potential to help change that situation, to help build the audience for dance.

There is a lot of talk about the critic's responsibility to educate the general audience about dance. Some writers seem to think that includes making scholarly references in their reviews to historical events or individual steps using French ballet terms. I am afraid I see this–and I am a dancer–as a kind of name-dropping. I question its usefulness to the general public. I would prefer that we writers focus on stimulating the layperson's curiosity about dance, for only then will they want to learn about it in a more in-depth way. And when that happens, I believe readers will be inspired to educate themselves to a degree that is appropriate to them. In fact, the idea of a

general audience looking at a dance performance with the amount of knowledge that we look at a dance performance with is rather revolting to me. It's certainly not my goal as a writer to endow the audience with that degree of insight. There is a lot to be said for not knowing too much and just allowing oneself to feel when one goes to see dance. I often wish I could enjoy performances with the more innocent eyes of my youth–eyes that don't see every sickled foot or poorly balanced pirouette. The only thing that seems important to me is that each member of the audience is able to take away something from the performance that directly enriches his or her life; if my writing about dance helps them do that, then I will feel my work has had a positive impact on this art form I love so much.

How can we as dance writers help to build the audience? I would suggest that we try to convince our editors to publish more articles aimed at those who generally do not attend dance performances, who know little, if anything, about dance, persons for whom dance seems totally irrelevant. Our purpose would be to stimulate curiosity to such an extent that readers might purchase a ticket to a dance performance and, armed with the information we've imparted, be able to enjoy that performance far more than if they had walked in cold. To my mind, this type of writing–what I call "throwing out the hook"–generally comes in two categories. The first is human interest stories about dancers and choreographers that demystify what they do and make it possible for the layperson to relate to these artists as human beings. One reason these stories are so important is because only a very small percentage of the general population has actually had any experience participating in dance. Think about it. Almost every North American child plays some kind of sport, creating in them a lifelong interest in sports. Because they enjoyed doing it, because they know the rules and the challenges inherent in these activities, they are a knowledgeable, enthusiastic and frequent audience at sports events. But dance is something that only a relatively few people–the majority of whom, unfortunately, are female–have experienced. There is a vast sea of people out there who cannot, for lack of experience, relate to dance at all. Human interest stories are the only way I know to spark curiosity in them to attend performances and learn more about dance. And I'm almost sure that once they experience the excitement of a good dance performance, they will be back for more. The second kind of writing that I feel has the potential to help build audiences is writing that seeks to place dance in the context of contemporary life. Currently, I think there is one dance writer who does this extremely well, and even if he were not the moderator of this panel, I would take this opportunity to sing the praises of Richard Philp. I always look forward to the way Richard weaves current issues in politics, environment, health or fashion to name just a few, into his *Dance Magazine* column. I regret only that his important and insightful commentary appears only in a publication that is preaching to the choir. His perceptive comments deserve a wider audience. What Richard realizes, of course, is that the way dance is created, performed and viewed today is undeniably influenced by the events surrounding our daily lives. I believe we writers can help to increase our dance audience when the writing demonstrates that dance is relevant to everyone's life–that it has the potential to be much more than just some tasty, elitist snack that is occasionally, or maybe never, popped into people's mouths.

MICHAEL CRABB: I can't remember who it was, but someone once described a critic as the person who waits in the mountains while the battle rages and then comes down afterwards to shoot the wounded. I have been on a number of panels with critics where the audience is filled with disgruntled dancers and choreographers whose sole purpose is not even to leave any wounded. I am glad to see that is not the case here.

I think we are using the word "critic" without really defining it. An important distinction has to be made because most of the people who write about dance, to my mind, are not critics and most of the dance writing (if it is even worth calling it that) is a kind of consumer-guide type writing which is called reviewing; it is placed in newspapers in decreasingly smaller and smaller quantities. If you are talking about a critic, surely you are talking about someone who is engaged in a continuing discourse about an art form. That is often a very difficult thing to accomplish in the context of a daily newspaper. Where it is possible, of course, is in the context of a serious dance magazine and especially a dance magazine that allows that kind of discourse to continue. Then you have a critic and that is where the societal role and responsibility become rather different than when you are a reviewer.

I mostly consider myself a reviewer. I don't think I would particularly define what I do as "criticism." Even so, I do start from certain basic points. First of all, I have a responsibility to the art form, which is not quite the same thing as having a responsibility to the practitioners of the art form, because they are born, live and die, while the art form continues. I have a respect and a love for dance. If I didn't, I shouldn't be writing about it. I consider myself a professional audience member. I see my responsibility to be a kind of a bridge linking the art form, its practitioners and my readers. But I am writing for myself more than anyone else, because I like doing it. If somebody wants to buy my work and print it–even if they want to pay me a paltry sum–that's fine. I couldn't support myself on writing, which is why I have a full-time job at the CBC.

Because I like dance and am enthusiastic and sometimes get angry about it, I want to share my emotions. That can become very self-indulgent, so I have to stop at a certain point and say, "Wait a minute. People may read this and be influenced by it. What is my obligation?" First of all, I am not a publicist for particular events or choreographers or dancers. I am a propagandist for the art form in the biggest sense, but I am not a publicist for it.

In sharing my own enthusiasm or objections to something, I may twig somebody else's interest, but I should do it in a language that is direct and respectful. Editors seem to like criticism that is negative and gets people angry, because that sells newspapers. I don't see any point in deliberately going out to insult individuals: even if you think something is bad, there is surely a way of qualifying or putting what you are saying in a context.

Another societal responsibility is to place dance within the broader context. One of the problems with dance is that it exists in a sort of vacuum and dancers live in a kind of hot house environment where they seem to be underexposed to what is going on in other art forms. They are sometimes not even aware of the way they seem to pick up on energies and influences in society which are clearly manifesting themselves. I think, as far as possible, it is important to make those connections for an audience, so they may see more of the relevance of dance. It might be difficult to make anybody understand the relevance of *Sleeping Beauty* but when you can look at something like James Kudelka's new *Swan Lake* and actually see how a choreographer can take a museum piece and, without destroying its traditional values, present it in a way that could be read as having contemporary vibrations and resonances, that point needs to be made.

We are living in an entertainment environment where everything is becoming bigger, louder, bawdier and more expensive. Of course, that is not necessarily the environment that creates good art; entertainment is the wave that carries the art. Just because something is small or refined or not necessarily virtuosic or might appear from the outside to be unspectacular, it may contain something that is emotionally extraordinary. Finding the language to share that knowledge with readers in the hope that they might be so intrigued they will go and see it, seems to me to be increasingly important. The big flashy performances can sell themselves; they don't need any coverage.

PAULA CITRON: When I started doing a lot of work for William Littler for the *Toronto Star*, I would phone him up and say, "Blank company, blank independent, blank person looks like they are having a really interesting show. Can't we give them an advance feature?" And William would say to me, "A newspaper is not in the business of selling tickets. We are in the business of selling news." I still haven't come to grips with that because my passion for dance is such that I want everybody out there to know that in some church basement somewhere, some independent toiling away is of such interest that all the twenty seats in that house should be filled. I guess it has always troubled me—the layering system that goes on about who gets in the papers.

My first point is that dance writers do sell tickets. I can

give you a stunning example from the *Globe and Mail*. I happened to be sent to review a performance of *Taming of the Shrew* with Karen Kain dancing with a new partner because her regular partner, Rex Harrington, was ill. I was so entranced with what Robert Conn did, I wrote that he was wonderful and brought Karen alive. The performance was sold out by the next day when they hadn't been sold out before. A lot of people were thinking, "Oh, Rex isn't dancing, do I want to go?" So, yes, dance writers can put bums in the seats. Don't think for one minute that we don't have that power. I am taking exception with Gretchen, because all the bums we put into the seats with our writing or our enthusiastic reviews or our enthusiastic advances are people who are in the choir too. I refuse to believe that the extra two performances that were added to *Swan Lake* came about because every single critic but one who gave it a really good review brought in all kinds of people who weren't in the choir. We have tremendous power and don't forget it. We may not be in the business of selling tickets, but we do.

The second thing I want to say is that we can create the stars. If we keep on mentioning the name of one dancer often enough, then that person is going to become an icon. If you look at companies, dancer X may be equally as good as dancer Y. But for some reason, the critics like X and Y is going to slip into the background. No matter where you are or what kind of dance you deal with—contemporary or ballet—you know that principal ballerina Y is terrific and she has her own little cult following, but she never became the icon because for some reason the critics gave X that push. I'm not so sure if what I am describing is a responsibility or a privilege, but it certainly has incredible ramifications. Often the icons we isolate become the icons in the popular press as a whole. Rudolph Nureyev jumped into the arms of the police at the Paris airport. Good for a story that day. But the critics kept on saying what a marvelous performer he was—how he was transforming dance and giving the male dancer the same status as the ballerina—and it began to impinge into the consciousness of the population as a whole. So that if Rudolph Nureyev came to your city, you got up off the couch, turned off the football game and maybe actually went to see him. The same is true for Mikhail Baryshnikov. There are all kinds of people who go see a Mikhail Baryshnikov performance who have heard about him, but aren't necessarily dance fans. Often we are responsible for pushing certain dance people into the popular consciousness. That is an enormous amount of power.

We also define the art by singling out choreographers. We have almost the same power as an art curator or an art critic: two people are painting, but this guy can really paint, hence he is going to get the historical note. Because we single out certain choreographers, in a way we are also defining the art form, because the art form is defined by the choreographers. The people who we decide to give a specific following to are the people who are going to define the art—which is not to say that there aren't a great number of other people out there who don't deserve it. There is a lot of power that goes with the job of reviewing or criticism.

We also create dance history. The scholarly writers among the dance critics and reviewers will write the dance book that future generations will read. And, we decide the trends. For example, very little has been written about black dance in Toronto, which is entirely different from black dance in the United States. It is a Caribbean/West African based dance, fused with ballet and modern. I happened to write an article on it for *Dance Magazine*; in a way I was defining what black dance was, after talking with these people. I therefore have set the tone of what black dance is. When we are identifying trends, in a way we are defining the art form and part of its creation, although we are not the creators. When a new kind of dance is being done, if we resist it or don't see its importance, we can squelch it. We can also be very dangerous by being too cute for words. The reviewers or critics I dislike the most are those who put themselves first and not the artists they are reviewing. That drives me crazy. The nicest thing you could ever say to me is, "You are fair." I may not like something, but at least I can say why and maybe even make a suggestion as to how it could be better. But writers who just trash something out of hand and are witty about it drive me to distraction.

I also worry, in my own personal case, that I am not talking enough about issues such as anorexia. Although I may think, my God, dancer X is looking really emaciated, maybe I have to write that down so I can help the health of the art form. Or I've got to say, Y has just danced too long. He's got to find something else. But I have got to couch it in words that aren't cruel. Maybe I have a responsibility for the aesthetic look of the art form and for the health of the dancers. There are very few women choreographing in ballet—lots and lots in contemporary dance—and maybe I have to speak up about that. Maybe I am not taking enough responsibility for what I can do with the power I have as a dance writer.

WILLIAM LITTLER: I don't think we create stars. I think we observe stars who create themselves. We merely report an observation of what should be obvious. I think we are witnesses. We are not the people who direct where the art is going. We are the people who are there to watch where it is going and to document, in some form, our reaction to it. We bring what our colleagues in the ministerial profession might call the good news. It isn't, of course, always good, but I think our position is, nonetheless, one on the sidelines. I think that is a healthy attitude to take rather than a preoccupation with the power that is implicit in the situation.

There are a lot of power games to be played in dance, as we all well know. I don't think there is anyone who is going to deny that a devastating review is going to have a short term effect on the artist it concerns. At the same time, I think we use it to wrap fish the next day, and many of us, even if we write for the quarterlies, end up going out with the garbage eventually. It is not a judicial verdict that we have to offer. We are not up there to decide what is important and what isn't. I take solace from advice one of my editors gave me a long time ago: "What I look to you to do is to take us to the event." Rather simple advice and not very easy to achieve. In other words, we are there for the people who weren't and we have to try to bring alive some form of an effervescent art form—an art form that disappears before our very eyes. We know that notation is becoming more sophisticated and various technological media exist for recording dance, but dance happens in images that disappear as you are watching. That is a very hard thing to try and recapture. What little we know of the romantic ballets is through the wonderful words of Gautier but you still won't find much about dance structure in his writing. He was able to offer a poetic evocation of the feeling that the ballet gave him in Paris in the 1840s. But there is little of the dance in his reviews, as gifted a writer as he was.

We are only there as witnesses to offer some testimony of a much richer and bigger experience. I think if we have skills to offer, they are skills of description and some degree of analysis; then we leave it to the people who read us to want to sense what we sense and go themselves. We don't replace the dance in any sense. I don't believe we record the dance in any but the most primitive way. We are merely witnesses to its existence and hopefully to its flourishing. The ability to sell tickets is a consequence of communicating our own enthusiasm but the object isn't to sell tickets. The object is to write about what we see and experience. If it has that effect—and I don't think we would be writing about it if we didn't hope it had that effect—then we have earned our paycheque. A good review will sometimes fill a house. A good review will sometimes have no effect on a house. It is a very mysterious process. I think the fact that attention has been paid means, as Linda Loman says in *Death of a Salesman*, that people know something is happening. We can hope that people will want to investigate it themselves. But I don't believe in saying, "You've got to go and look at that." You only say what you thought you experienced and leave it to the readers.

FRANCIA RUSSELL: I think the critics who are most effective are the ones who report the event clearly and accurately and give their own personal opinions, but as opinions, not as pronouncements. Paula, would you like to move to Seattle, because we could sure use the sentiments you expressed? It is not about a feeling of power, it is an awareness of the power that is inherent in the position and the sense of great responsibility. I do think it is really important for all the people writing about dance to care about dance and to make that come through in every review, whether positive or negative, because it is usually not either one all the way through. Our civiliza-

tion will be judged more by our culture than by anything else we do and any word you or I write is going to be here a lot longer than we are. It is very, very important.

JOHN ALLEYNE: When I was a dancer and a choreographer, I didn't read the reviews. I didn't read the good and I didn't read the bad. I felt they were just one person's opinion and had nothing to do with me or my relationship with an audience. Since I have become a director I have been forced to build relationships because, yes, you writers do sell tickets.

LINDSAY FISCHER: I don't think dancers live in a vacuum. Most of the dancers I know are also avid film critics, for example, or play an instrument or think of themselves also as actors. Many of them make a special effort to have a literary connection with what they are doing. Basically all of us are critics. We don't go to ballet and sit there with a blank palette. We go and we criticize. That's how we improve. Dance criticism is in its infancy. It has a long way to go to catch up with criticism that is written about literature or visual arts or music. I was in the New York City Ballet at the time when I saw what I thought was the crucifixion of the company by critics. Hearing Paula make her comments and mention the responsibility that is incumbent on her as a person of power makes me feel a lot better about that. I think that kind of acceptance of responsibility and power is vital to the maturation of dance criticism. To respectfully disagree, as a teacher I have power. As someone who sits on an audition panel, I have power. If I pretend I don't have any power I am only fooling myself and doing a disservice to people who depend on my expertise. I am taking away my opportunity to do something which I believe is important. If I don't believe I have power or I don't want to exercise that power responsibly, then I should stay home. I would like to see dance criticism evolve towards a form where it is comfortable saying, "This is my qualitative evaluation. This is how it affected me." I think this is what Gautier did. He didn't write about what happened, he wrote about what he felt. That is why we still read him and that is why it is poetic. We need to get back to that. We need to know what we feel—not what can be quantified.

COMMENT: This is not an ideal world. I think we have to

accept the responsibility of the power, but how do we use it? We can either be cute with words and destructive, or attempt to be fair and build the art form by encouraging new artists and audiences to come to dance.

There are many critics/reviewers who do not get on professional terms with the dance community. They feel that if they get to know dancers in any real way, it will compromise what they do. I want to state here and now what I believe. The more I talk to dancers, choreographers, artistic directors, publicists and administrators, the more it broadens my knowledge of the art. I am not privy to the politics in a dance company. Often, it's helpful to understand the context. I am not talking about gossip here. I want my relationship with every dance professional to be on such a level that we can be very honest with one another. That way we are growing in the art together. I believe we can strive for some degree of trust. I do not think this compromises me. If I have a good relationship with the National Ballet, and yet I am not happy with something I saw on the stage, it will not compromise me to say that I did not like what I saw and why. I have just fallen into that pattern in my writing life and it certainly has helped me in my craft. What is the relationship between a critic and the people that you are reviewing?

LINDSAY FISCHER: I think what you are saying is that we are all part of a system and if you acknowledge your place in the system, then you can have a beneficial effect on the art form as a whole. I agree with you.

WILLIAM LITTLER: I think there is a very important critical point of view. You have to care more about the art form than you do about the people who practice it. You have to be willing, if necessary, to hurt the feelings of the artists to further the art form. It is a question, I think, of temperament. There are those who are clubby and thrive in a situation by being part of the milieu; that doesn't necessarily mean they are compromised. And there are those who thrive on distance, because of the perspective that gives them; they are not necessarily less effective. We are not coming out of a standard mould. We have different personality types, different backgrounds, different perceptions, different attitudes. I think we ought to celebrate our plurality as witnesses instead of assuming that there is a prototypical model that we have to subscribe to.

MICHAEL CRABB: We are professional audience members. For example, I know the Royal Winnipeg Ballet very well. I just dumped all over this horrible David Nixon *Beauty and the Beast*, which they misguidedly staged. But I don't believe for a moment that my criticism will have any effect on its success. Let me tell you, it will sell out across the country and I'm glad it will. All I'm doing is putting it on the record that I think this ballet is selling out to focus groups–because it was designed as a market-driven production—-and I thought it was hideous. I don't believe that critics actually sell tickets. I remember Steven Godfrey–God bless his soul–the former dance critic of the *Globe and Mail*, and I coming out together from a mixed bill at the National Ballet. We were just so thrilled by this program. I gave Steven a ride to the *Globe* before I went to the *Star* and we were just bubbling over with enthusiasm. We actually said, we've got to get people to come and see this show and wrote the most enthusiastic reviews. It didn't make any difference to sales. None at all.

PAULA CITRON: A good review can put bums in seats. A good review may or may not put bums in seats. A bad review will never put bums in seats.

QUESTION: You haven't mentioned anything about your responsibility to the artist. The only way for them to grow and change is through feedback, which doesn't happen in the newspapers. Can you talk about that?

GRETCHEN WARREN: I don't think you can create a good choreographer–God creates a good choreographer–but if I was in training as a choreographer, the only people I would want feedback from would be my colleagues at university who, every day, give classes and know how to guide a person through the basic rules that make for good choreography. I don't think any critic has the ability to do that.

COMMENT: Virgil Thompson said to one of his colleagues, "If you want to write to the artist, buy a postage stamp. We are not adjudicators. A review is not a classroom." That specific kind of help comes from your colleagues and your peers. It doesn't come from a reviewer who is sitting on the aisle and responding as a member of the audience. If you can get anything useful from a review, fine. That's a bonus. But we are not writing for you. We are writing for the general public.

MICHAEL CRABB: I don't write for dancers. They are the last people I am concerned about.

LINDSAY FISCHER: Our primary reason for dancing on stage is to communicate with the audience, so yes, if you are writing as an audience member, we care about what you write. Why shouldn't we expect some level of accuracy in response from you? You don't write, "Other people were there and they felt..."

WILLIAM LITTLER: We are not representative of the entire audience; we are members of the audience.

MICHAEL CRABB: There is the matter of simple reportage. For example, I hated David Nixon's *Beauty and the Beast*, but I said in my review that people stood and cheered and the house was sold out. But I am still entitled to my opinion, which was based on concerns about what the performance meant for the art form. I remember watching *La, La, La* and seeing what was done to the dancer. I felt the pain myself and thought, the audience is getting off on this, almost like it was a bullfight. I wrote a really tough review on it, not from the point of view that it was good dance or bad dance, but about what it was doing to dancers. Is *La, La, La* the right direction for dance?

PAULA PAULA: Dance writers have the power to define excellence. When I am writing my reviews, I am writing to the general audience as well as the dancers and the choreographer. There is another way we have power—in what we choose to review. Generally speaking as an independent choreographer who does maybe one show a year, your chances of getting an advance feature are practically nil. Your chance of getting a review if there is a lot of high-profile stuff going on around you is slim. It would be nice if newspapers and radio could balance it out a little more.

GRETCHEN WARREN: What we are talking about is respect for the artists on the part of the critic. I don't know how you respect something unless you educate yourself about it. How do you have any value for it unless you know what's involved in it? I would like to see critics show up to more rehearsals to see the hours and hours and hours that go into a production because I think then they wouldn't write flippantly without an idea of what goes into producing one minute of dance on stage.

RICHARD PHILP: What do you think are the basic ethics that a dance writer has to possess?

LINDSAY FISCHER: I certainly have had the best and most honest criticism from my wife. Being personally close never stopped her from giving me very difficult, painful criticism.

WILLIAM LITTLER: We all have horror stories. Gautier not only wrote well about dancers, he also kept amorous company—some say that inspired him and others say it prejudiced him. I am less concerned about whether people are right or wrong than whether they are interesting. I think there are certain ethical standards we have to accede to as human beings. We have to abide by standards of decent behaviour in relation to other human beings. I don't think those who are in the business of needlessly inflicting cruelty earn much of our respect. This is not only specific to dance criticism. You have a certain duty to acknowledge your fellow human beings' right to a certain measure of respect. I am not one of the milieu. I sit on the aisle and learn as much as I can through experience. I acknowledge that I would not feel comfortable with the level of acquaintance with dancers that many other critics have. I think that if we are honourable human beings, we have a right to write, but if we behave dishonourably, we lose that right to write.

Afterword

Photograph on previous page:
Dancer: Desmond Richardson
At: Holland Dance Festival
Photographer: Antoine Tempe

AFTERWORD
DEBORAH JOWITT

When I was first invited to participate in the extraordinary global conference embodied in this book, I thought I understood the title. How smart, I thought, how refreshing! "Not Just Any Body," but a particular body–my body, your body, her body, his body. This implied way of thinking could enrich the scenario endemic to Western dance training; ballet has traditionally set a dancer's personally shaped and genetically coded body in opposition to an ideal body that he or she must strive to acquire–a body that is stronger, leaner, and more flexible than that of the average human being. To acquire that body via extremes of discipline and endurance–with the goal of successful career and the prospect of occasional rapture–often demolishes both individuality and joy. And, of course, many fascinating presentations at the conference dealt with how not to abuse this body, how to make training more efficient as well as more sane and more personalized, how to deal with injury.

It's possible, however, with a small stretch of syntax, to read the title as "Not Just Any Body." To do so opens–as the conference did both implicitly and explicitly–the worn-hinged Pandora's Box containing that old mind-body split: our souls are temporarily housed in an unruly, appetite-driven body, controlled (so theologians fervently hope) by our soul-inspired minds. Current scientific thinking has presented another image–one that differs even from the picture of the brain as a pilot, up there in control central running things: On the cellular level, we are networks of brain power. "Soul" runs through us, sails in our blood. Whether or not one believes in an afterlife is not the point; for the time being, we are our bodies; our bodies are us. Especially in dance.

At least two conference speakers alluded to Michel Foucault's *Discipline and Punish* and his term "the docile body." In hallowed tradition, the student dancer and company dancer alike do not "talk back," do not ask "too many" questions, and are not encouraged to spend time cultivating interests outside the studio and theatre. At worst, the docile acceptance of severe criticism and willingness to live with a constant high level of stress are deemed a prerequisite for excellence–a notion represented at "Not Just Any Body" as being unsound on just about every level, from the scientific to the economic to the profoundly personal.

The dancer and the athlete have much in common (pay not being one of them), but among the arts, dance is unique. To the teacher, inevitably, the young dancer-body is clay to be moulded; to the choreographer, an element to be shaped and placed in a composition. The dancer comes to view himself/herself with an equally detached and critical eye. One of the points made repeatedly in this book is how poorly these bodies-as-instruments are often dealt with by teachers, choreographers, company directors, and the dancers themselves. The heartening message is that this situation can change, is changing, must change. No violinist treats his instrument shabbily, no craftsman manhandles his best tools, and these–however expensive–are replaceable. That body-self is not.

A new ideal image glows from these pages: that of the empowered dancer, the dancer not afraid to take responsibility for his/her state of mental and physical health, the dancer who can feel like a collaborator within the acknowledged dictatorship run by a choreographer.

The image, of course, requires changed thinking on the part of teachers, choreographers, and company directors: a certain degree of stress, challenge, and ordeal produces champions; too much does not. That November 1999 weekend in satellite-linked Toronto and The Hague was filled with heady ideas. How many pliés are enough in a lifetime? Why not cross-train like athletes–ballet one day, maybe yoga the next? A Jacuzzi in every company? Does it always make sense to save the hardest steps for the end of class? Is muscle memory so slow-witted that it can only retain information through daily repetition of the same steps? One could sense harumphs and whispered expletives at some of the more radical thoughts. The three days were also rife with sobering facts: tests for osteoporosis have revealed some very young, extremely thin dancers to have the skeletons of sixty-year-old women. But, as the statements in this book reveal, the aim of "Not Just Any Body" was not simply to promote the health and well-being of the dance community, but to investigate the possible links between them and greater excellence, deeper artistry, career longevity, and joy.

A year later, as I read the accounts of workshops, and the transcribed speeches, discussions, and questions that made the conference so profoundly stimulating, I am impressed all over again. The book documents a profession at the verge of a new millennium, querying its own standards and methods, evaluating the risks of change. The voices are, in the main, not those of critics and historians but of dance practitioners–those in the thick of it. And the dancers who speak so eloquently on these pages testify to the integration of "the body"–their bodies–with whatever else makes up a dancing-thinking-feeling person.

Deborah Jowitt
December, 2000

Appendix One
Workshop Reports

A summary of sessions from
The Hague and Toronto
Not Just Any Body, November 1999

REPORTS FROM THE HAGUE
Body Image
Anna Aalten
Moderator–Gaby Allard

Anna Aalten talked about body image and body politics: what kinds of body image dominate and under what circumstances are these images created? As an anthropologist, her chosen method of research is listening to the stories of classical dancers.

The body is an unnatural surface on which ethical rules are inscribed and through which cultural roles are performed. Photographs from Africa show scars–expressions of beauty and status–on women's backs. The codes of this culture reveal that these women are mothers, because scarring is started only after the birth of the first child.

What is inscribed on the bodies of Western ballet dancers? They are looked on as objects that can be moulded and shaped to suggest lightness (the illusion of weightlessness) and verticality (movement is always upwards from the central spine). These effects are created mainly through training in dance schools –where young students, particularly female, have to meet strict audition criteria and specific physical demands–and dance companies. In ballet, the school structure is strongly hierarchical and the aesthetics are set. It is not easy for dancers–often compared to paintbrushes in the hands of a painter–to find their own space.

The following questions were discussed: Is ballet really resisting all influences of changing times? Or has ballet been married with modern dance since the 1950s? Thin or too thin: what is behind eating disorders? Should regular and hard training be enough to keep the body thin? Why are dancers concerned about weight and eating? Is it the responsibility of staff to remove pressure from young dance students? Can we redefine beauty and strength?

It is necessary in dance education to work on respect and the happiness of individual students; we must try to put them in the right place for who they are and what they need and want. It would be interesting to think about what we are doing instead of why.

Lifestyle
Ton Simons and Cees Vervoorn
Moderator–Linda Yates

Dancers can learn the following from athletes and the sports community: discipline, physical training, professionalism, keeping an open mind, developing a talent program, listening to the body and resting–the most important part of training.

Athletes are better organized to take care of their bodies than dancers, who only listen to their bodies when they are injured. Stiff competition–pressure not to lose a job or a role–discourages dancers from admitting to or dealing with injuries.

CEES VERVOORN: Consider these attitudes: "If you don't make it, you don't make it" (dance) versus "we will help you to the top and cannot afford to lose even one single athlete" (sports). "All on your own" (dance) versus "a whole team of specialists" (sports). Sports athletes are stimulated and provided with training programs. They are tested and evaluated regularly by physiologists and psychologists. More specialists should be brought in to work with dancers. Physical tests show that the cardiovascular state of young dancers is worse than that of the average person. "Unhealthy lifestyle" (dance) versus "healthy lifestyle" (sports). Scientific research programs and neuro-endocrine system surveys have proven that people should not be pushed beyond their limits. Dancers have to give priority to rest and resist overtraining; they must also remain goal oriented. It should not be forgotten that the most important aspect of being successful is to have fun during the process; this will certainly show up onstage.

COMMENT: Aesthetics in dance are used as an alibi to neglect the state of the dancer's body.

TON SIMONS: Dancers start dancing at a young age because they love it; because of that love, which sometimes turns to hate, dancers are often inclined to suffer. Schools should start making young dancers aware that this is a fashionable, romantic idea from the last century; it is no longer the right way to treat body-mind. Artistic directors should come together and change their demands on dancers. The links between the different levels of education should be strengthened.

Talented in Dance: Detection and Development
Jacques van Rossum
Moderator–Jeroen Fabius

In his presentation, Jacques van Rossum provided the attendants with the results of his research among students and teachers of different dance academies in The Netherlands. This research was focused on the development of dance careers of talented individuals. Van Rossum discussed some issues that appeared to play an important role in the dance career.

In accordance with the Bloom (1985) study on talented individuals in science, art and athletics, the career of a professional dancer can also be divided into three phases, from the first dance classes at the local school (stage 1), via the academic training (stage 2) to a professional career (stage 3).

Within this framework of different stages, several questions can be posed and answered about the role and behaviour of parents, of dance teachers, and of the talented individual. These questions are all embedded in the central problem of why some will reach the goal of being a professional dancer while others, seemingly equally talented, quit or drop out.

Within the context of scientific research on expertise, it has been stated that individuals who have reached the top level within their domain (e.g., scientists, musicians, athletes) did spend more hours practicing than those who failed to reach that level. As a rule of thumb it has been ascertained that top level expertise "needs" ten thousand hours of deliberate practice during a period of about ten years.

Further, scientific work on the role of motivation in talented individuals (how one is able to spend that number of practice hours over such an extended period of time) has indicated that being intrinsically motivated is a key issue. Becoming too much attracted over the years to the extrinsic aspects of the task (fame, money, trips abroad, popularity) must be considered a fatal risk, especially for individuals in the first two phases of their career. The role of the teacher in this process must be considered primal, from the data gathered in The Netherlands, especially since many of the young talented dancers indicated not being from a "dance family"–the dream of becoming a professional dancer might then easily turn into an individual enterprise. The teacher should provide a rich learning environment, in which the talented dancer is challenged to grow and develop, motivated by the central intrinsic experiencing pleasure doing it (the sheer fun of moving/dancing).

As a summary, van Rossum referred to the "Manual for Talent Development" which is published by the Dutch Olympic Committee and is in use by Dutch Sports Associations. The following elements are relevant: intrinsic motivation of the dancers is the primary and most important drive, and should be supported; the explicit choice to attain a top level should be made by the individual; significant others near the dancer should provide a rich learning environment (e.g., other talented individuals, inspiring trainers and coaches, no unnecessary specialization at too young an age); sufficient information on all the aspects of dance training, health risks, and the specific talent development requirements should be available to everyone involved to enable them to create a common strategy and cooperation in the guidance and support of the talented individual.

Awareness of the fact that children who are selected as talented individuals are children with different, more advanced but also complicated patterns of learning. Teachers and coaches should adapt to these patterns as much as possible. If such provisions are taken, the development of a talented individual into a professional or expert might become a matter of planned action instead of just lucky chance.

FACING TRANSITION
Suzie Jary
Moderator–Annemieke Keurentjes

Suzie Jary briefly spoke about her ballet and musical theatre background, her decision to go back to college to study counseling and her involvement with Career Transition for Dancers (CTFD) in New York. She recalled personal anxieties connected to her transition phase and stressed that transition is an organic process of moving through life. Summarizing the history and goals of CTFD, which started in 1985 in America to help professional dancers deal with both the psychological and pragmatic aspects of transition into a new career after dance, Jary said the organization provides dancers with a framework in which they can begin to think, speak, be listened to and create a future. It is essential that the economic, educational and personal sacrifices the dancer has made in the past to master the art form are re-assessed in the present.

Participants then introduced themselves with personal definitions of transition that included: dancers transitioning between companies or to the independent sector; transitions from training to professional careers; transitions after injury; and constant transitions among different roles in dance, e.g. dancer, choreographer,

teacher, activist, businesswoman/man.

Jary distributed a drawing of a flower with twelve petals each representing an area of life: the right side related to "doing" and the left side to "being." To balance one's life, one should identify what one tends to overemphasize or neglect and slowly try to allow tendencies to come or go. Dancers may think there is never enough time to improve their technique so they feel guilty when they engage in leisure and play. The responses of the group confirmed this: the pattern is established in early dance training. According to one participant, dance attracts passionate people who develop extreme relationships to dance. Training and culture perpetuate this: dancers are constantly called on to prove their devotion to dance. As a result, they may have a weak connection with the real world. To change this attitude, teachers need to expose students to other areas of culture, society and art. Teachers should also stress the importance of connection/application. When teaching a specific technique, they should not claim it is "the whole truth," but should stimulate an application of the information they provide to other aspects of life or to other dance techniques. If dancers acknowledged and cultivated a multi-faceted personality, any transitional phase would be less associated with anxiety. Jary wound up the discussion by reminding the group that each individual is their own best expert.

HEALTH, WELL-BEING AND SAFETY IN DANCE COMPANIES
Toine Schermer and Els Frankenhuijzen
Moderator–Barbara Leach

Can health, well-being and safety plans take into account the nature of the dancers' working environment, schedules and specific training needs? What are the challenges of introducing new systems?

Els Frankenhuijzen and physician Toine Schermer advise dance companies about safe and healthy working environments in Holland. Curing individual physical problems is not enough because the problems are often created by the work conditions in the company. They have developed a Risk Inventory and Assessment (RI&A) to determine how working conditions can be optimized. Focus points of the RI&A are: safety and health procedures; absenteeism procedures; general facilities: floors, dressing rooms, stage noise, lighting and climate conditions; physical stress (e.g. how much time to learn something new); and welfare which includes job content, work load, support and working hours.

They saw a similar picture in all dance companies: none had a safety and health policy; internal communication (social policy) needed to be improved; safety was not sufficient; and physical stress for dancers was very high. They concluded that the situations in Dutch dance companies were not very good. The staff commitment to the health and safety of dancers is very important. A number of dancers were very reluctant to give information about their working conditions (probably because they were afraid of the consequences for their career) and they noticed that improvement was sometimes hampered by clinging to traditions. Adrian Schriel said the choreographer or artistic director is the person dancers have to work with. If he /she is not committed to the dancers' health, there is nothing that can be done. It is a matter of power. Patricia Kapp wondered whether health rules would limit artistic product as the choreographer often has a brilliant new idea at the very last moment. Toine Schermer replied that there are often risks; it is important that the people involved know about them. Communication is very important. Richard Alston did not agree. He said that the health and well-being of his dancers are more important than high-tech stage designs. Safety will not limit aesthetic creativity. He also mentioned the important role of Dance U.K., which is similar to the ARBO-dienst. Deborah Bull said that dancers themselves could make a difference as well: they can decide what they want and do not want to do. Jane Lord said that the dancers live very much in the here and now and do not think about five years from now. Jean Geddis mentioned the importance of education. Fay Nenander agreed and said dance education should teach students verbal skills, give them the ability to choose and encourage them to know about responsibilities. Kirsty Lloyd wondered how the RI&A is checked. Toine Schermer explained that this is checked by the Labour inspection.

Ronald Klaassen was surprised that the list of focus points did not include the mental stress of a dancer. Toine Schermer and Els Frankhuijzen explained that for a complete mental check the questionnaires would have to be extended; however, they include

questions about stress. They emphasized the fact that mental stress is also related to the working environment.

PSYCHOLOGICAL SKILL TRAINING
Britt Tajet-Foxell
Moderator–Paul Bronkhorst

According to psychologist Britt Tajet-Foxell, injury recovery has a lot to do with the psychological state of mind of the dancer. She formulated a model for injury management using and adapting research done in sports where more money is available for research on injury recovery. The dance and sports fields have a lot in common: both involve training from a young age; both work with highly motivated people; both have high injury risks; and both dancers and athletes need their bodies in order to be able to perform professionally.

Tajet-Foxell focused on how stress and anxiety can influence injury recovery and how psychological skills can be used in this process. Stress response activates the nervous system and causes a psychological response. Stress can be described as a series of events: demands put on the individual; the individual's perception of the demands; the actual response to the demands; and the consequence resulting from the response.

Research provides confirmation of a strong correlation between stress and anxiety that affects injury recovery. The body has chemical and physical responses: blood pressure becomes higher, adrenaline is released, there is a higher pain resistance, etc. If stress becomes chronic, it will have a destructive effect on the dancer's health. The nervous system is triggered by thought; the level of stress depends on the dancer's evaluation and expectations of the situation. In the dance field, most people focus on things they cannot do instead of what they can. This attitude affects the mind and body negatively; the stress level rises too high and becomes destructive. So, dancers should use their minds to affect their psychological confidence: "I can do it" will change the perception and evaluation of the event. Dancers should break the cycle of negative thinking and challenge their thoughts in a positive way.

SPORTS MEDICINE
Robbart van Linschoten
Moderator–Arthur Kleipool

Dutch sports physicians have been trained as specialists since the 1980s, focusing on the care and cure of injured athletes. In 1999 there were sixty sports physicians working in hospitals, sports medical centres, private practices and national sports organizations. Dancers, like athletes, are relatively young and injury prone; they have a high risk of overuse and injury of specific body parts and their drive to perform at a top level is high. But the method of training, as well as the whole mindset of dancers, is quite distinct. Dancers view their bodies as instruments to express artistic meaning and the enormous pressure to perform continuously well makes them extremely vulnerable to injuries. At the same time, this different way of thinking about and treating the body impedes dancers from finding the right medical advice. Even though sports physicians are specially trained, very often the advice they give dancers is contrary to what they themselves or their dance teachers think is the right cure.

What can a sports physician offer dancers? Biomechanical knowledge, which is improving along with medical technology, can be very valuable. As Richard Alston commented, "Knowing that knee joints can only do a certain number of grand pliés until they get worn out will change the dance teacher's idea of what should be done in training."

What do dancers need from doctors? The dancers who attended this session were clearly in favour of a more holistic approach–a collaboration of spiritual and physical strengths to achieve a specific goal–than is usual in medicine. They asked for an understanding of dancers as physical artists under pressure to keep going. Dancers are usually less replaceable than team athletes and they have less financial backing. Boni Rietveld stated, however that the artistic aspects of dance should not justify living an unnecessarily unhealthy lifestyle.

It became clear that there is a need for integration and interaction between the medical world and the world of dance. The suggestion was made that physicians take dance classes and dancers take medical classes.

EMOTIONAL ASPECTS OF DANCE TEACHING
Julia Buckroyd
Moderator–Suzie Jary

Julia Buckroyd gave her workshop the title: "The body, the self and dance training." Her aim was to explore how the sense of self is created first via physical handling and holding, and then by all sorts of physical experience such as increased co-ordination and strength and then to explore how that original sense of self is affected by dance training.

The dance trainee's sense of her own body/self has already a significant history by the time she becomes a trainee. Her body "story line" develops through infancy, childhood and adolescence. During infancy, the handling of the baby by the mother will be influenced by the mother's experience of the act of birth. Similarly the mother's attitude to taking care of the baby, has a strong impact on the sense of self that the baby develops. This sense of self, this first identity, is a body-self and will be further developed by the child's gradually increasing physical competence. The child has none of the accomplishments to create a sense of self (eg job, house, partner) that an adult has. The only self available for the baby/child is a body-self. In dance training, the trainees' pre-existing sense of self is met by the attitudes towards her/her body of the training institution. A good sense of self may survive a critical environment. A poor sense of self will be further undermined. The result of this chemistry is important.

Good self-esteem is of great importance for the dance trainee. Good self-esteem will enable her to take appropriate care of herself. Poor self-esteem will prevent her from doing so. Poor self-esteem can be the underlying cause of injury, inadequate nutrition, illness, eating disorders, misuse of alcohol or recreational drugs and dangerous sexual behaviour.

The learning environment has a huge influence on the development and maintenance of self-esteem. Learning progresses through encouragement rather then negative criticism.

In dance education encouragement is sometimes thought undesirable, if a student appears to lack the ability to pursue a career as a dancer. However, since only about 5 percent of trainees become professional dancers, the training justifies itself by other criteria also; it has to stand on its own as a good basic education. All dancers can be encouraged to make the best possible use of the training. Similarly good self-esteem is fostered by the concern shown by the training institution for the welfare of trainees. It is the responsibility of dance schools to train healthy dancers. For example, it is unethical to allow a dancer to perform if she is unable to maintain menstruation.

Justification of training methods which are damaging to self-esteem are often based on ideas about what "dance" requires–a particular aesthetic, for example. We must remember that dance is our own invention and can be what we want it to be. There can be no justification for dance training which teaches young people to think badly of themselves and erodes their capacity to take care of themselves.

Gender Differences: The Effects of Heredity and Training in Dance
Yiannis Koutedakis
Moderator–Eileen Wanke

Yiannis Koutedakis described his background as, "one foot in sports and the other in dance. The only difference between dance and sports is the outcome since both share the same engine: the body."

In the 20th century, women have shown a dramatic increase in levels of physical performance compared to men. Statistics have shown that, in terms of speed, for example, women have made twice the progress, causing a gradual decrease in the difference in physical achievements between men and women. These increases are the result of better female machinery and changes in society, not better training methods. Some decades ago it was unthinkable for women to work or go out of the house and the male body became stronger because of physical exercise. Women are now back in action.

Women also have a higher percentage of essential fat because of childbearing; there can be a number of potential problems when fat is reduced. When training harder and/or eating less, a woman might face menstrual irregularity, loss of bone strength, osteoporosis or even early menopause. Tests have also indicated a delay in menarche in girls who trained too hard.

Finally, graphs connected with the cardiovascular system confirmed that the difference between men and women is significantly smaller when comparing trained as opposed to untrained individuals, even though the size of the heart in women is smaller.

Group Dynamics in Dance Companies
Margreet Kooistra, Jane Lord and Nanine Linning
Moderator–Paul Waarts

Former actress Margreet Kooistra is now working as a business management trainer in the area of team building where she makes use of two strategies:

A. TEAM BUILDING
• Forming: define what roles you need in an organization and fill in the gaps;
• Storming: take a position within the organization, define one's personal role and the pecking order becomes clear;
• Norming: set goals for the organization, share ideas and the team will take shape;
• Performing: work as described above to operate efficiently and effectively as a team.

B. TEAM ROLE MODEL (developed by Meredith Belbin) defines eight functions that are needed in any organization:
1.Chairman: coordinating, charismatic, communication skills, procedures, leader.
2. Shaper: competitive, goal-oriented, ego-oriented, willpower.
3. Generator: creative, distant from the team, critical and individualistic.
4. Monitor: objective, analyzing, serious, asks "why?"
5. Company worker: commitment, practical, conservative.
6. Research investigator: networker, brainstormer, extrovert, outside the team.
7. Teamworker: people relationships, harmony, avoiding conflicts.
8. Complete finisher: absorbs stress, warns, perfection, details.

Jane Lord (First Soloist and Chair of the Dancer's Council of the Dutch National Ballet for twenty years) said that the group has to deal with hierarchy and age differences. Dancers are growing older and being promoted, but criteria for promotion are not properly defined. The more experienced dancers might guide the younger ones in this process, but since these younger ones are rivals as well as colleagues, it is a delicate support system possibly resulting in undermined physical performances. Staff should give clear direction; individual interests should not overtake the organization. Communication is essential to group dynamics and the following facets must be taken into account: expectations, responsibilities, rewards and (lack of) attention.

Nanine Linning, a young dancer/choreographer who recently graduated from Rotterdamse Dansacademie, wants a company for herself. She finds starting over again and again in new projects with different people does not give her the opportunity to develop creative work. She is not in favour of a hierarchical setting because she wants information from her dancers and does not want to work from an ivory tower even though this makes it much more complicated.

Onno Stokvis would like to know why it takes the Dutch National Ballet and similar companies a lot longer to become democratic than the rest of society. Jane Lord suggests that changes need to be implemented by the staff; if the staff is not keen on democracy in a company, nothing will change.

Jack Gallagher mentions the intensity of the job and thinks time management is an important issue: if there is only time for rehearsals in a company, you can't develop a culture where discussions are a regular part of the process of group dynamics. He also emphasizes the top-down approach.

Dragan Klaic states that this top down approach is not very likely to happen because the artistic management of a company is conservative. Dancers are trained to be submissive and fragile. They don't speak up very easily. Pathological changes are needed to implement changes. Maybe cultural diversity will force a breakthrough in this impasse.

Jane Lord agrees that it is valuable if dancers get extra training outside the company and she encourages dancers who have been working with other companies to come back and share their experiences.

Jean Geddis Zetterberg says the training—especially communication methods—should start at school. Don't teach "shut up and do as I say," because this will create a submissive attitude.

Thea Barnes adds that in a smaller company with a contem-porary repertoire, conditions are sometimes the other way around: everybody has a different background and a different view on everything and it is hard to give direction. Management feels that if you give the dancers an inch, they will take a mile.

Jeroen Fabius says the role of the business team and the position of the company in the market are very important. When the Frankfurt Ballet operated a bit outside of the limelight, they were able to develop in the way they did. When technically perfect dancers with no personality or brains came to audition, William Forsythe always said they had forgotten to bring their personality. He emphasized the importance of general education and personal growth.

Barbara Leach asked, even though dancers in the Dutch National Ballet company accomplished a lot, how could a role model like Belbin be implemented in a non-verbal setting since communication for dancers is a physical matter?

Annemieke Keurentjes told of a team of music schoolteachers who did role model training by physically taking positions representing the hierarchy; however, the model is more demanding for trainers because they have to pose the right questions to make everyone aware of positions and needs.

Jacques van Rossum said that in sports it is virtually impossible for a situation similar to that in dance to occur, because athletes are accustomed to discussing and taking responsibility for their training programs. He stressed the important of education in this aspect. Volleyball experience reminded Ruud van Imhalt that mature athletes will build team experience and responsibility. Margreet Kooistra suggested a lot of insecurity can be reduced by emphasizing that the roles in the team building model are functional roles, not personal characterizations. Krisztina de Chatel said it is very valuable for her to discuss artistic items, to share her ideas with the dancers and share ideas about creation in order to develop the artistic product.

Guido Severien concluded that the structure and culture of a company are partners in crime concerning the restriction for individual dancers. The decision-making system needs long-term revision and it is essential that dancers are involved in reshaping it.

NOT JUST ANY BODY

Jasmine Challis
Moderator–Anna Aalten

Jasmine Challis, a nutritionist working with dancers and dance companies, explained that nutrition is a new science developing very fast in light of new research.

What is the optimal diet for a dancer? A balanced diet for everyone has 1/3 fruits and vegetables, 1/3 breads and cereals, 1/3 different meats plus food containing sugar and fat, milk and dairy products, but dancers also need more fluids, nutrient-dense food, higher carbohydrate intake, lower fat intake, more fibre, more protein and slightly more vitamins and calcium. Fluid replacement is very important to prevent the adverse physical and mental effects of dehydration. With physical exercise, dancers lose 1/2 to 1 litre of fluid in an hour. A suitable fluid during classes is one with isotonics. Try to avoid juices or fizzy drinks.

Challis recommends that dancers be hydrated at the start of the dance session, have a good warm-up to reduce urine formation, get used to taking fluids during exercise, plan fluids breaks, rehydrate after exercise, avoid salt unless prescribed, acclimatize when possible, wear clothing that allows the body to breathe and the sweat to evaporate, reduce humidity in the studio if possible, and do not rely on thirst!

Challis mentioned that even though dancers are physically very active, they need about the same daily calories as everyone else because their body weight is usually lower. Therefore, to stay slim, dancers need to lower fat intake and increase fibre. If a dancer needs to lose weight, it is better to find alternative ways of exercising to optimize energy output instead of eating less. A higher intake of carbohydrates is demanded, especially within an hour after intensive exercise, to help the muscle glycogen. Also, dancers need slightly more protein, especially if they are recovering from an injury or if they have a muscle turnover. Meal planning is important: dancers should spread meals evenly over the day to allow energy replacement and make sure they get all necessary nutrients and calories.

CHOREOGRAPHERS
Richard Alston, Bianca van Dillen, Roland Schankula and

Michael Schumacher
Moderator–Derrick Brown

After introducing themselves as choreographers with additional involvement in dance, the presenters engaged in a discussion guided by questions posed by the moderator.

How do choreographers keep themselves sane and healthy during the exhaustive process of creating a piece? The presenters all agreed that it is important to take good care of oneself, and that the actual pressure depends very much on the working circumstances. The choreographer can usually choose his or her own way of working. Besides avoiding the "tortured creative soul" to keep oneself sane, there is also the issue of the health and well-being of the dancers who choreographers work with. It became clear that the most difficult situation is the one in which the creation of the piece is dependent on a large group of dancers. When communication between choreographer and dancers is bad, both sides may be taking too many health and safety risks.

There are different ways to negotiate the performance of a particular movement with dancers. Some choreographers demonstrate with their own body; others do not. But the most important thing to performing a certain movement or even a whole piece that demonstrates the well-being, health and excellence of both the choreographer and the dancer is the sharing of ideas, intentions and opinions.

It is impossible to teach dancers and others how to be good choreographers according to Gunnar Alexander from Sweden. Even if one goes to a choreographers' school, one will only be provided with the tools. Whether someone uses them well depends on many things including a feeling of responsibility towards oneself and others and an adequate level of communication.

Empowering dancers to take responsibility when it comes to putting their bodies at risk is not always easy, Michael Schumacher said. The relationship between the choreographer and the dancer is not the biggest threat to the dancers' well-being; it is the financial, economic and bureaucratic state in which the dance world finds itself. We should address the pressure, hard work, inadequate financial support and inadequate insurance for the specific demands of the dance world.

TEACHING SKILLS
Francis Weyts
Moderator–Ted Willemsen

Every child, to a greater or lesser extent, has an inner urge to move and dance with complete freedom. It is vital that the transfer of ballet technique does not drum that inner force out of the child. How can we maintain the natural, internal movement of children?

There are problems with using a mirror at the front of the class to learn ballet. The mirror does not warn young dancers against excess tension in the body. In particular, Weyts used the term "cramping"–the result of a chain reaction of wrong corrections from either watching the mirror or the teacher–to describe a sort of tension that restricts freedom of movement. The Achilles tendon, a vital shock absorber in more advanced ballet, and the muscles around the hip joint are particularly vulnerable to cramping. Other common problems of young dancers which can be improperly corrected are "rolling in" the feet (usually traced to a misalignment in the pelvis) and overuse of the quadriceps which pulls the leg back into the hip socket.

Weyts sees the full use of the natural turnout as one of the keys to finding freedom of movement. This allows for pelvic stability, best found by letting the student lie on their back and relax the legs completely. Another key is using imagery to describe the exercises. An example from Naomi Duveen: In order to avoid excess tension in the Achilles, she speaks of pushing the talus forward so the line of the foot automatically follows the line of the leg. In this way, the toes can be felt as the last action in the point.

There is a necessity to strip ballet down to the fundamentals–the tendu and the plié–the starting points from which smooth, free movement can follow. At its very simplest, the tendu is a shift of weight and the plié is a sort of relaxation. Working on these, young dancers can find a state between relaxation and tension that can be described as "alertness" or the "image of movement."

Participants were mainly after practical tips in teaching their dance students. Weyts advocated learning about the bodies of individual students which requires more dedication and time than might at first be apparent. It may even be necessary to seek another opinion from, for example, a physiotherapist on the problems of a particular student. Progress may be slow.

GROWTH SPURT
Rachel-Anne Rist
Moderator–Jacques van Rossum

Rachel-Anne Rist's ideas about growth spurt are changing, shaped by new sources of information; they are based on her own experiences and observations, not scientific truth.

A young person's growth spurt often happens after a holiday that combines relaxation, sun and food: for girls, around age eleven to fourteen, and for boys, age twelve to fifteen. The bones grow very fast, much faster than the muscles, causing a lack of muscular support and making the bones very vulnerable. During the growth spurt one sees, first of all, knee injuries, then pelvis injuries and finally back injuries.

Added complications include: psychological problems caused by the transition from child to young adult coinciding with added academic pressures (at this age, children have to do much more homework); peer pressure and sociocultural pressure (i.e. the idea that young girls can only be beautiful when they are thin); decrease in self esteem; and dramatic hormonal changes.

Signals of the growth spurt include: rapid change in height; loss of control of leg extensions; loss of balance; loss of flexibility; loss of stamina; loss of general control; loss of ability to do things that were previously simple; feelings of inadequacy; increase in injury rate; and increase in "dropout rate." Combined with this is the fact that the pupil is very aware of the fact that he/she is having an expensive education for which their parents, sometimes with great difficulty, are paying. Therefore, the counseling skills of the ballet teacher are very important.

If a ballet teacher notices students suffering from growth spurt, he/she can make the class less physically stressful, saving recovery time later. Rachel-Anne Rist suggested the following modifications:
• Re-examine pliés and placement. Those movements cause a lot of stress on young knees and there are other ways to get the same results.
• Reduce the amount of impact work in allegro, especially on one

leg as well as the number of repetitions.
• Increase the time spent on postural modifications.
• Reduce the amount of pointe work.
• Increase the time spent on body conditioning and fitness training (e.g. swimming or cycling, not running).
• Decrease the time spent on movements in which the knees have to bear a lot of weight (modern dance, jazz dance).
• Increase the time spent on acquiring proprioception skills (i.e. being conscious of space). This is about how to use and adapt the body and is very good for balance.

The challenge for the teacher is to recognize and discuss physical changes with students. Remembering that each student is different, the teacher should combine normal class for some with an altered class for others. Some students may even have to stop lessons and do their own thing for awhile. Teachers should make sure they still feel involved, reassuring them that this is a transitional phase. Students should be given a time-scale so they have an idea as to how long this situation can last. While students should be encouraged to take personal responsibility for their growth spurt, it is very important for teachers to recognize their new adult status.

Teachers should also: look at the footwear worn outside the class (platform shoes are very bad for their balance); check for symmetry of spine during transition; check for equal leg length; try to establish a support system, including a doctor who knows about dancing and dancers, for medical referral and, if possible, psychological support; establish body conditioning from an early age; and encourage development. All the dance teachers for each student should have a consistent team approach. Expert help should also be available for teachers.

Rachel-Anne Rist stressed that it is important to make changes when a young dancer is in the growth spurt to prevent knee, hip and spine injuries. Good dialogue with parents will lead to understanding and gratitude, encouraging students to take responsibility for their own physique and technique.

All participants agreed that acknowledging this period in a dancer's life is very important. There were questions about how to deal with exams for students in a growth spurt. Rist said that either exams should be banned or assessments–including cate-

gories such as commitment and understanding in addition to dance technique–should be improved. It is important to inform the examiner about the specifics of the growth of the student.

Rist said that although it is particularly important for boys to have good male role models. She thinks that the main problems are the same for both sexes–although she would like to do more research on this subject. Several participants agreed that lifting too early is very bad for boys' backs.

Would these changes would make the students better dancers? Rachel-Anne Rist said she didn't know, but she was convinced they would be better informed dancers and better adjusted individuals.

Successful Implementation of Prevention
Chrétien Felser
Moderator–Toine Schermer

How can we overcome resistance to the successful implementation of injury prevention programs at the individual, group and organizational levels of dance companies? Bad conditions might include: lack of attention to the dancer; bad management; poor physical working conditions in the floor, shoes, climate, dry ice or lighting; and overloading dancers through bad training or technique. The primary action would be to take away the source of risk, e.g. replace an inadequate floor. Secondary actions involve leaving the source of the problem but reducing its effect through, for example, additional warm-ups, cool downs and healthy working schedules. Tertiary action would be to accept the damage that is already done and prevent it from getting worse.

The cost of work-related losses in The Netherlands (working population of 6 million people) with 80 percent of absentees back at work within a week and 6 percent (350,000 people) absent for a longer period due to physical and physiosocial problems or accidents, is 12 billion Dutch guilders a year. There is now a movement to shift the financial responsibility for disabilities from government to employers. At this time it does not seem that health and safety issues are reasons to change jobs; the main reasons are financial, time and personnel resources, and job satisfaction.

Bad work situations still exist after illness, accident or injuries have occurred. It makes sense to make prevention a priority and this is often the sole responsibility of the individual. Health services and health care are generally provided away from the company, leaving dancers alone and cut off. When the source of illness lies in the organization and a dancer gets well outside, the illness will recur once the dancer returns to work. Dancers often blame themselves for injury. No longer part of the daily routine of the company, they can experience being left alone to heal as a kind of punishment.

The following list details obstacles for implementation of a prevention program: denial; declination; compensation; conflicting interest; culture/values; formal/informal organization; short term oriented; no drive from inside; money and time management. These obstacles can be improved by: adequate problem analysis; a combination of measures directed to work environment and workers; worker participation; top management support; more information for freelance dancers; management and artistic directors; and accessible facilities for small dance companies.

The last question during this session remained unanswered: Doesn't it all come back to education and the willingness to change?

THE INDEPENDENT DANCER
Gill Clarke
Moderator–Guido Severien

The advantage of being an independent dancer is mainly the remarkable freedom to try to incorporate new ideas into dance, sometimes even approaching a choreographer instead of waiting to be approached. The problem appeared to be how to put these ideas into practice within the independent dance sector. Gill Clarke made clear the drawbacks of independent status are linked to the lack of recognition which results in much less financial support, smaller wages and fewer provisions for health insurance, personal training and even transport of luggage when travelling. These are all factors that threaten the independent dancer's health and the quality and pleasure of their performance.

Participant Imogen Claire, member of the International Federation of Actors, strongly advised independent dancers present to get in contact with her union as it could provide flexible solutions. Not everyone seemed too sure, apparently because of

previous bad experiences. One of the reasons so many independent dancers were not members of this union was the demand for an employment contract. Sometimes independent dancers don't work with contracts. How about signing a contract with yourself when working on an independent production?

The idea of creating an international membership passport for independent dancers that would provide access to the basic needs for an excellent and healthy performance anywhere was presented.

After a discussion about the situation of independent dancers in different countries, the session concluded by stressing the need to take the independent dancer seriously, and suggesting more exchange between the dependent and independent sectors.

AEROBIC FITNESS FOR PROFESSIONAL DANCERS: THE CHALLENGE
Eileen Wanke and Ted Willemsen
Moderator–Ronald Klaassen

Ted Willemsen focused on the physical condition which he defined as the ability of the body to adjust or adapt to a working load. This varies from person to person and dancers have variable endurances and abilities to cope with working loads. Willemsen described loading capacity, which is the ability of the body-tissues to cope with force. Training (soft aerobic fitness, quantity training or cardiovascular training, which is what dancers usually cannot find the time for) can increase the loading capacity. This is the crux of the conflict between the athlete and the artist. Dancers are athletes first, because degeneration of the body stops us completely in our tracks as artists. Athletes do not always train at 100 percent of their working load and they allow their bodies to rest as a performance approaches. The opposite is usually true for dancers, who tend to work harder as a performance approaches.

Ted Willemsen looked at non-building muscle strength training, which is part of the ideal injury prevention training of a dancer. Connective tissue adjusts to an increased working load, although the change of training and a setting in period between working load and perceived effect is actually a high-risk period when one is susceptible to injury. Dancers can genuinely increase the blood supply of their muscles and can benefit from training in the recovery time.

Eileen Wanke compared the dancer to the power athlete. She focused on the integration of endurance training into the daily class. The time restrictions might make this an ideal compromise solution to increase the cardiovascular work. In ballet class, waiting should be eradicated. The snag is that dancers lose concentration and co-ordination at the point of fatigue. This is the point at which injuries happen.

"Dancers do not like to run" and most often their contracts do not allow them to be engaged in sports because of the so-called risk of injuries; therefore, other solutions to increase the aerobic fitness of dancers must be sought. Modified training aims to minimize breaks between the exercises. The notion of training choreography, based on three and a half minutes of foundation or basic principle technique, enables non-stop training.

Wanke tested dancers in order to establish an ideal modified training consisting of a ballet class without a drop of heart rate to resting levels with the only breaks coming after the ronde de jambes and grande battiment exercises. Participants in the test modified training and increased their endurance capability. Wanke finished by pointing out that traditional ballets can push dancers to an aerobic respiration anyway so the endurance is actually useful even within existing demands on the dancer. Dancers also feel less tired after a few months of modified training. The fitness is thus achieved outside of a need for running, cycling or swimming.

Winter (out of season) training is most suitable for modification. Dance specific or integrated endurance training can be a key to the powerful dancer becoming less susceptible to injuries. Twenty to thirty minutes of continuous activity is needed for real benefit to fitness. Maintain diversity even in aerobic training so that a whole body workout is achieved. Modified training is best when this comprises 40 percent of the training for the professional dancer.

Questions were asked concerning the application of these guidelines to the training of dance students. Can we modify improvisation training as well? Wanke replied that twelve to thirteen year olds can start to work this way. Corrections cannot really be given during a modified training. The dancer can become

more responsible as the energy saved by the body is significant. Lack of alignment will possibly become more evident in an aerobically working body. Modified training can increase in intensity as the dancer's ability to cope increases.

Prevention of Physical and Mental Overload in the Dancer
Arie Koops and Kitty Bouten
Moderator–Yiannis Koutedakis

All training is specific and individual. The training of today is not the training of tomorrow and the training for one person is not the same as for another. It can range from a basic exercise routine to overload, overreaching and overtraining. Exercise alone does not ensure progress. Overtraining will cost the performer weeks or months to return to a high level of performance. The art of training is to find the optimal training load–large enough to challenge and small enough for the performer still to be able to adapt. This is where growth towards excellence happens.

What is the right amount of training? This could mean working harder and harder–but it could also mean working smarter and smarter. Avoid monotony. If one has to train over a long period of time, one needs to play with the volume of the training in relation to its intensity. This interplay should be coordinated to the performance schedule. A preparation period can have more training volume, whereas a performance period should have less, but a little more intensity. These fine-tuned adaptations will avoid overload and support excellence.

How do dance companies adapt this valuable knowledge from sports and other fields? Kitty Bouten lectured on the prevention of mental overload in the dancer from the perspective of a movement scientist who has done a study on mental stress with twenty-one dancers in a Dutch modern-ballet company during a rehearsal and performance period of about six months. Weekly interviews and questionnaires such as the Rand Mental Health Inventory (RMHI) and the Anxiety Scales (STAI) determined that physical overload by itself had barely any influence on mental stress. Anxiety, however, did have a lot of influence and, interestingly, statistics showed that the sensitivity for anxiety had more influence on mental stress than the actual anxiety itself.

Dancers have very little control over the high psychological demands of their work situation. This is considered to be the most vulnerable and stressful condition, as compared to the thriving workplace combination where staff has a high measure of control and high psychological demands. Dance staff, including teachers and directors, often have dance backgrounds themselves; this adds to the communication and management challenges in dance companies.

Sources of Injuries among Classical Ballet Dancers
Ferenc Mády and Irén Ballya
Moderator–Moira McCormack

Ferenc Mády gave a funny but shocking lecture, illustrated with slides, about the sources of injuries among classical ballet dancers in Hungary based on his research at the Hungarian State Opera between 1984 and 1999. There are 113 dancers in this company with 178 injuries in that time. The average age of the dancer (male or female) with an injury was 30 years. Making a distinction between class, rehearsal and performance injuries, Ferenc Mády showed several diagrams with sprains, wounds, fractures etc. He also showed a chart indicating that January is the month when most injuries happen due to the heaviest workload for the dancers and the fact that January is the coldest month of the year.

Mády noticed a lack of warm-ups in the class. The warm-up is important because it stimulates the blood supply; missing it can lead to injuries such as spine problems. During rehearsals, some dancers are dancing and some are watching. The watchers should be warming up to be ready when they start dancing. It is also important to have long, precise exercises when it comes to preparing for fight scenes which are riskier than others. Choreography should include a short time of relaxation. New unknown techniques can lead to injuries. The choreographer should choose a dancer who is suitable for the job. It is important for dancers to rest for three hours after class and rehearsal before an evening performance. Dancers also need an additional hour to prepare for the role and warm-up. The light on the stage and the darkness in the wings can be very bad and confusing for the eyes of the dancers. The edges of the stairs have to be made clear with tape. The structure of the floor can cause ankle and foot injuries. It should have a good elasticity and the plastic on top of it should not be slippery or just painted. It is important that the scenery allows enough space for the dancers to move properly; they should have lots of opportunity to practice with the scenery elements in place. Participants wondered how much influence Ferenc Mády has on all the aspects he mentioned. He explained that he doesn't have any influence on the production but he tries to communicate with all parties (stage management, artistic staff and, most important, the dancers). The lecture and the discussion afterwards made it clear that there is a big difference between the situation in Hungary and the situation in the Western world when it comes to facilities, safety rules, medical staff, financial means and ways to treat a patient. For example, Mády sometimes shows a patient Hungarian hospitality by inviting him or her home to have dinner with his family.

Limits to Responsibilities
Tim Persent, Maurits Ypma and Naomi Perlov
Moderator–Lucia van Westerlaak

Naomi Perlov, as a teacher and rehearsal-director with large companies, has seen many different dancers. She thinks the pressure on dancers in the smaller companies is enormous. Saying that you cannot dance one night might mean the performance has to be cancelled, whereas The Paris Opera always has a second, third and sometimes even fourth cast waiting in the wings, ready to replace dancers who get injured. She considers this a good way to diminish the pressure on the dancer. Deborah Bull disagreed: Having young people ready to replace you puts pressure on the dancer who might decide to continue with the risk of an injury. Perlov gets tired of working with very young choreographers and dancers because they have problems taking responsibilities.

Tim Persent started as a dancer in a mid-large company at a very young age when the only thing he had on his mind was dancing as much and as well as possible. It took him many years to discover his own limits. He now knows how far he can go and dares to tell the choreographer what HE wants. He chooses the people he wants to work with and notices respect coming from both sides, although it is easier to communicate artistic direction in a small company.

Maurits Ypma has worked as a physiotherapist with a lot of dancers, including young ones. He feels it is hard for young people to know their body and take responsibility for it. In some cases, dancers want him to make decisions, because they are afraid to decide for themselves and have problems communicating with the staff choreographer.

Tim Persent points out that as a dancer you are prepared to be an instrument—the inspiration for your choreographer—and you do not want to complain too much although he feels a lot has changed in the last five years, just by communicating.

In general there is still the feeling that you might lose your job if you open your mouth, which makes it difficult to be persistent in making your own choices. Deborah Bull thinks it is important to give dancers freedom, even when they make a decision to jump out of the window, but dancers need a lot of knowledge to make the right decisions. Athletes are much more aware of their own bodies and their bodies' needs.

All the participants agreed that change has to start with education particularly since most artistic directors/choreographers were educated as dancers themselves. Jean-Christophe Maillot said it is part of the dancer's job to go beyond the limits. There is no generality, only unique cases. Maillot thinks the biggest problem is with artistic directors who do not want change, especially those who did not make the effort to come to this symposium.

Korry Perigo emphasized that there is big responsibility for dancers to create change now, instead of waiting for the next generation. Cisca van Dijk-de Bloeme felt that counseling opportunities at dance schools are very important. Students need someone they can trust who can guide them. Dancers have to learn how to find their talents. One of Cisca's students has had difficulties finding a job because dance companies are not ready for self-conscious, independent dancers who are able to express their feelings.

Philippe Braunschweig said although there is an enormous difference between sports and dance, some dancers could learn from sports results. In particular, sports organizations have much more money and resources for research.

Choreographers need more knowledge of human skills, social behaviour and teambuilding. Onno Stokvis advised dance academies in Europe to work together to create one system.

In conclusion, this discussion was a very heated one involving more or less all the different professions in the dance world: teachers, choreographers, directors, representatives from the Ministry of Culture and the union, dancers and former dancers, rehearsal directors and Maecenas. A whole tradition is not easy to change when there are still so many conservative people in important places.

Iyengar Yoga as a Dance Training Supplement and Health Promoter
Krishna Lee Hanks

In this workshop, Iyengar Yoga was presented as a supplementary training for dancers. The seminar focused on using yoga postures for injury prevention and recovery. This training has also been proven as being beneficial to a dancer's body alignment, breathing patterns and concentration.

Gyrotonics Expansion System
Hilary Cartwright

Gyrotonics Expansion System is a unique form of exercise especially developed for dancers based on principles drawn from yoga, dance, swimming and gymnastics. It combines a repertoire of exercises performed on custom-designed equipment. This workshop focused on how dancers can benefit from the system.

The Alexander Technique
Tom Koch and Daniela Graca

The Alexander Technique is a process for recognizing and changing harmful tension patterns that hinder freedom and confidence in movement. The basic principles of the technique were introduced and their application to various dance techniques and styles were explored.

The Mensendieck Method
Karina Bolger

Mensendieck is a practical therapy for prevention and cure that stimulates awareness of the body and teaches how to use the body correctly in daily life and in dance. Exercises were offered to balance strength, mobility and coordination. The starting point of this therapy is that each individual has his or her own specific posture and way of moving.

* * *

REPORTS FROM TORONTO
THE DANCE OF PERFECTION
Marion Woodman, Sorella Englund, Kathleen Rea, Mikko Nissinen and Niva Piran
Moderator—Lori Finklestein

This session addressed the crucial issue of perfection and its role in dance. Questions such as: What is perfection? and How does perfectionism affect the dancer in her/his striving for excellence? provoked an incredibly dynamic discussion of issues which have long awaited public acknowledgment and attention.

To begin the session, each panelist spoke with honesty about their own struggles and/or understanding of perfection and the lurking realities and deadly consequences that it has on dancers. Marion Woodman spoke of the importance of staying physically, mentally and spiritually connected. She referred to perfectionism as a deviation of the body from the mind, suggesting this addiction is ultimately a death instinct.

Sorella Englund generously shared her experience with perfectionism as a dancer struggling with an eating disorder. She posed thoughtful questions such as: "What really is perfect?" and "Is the goal of art perfection?" Englund stressed the importance of encouraging young artists to develop who they are as individuals as opposed to becoming images of some perfectionist ideal.

Mikko Nissinen reflected on the valuable resources we have as an artistic community to produce excellence in dance. He spoke with confidence about positive ways to provide structure to young dancers without oppressing their curiosity, love and enthusiasm for dance.

Kathleen Rea shared some personal experiences of her struggle with perfection in her dance career. She asked, Is perfection necessary for excellence? Rea made reference to the importance

of connecting mind, body and spirit in order to clearly channel creative energy.

Niva Piran spoke about the active role of preventive methods in educating dancers from an early age to develop a healthy self image.

All of the panelists unanimously promoted the importance of striving for excellence in dance. They acknowledged the destructive physical and spiritual consequences of perfectionist tendencies. The session was heightened as emotionally charged members of the audience elaborated on these issues, creating a dynamic interplay of energies and marking a groundbreaking public awareness of the dance of perfection.

PREPARING DANCERS TO MEET THE DEMANDS OF TODAY'S CHOREOGRAPHY
Serge Bennathan, Penny Flemming, Allen Kaeja, Aminurta Kang, Brian Macdonald, Susan Macpherson and Sara Porter
Moderator—Paula Citron

How do we prepare dancers for a dance career with no boundaries? Panelists agreed that the demands on dancers today are immense. The growing breadth of dance choices is both a luxury and a burden for young students. Panelists presented many ideas for young dancers to enhance their dance experience including: a classical training as a foundation, neuromuscular training, mélange technique classes, and sport medicine applications to build core strength. Most of the panelists agreed that classical training created a strong foundation of stamina and strength for future explorations in dance. Allen Kaeja asserted that being a brilliant mover is not enough anymore, and that dancers are now creative partners in the choreographic process and need to flex their imaginations as well as their muscles.

Have we educated our young dancers sufficiently to make responsible training choices? The panel encouraged curiosity, exploration, experimentation, confidence and awareness in students. In order to make the right choices, they suggested mentoring and counseling for students to better facilitate the learning process. The panel also hoped to teach by example, encourage their students to listen to their instincts, and demonstrate a passion for dance. By doing all of these things, hopefully, students will be empowered to experience dance completely.

Professional Career Longevity and Facing Transition
Carol Anderson, Karen Kain, Darryl Ogilvie-Harris
and Joysanne Sidimus
Moderator—Linda Hamilton

Why are people compelled to study dance professionally? You don't choose dance, rather dance chooses you. Common among the panelists was a visceral reaction to music and a need to physically move in its presence. As a child, Karen Kain danced to the music available to her on her parent's record player—Scottish waltzes.

Who should become a professional? A dance career should be undertaken only if dance is something that you can't not do, according to Joysanne Sidimus. Other attributes required are physical propensity, emotional fortitude and a willingness to work very hard. Darryl Ogilvie-Harris suggested that a dancer must take the "punishment to learn the discipline for dance." The ability to take what is given, in terms of personal attributes as well as experiences, and turn this into positive experiences, is often a quality of the professional dancer, says Carol Anderson. Mentors and role models can also be a factor.

Is dance a career (defined as either a field or pursuit of successive achievement, especially in public, professional or business life) or a calling or a vocation? Carol Anderson suggested that dance is more of a "mosaic." In the course of a dancer's life, he or she might be a teacher, rehearsal director or a critic as well as a performer. Darryl Ogilvie-Harris asserted that sometimes only a retrospective diagnosis would say whether a person had experienced a career in dance.

Once a professional, how do you care for yourself? Diet, cross-training and prompt attention to injury were key points for Darryl Ogilvie-Harris. Linda Hamilton bemoaned the predominance of smoking among professional dancers; as well as lowering cardiovascular performance, smoking also makes bones soft. Looking after one's psychological well-being can reduce injuries and make for a happier, better adjusted person and performer, says Joysanne Sidimus. Karen Kain stressed that dancers must

address psychological issues because the stress and expectations surrounding performance can wreak havoc on the most capable of performers.

People say, "Get a life!" How? Associating with people outside the dance world and having other interests are crucial. Life is not a tendu, says Sidimus. Ogilvie-Harris wondered, not entirely facetiously, if all great dancers are unbalanced. Response from the other panelists suggested this may have been the case in less informed times, but new attitudes and resources exist so that it need not be the case anymore.

An audience member suggested that the real difference between an amateur and a professional is making money. Are schools teaching dance students how to earn? Panelists suggested that in Canada, because there is so little chance of a dance career being a money-making venture, this aspect of "career" does not even enter into discussions.

An audience member suggested that institutional training could become more rounded, perhaps spending less time on technique, and more time developing a more fully functional human being. Most children, however, when asked whether they aspire to be a well-rounded human being, or the next Karen Kain, will invariably pick the latter.

The Psychological Well-being of the Dancer
Mihaly Csikszentmihalyi, Marie Herbert, David Popalisky
and Bonnie Robson
Moderator—Richard Meen

Bonnie Robson, who has spent years studying students in dance and theatre, began by introducing the support services she has created for young dancers where she facilitates discussion groups, not therapy sessions. She has found that being special—being in an intensive dance program at a young age—has risks such as social isolation. And she talked about competition as being, in the student's eyes, "a way of life." Robson's research, conducted over five years with students from a variety of schools, showed that 24 percent of arts students, 13 percent of intellectually gifted students and 10 percent of students not in intensive artistic programs, sought counseling. She noted that talented children didn't tend to suppress anxiety the same way other students did.

David Popalisky and Marie Herbert explained the creation of their innovative, long-overdue program at Santa Claire University dedicated to educating dance students about health issues in a post-secondary setting.

Finally, Csikszentmihalyi, reacting to what he heard from all the panelists, expressed his pleasure with the "curriculum innovation" Popalisky and Herbert were responsible for, but stated that we (dance enthusiasts) need to move towards a more positive view of what's going on in the arts: the arts should engender hope, optimism, wisdom and flow, which is what "nature is about." He appreciated the work done by the panelists, "giving people an opportunity to express and define themselves." But he emphasized that there was too much concern with what goes wrong in the arts, echoing Robson, who asked, "How far can you go without paying a price for perfection?"

BUILDING SUPPORTIVE MANAGEMENT AND ADMINISTRATIVE STRUCTURES
Valerie Wilder, Jane Marsland, Myles Warren and George Thorn
Moderator–Robert Sirman

Robert Sirman began with an overview of how the themes of the conference, health and well-being of dancers and the milieu, relate to the health and well-being of organizations. "We were trying to explore which concepts could be applied to institutions as well as individual practitioners. Just as we are looking beyond health as it relates to biology and encompassing psychological and spiritual health, so we are looking to the health of organizations beyond economic health."

Valerie Wilder discussed the need for more engagement and involvement at all levels. The connection with the community and the overall balance of the organization is now critical to its health. As dance is multi-disciplinary, for every performer there is a support team implying some level of organization, even if it is as basic as a studio, mirrors and a tape deck. There is still enough allure in the field to attract more dancers than there are spots for them; this is not the case in the organization itself. We must prepare for successions, for the future of the organization and provide more training in all areas of administration.

Jane Marsland spoke about the critical nature of the artistic vision that drives the organization. Staff is often there for meaningful, lifetime work and they value their deep connection and shared beliefs with the artistic community. If things are out of sync, problems must be dealt with head-on. Collaborative problem solving is key. Today we are also looking at new alliances and models of shared significance to accomplish our goals.

Myles Warren spoke about the paradox between artists finding new ways of working and having to relate to old models in the corporate/granting structures imposing expectations which don't enable artmakers to grow and develop, and don't support learning–they support the product. Mentorship support must be ongoing; we must discuss the life, not the career, of an artist. We must also look at how arts managers can continue to learn. How do the essentials get transferred without imposing old-school institutional constructs? Making art is about innovation and invention, not marketing and economics.

George Thorn works full time with various arts organizations around North America trying to help achieve healthy organizations. He acknowledged that we are working in environments ranging from volatile to hostile and raised ideas of how organizations take on challenges and move forward to healthier states. The arts are better than most sectors at solving these challenges because they deal with the creative process–planning, problem solving and decision making. Thorn recommends a dynamic balance which involves leadership, a sense of vision and a forward-moving decision-making process.

Questions from the audience sparked discussion on how institutions relate to communities; how independent artists can exist with many different examples and methods of organization; and how the roles and relationships of boards can evolve and change.

ENHANCEMENT OF PERFORMANCE: APPLICATIONS FROM SPORTS PSYCHOLOGY
Kate Hays and Tom J. O'Hara

The panelists, both of whom are sports psychologists, said that although dancers engage in a complex activity, sports psychology can be a vehicle to examine some of the psychological aspects affecting their performance.

Tom O'Hara spoke about attention control. Dancers must work to develop their concentration and self-awareness by identifying potential relevant and irrelevant areas in any class, rehearsal or performance setting; assessing their own concentration style; and using a variety of concentration techniques to maintain and regain proper focus. His formula for success is: Awareness + Control + Repetition = Positive Change. The best way for a dancer to begin a psychological training program is to start with his/her best performance: What were my thoughts before, during and after this performance? How did I feel? What worked? What didn't?

Attention is always shifting for the dancer and this natural phenomenon could become debilitating. How does a dancer find focus once it is lost? O'Hara showed graphs of how attention shifts and concentration errors occur, indicating a dancer's internal and external focus as either narrow or broad.

Kate Hays moved onto issues of tension and relaxation, asking "Where do you experience tension in the body." The audience responded with: the chest, the jaw, the shoulders and the neck. Then Hays asked about thought processes during a performance. Responses indicated the audience felt scattered or very tired; some experienced a loss of memory while others felt bombarded with doubts and worry. Suggesting a rating scale of 1 to 10 (1 = very low tension and 10 = very high tension), dancers need to perform somewhere in the middle. Very high or very low tension can be debilitating.

Dancers should become aware of their eating habits, limit their alcohol intake and refrain from smoking. They should also engage in cardiovascular exercise since dance does not always develop this. Some short term solutions included relaxation and breathing exercises. Hays also touched on self-talk and affirmations. Mental chatter is a key to positive (extremely useful) and negative (debilitating) thoughts. Since dancers are usually perfectionists involved in a competitive atmosphere, they must be aware of negative thoughts and work to eliminate them. She said it can be useful to chart thoughts–situation, automatic thoughts, responses–to become aware of thought patterns and eventually eliminate negative feelings.

Use affirmations which are short and specific, rhythmic, in the present tense, positive and stated with an expectation of success, such as: "I am ready." "My body learns." "I am the swan." "I am, thus I can." "Be calm my heart." Hays also spoke about Goal Setting. Smart goals are specific, measurable, action-oriented, realistic and timed.

O'Hara discussed mental imagery, a technique which puts the dancer into a desirable state. "What do you use imagery for? Arousal? To feel more confident? For mental practice? To create a desirable mood?"

FLOWER SEED DANCE
Peggy Baker

An in-depth study of the action of the shoulder girdle, devised by Irene Dowd. The class participated in the Flower Seed Dance, which explores the relationship between the shoulder blade and the movement of the arm within the shoulder girdle. They experienced the directional intention and counter force needed to create proper muscle tone and integrity of joint movement while keeping the torso independent of the shoulder girdle action. All participants experienced the sequences and questions were geared towards correcting the dynamics. The focus and concentration was intense and motivated participants to think along new paths.

RECENT ADVANCES IN POINTE SHOES AND FOOTCARE
Carol Beevers, Nicholas J. Durand and Mark Suffolk

Nicholas Durand opened with a slide show depicting common pathologies associated with dance and pointe work. Basic common injuries were outlined as well as more serious problems that occur primarily when minor conditions are ignored. Durand stressed that pointe work is not a natural practice and that the key to successful training is preventing and minimizing injury.

Carol Beevers outlined a brief history of the development of pointe shoes and pointe work, and then opened discussion on recent developments in pointe shoe manufacturing. She indicated that many changes in the pointe shoe industry are met with resistance as dancers tend to be conservative, wishing to protect the aesthetic of the pointe shoe as we know it today. Changes must occur gently, slowly, and with proper expertise backing them up. Mark Suffolk described the relationship between the National

Ballet School and Freed of London Ltd. Together they have developed pointe shoes that are more appropriate for recreational dance students, as well as accommodating the wider foot of today's dancer. Castings, used to determine how a dancer's foot differs in and out of pointe shoes, were passed around for the delegates to marvel at and potential problems were explored.

New choreography requires us to take a different look at pointe shoes and the way they function. Dancers are expected to perform an increased range of movements with increased physical stresses and fatigue.

Many concerns were addressed including the cost of pointe shoes, use of synthetic versus natural materials, new models and variations, use of aids within the shoes and the many varied uses and misuses of the shoes themselves.

Curriculum for Partnering Skills
Sylvain Lafortune
Moderator–Pat Fraser

Partnering is not only intended to enhance the female dancer; it involves two dancers working together. The lifted must trust the lifter completely; one does not perform without the other. Both must understand how to communicate with each other. The point of body contact, use of body weight, the laws of gravity and what preparation to use are key concepts. As well, dancers should understand how to press down on the point of support, direct the weight towards the centre, stabilize and hold the weight of the lifted against one's centre. The basic families of lifts are: dead weight lifts; counter lever lifts; assisted jumps; assisted jumps with a preparation; assisted jumps that travel; and catch lifts. The preparation for the lift and its dynamics are important influences that can change the nature of the movement. Both men and women must prepare themselves for partnering with strength training; the abdominals in particular should be trained daily.

Arts in Education: Enhancing Learning Abilities and Creative Capacity
Ann Kipling Brown, Susan Drake, Susan Koff and Norma Sue Fisher-Stitt
Moderator–Walter Pitman

While dance training depends particularly on skill acquisition, dance education combines technique with imagination, synthesis, reflection and an understanding of the world. It is the balance of creativity and skill that allows for effective self-expression through movement. This is the "meaningful encounter with the arts" stressed in the work of pioneer dance educators John Dewey and Maxine Green.

Dance education brings joy into daily life and is worth doing for its own sake, not just because it will improve standardized test scores. Unfortunately, these benefits are difficult to measure but, with the desire for quantitative results, dance testing (however elusive and value-based) has become essential.

The crisis in arts education, and specifically dance education, lies in the lack of not only effective curriculum implementation and assessment tools but also the acceptance of dance in the administrative world. In public schools, dance is the last art form to be included. One way of achieving recognition is by providing resources to educators. Many general elementary school teachers feel inadequately prepared to integrate movement into the classroom and avoid teaching dance completely. In addition to professional development sessions, a partnership between teachers and local artists can bring about a positive dance experience by working together and drawing on each other's strengths. Unfortunately, there is never enough funding to fully develop these resources.

The arts in education enhance learning abilities and creative capacity by providing students with tools for self-expression, reflection and exploration and helping to develop better citizens who have the strong communication and interpersonal skills required in today's job market. For these reasons, advocacy of arts education–through teacher, artist, and parental involvement–is essential.

Gender-based and Relationship Issues in Dance
Gail Lee Abrams, Darcy McGehee, Marianne Schultz, Clyde Smith and Claire Wootten

Although the five papers presented in this session varied in topic, many of the interviewees had experienced, described or were on the verge of rites of passage.

Claire Wootten's graduate research is on feminist pedagogy and ballet training ("the feminist meets the ballet teacher"). The students she interviewed at the National Ballet School identified a perceived inequality between boys (physically competitive) and girls (perfectionists). The female students didn't feel physical or powerful because of the restrictions of pointe shoes and classical roles.

Clyde Smith presented a part of his doctoral work on abusive behaviour in a modern dance conservatory in which interviewees characterized their training studios as prisons. One respondent felt that she would spend the rest of her life re-patterning her body to recover from her training.

Darcy McGehee wanted to understand the relationship between how we move and learn. She examined the movement similarities between her autistic son and her university students studying ballet, identifying tension in the foot and an inability to flex the upper torso as similar symptoms.

Gail Lee Abrams interviewed dancers about their experiences giving birth. Very few of her interviewees experienced lower back pain and there was a smaller percentage of C-sections than in non-dancing mothers. Many felt their dance training helped them both physically and emotionally to stay connected to their bodies, feel subtle changes in their bodies, use breathing to ease pain and endure long labours.

Marianne Schultz interviewed dancers as mothers, questioning how their lives and identities changed. The mothers' perception of self changed after giving birth. Many struggled with their place both in dance and in the real world. Some of the artistic directors interviewed felt that mothers became better dancers because they abandoned perfectionism and appeared more grounded.

Perfectionism was identified as a common female trait in this session. Implicitly trusting authority and consequent abuse of power also appeared as common themes. At the end of the session, an audience member lamented the title of the session. He had hoped there would be a discussion about both male and female relationships in dance. Panel members agreed there needs to be more research into the male perspective in dance.

The Dancer As Athlete: Next Steps in Body Conditioning
Roger Hobden, Sylvain Lafortune, Sarah McCutcheon, Mikko Nissinen and Betty Tate-Pineau
Moderator—Penny Flemming

Discussion centred on whether dance class, particularly ballet class, was sufficient to provide a dancer with all they need in terms of their physical training. Many panelists acknowledged that although class is an essential tool, it is only one among many that can and should be used to comprehensively prepare the dancer for performance and guard against injury. The panelists with medical training expressed concern about the large numbers of repetitive injuries they treat, and wondered how much daily technique class might be contributing to these occurrences. Sylvain Lafortune and Roger Hobden felt that importance should be given to training in other areas of fitness; cardiovascular endurance and strength should not be tacked onto the end of a dancer's busy and exhausting day. Suggestions ranged from throwing out the whole training model and starting again, to modifying existing classes to cover these training issues.

Encouraging and Developing Choreographers
Serge Bennathan, Dominique Dumais, Danny Grossman, Bengt Jörgen and Grant Strate
Moderator—Penelope Reed Doob

This panel was an informal conversation among some of Canada's key choreographers. Is choreography something that is innate in the artist or does it need to be trained and/or taught? Panelists stressed the importance of creating a positive environment for artists inclined to explore their limitless and often unknown potential.

Each panelist generously shared their own experiences of dance and choreography throughout their childhood, and how these desires and impulses emerged and matured into their professional careers. They described the many personal and pivotal influences in their lives and the experiences that ultimately encouraged, supported and helped form who they are as artists. While noting the struggles and the risks that the choreographers took when first presenting their work publicly, they all expressed gratitude for the many opportunities for their choreographic needs to fulfill themselves.

Included in the discussion was an awareness of the role that women choreographers have played throughout the history of dance, and also of the predominance of male choreographers–particularly in classical ballet–in today's society. The importance of exposing oneself to other disciplines of dance and, more broadly, to all the many different mediums of art was also addressed.

The importance of choreographic workshops was stressed both by the panelists and the audience members. It was noted that having the external support and creating the opportunities for artists to craft, develop and discover their own unique process were of utmost importance for choreographic development. This mandate was a responsibility of educators and of the art world at large.

PHYSICAL AND INTELLECTUAL PREPARATION FOR PERFORMANCE
Peggy Baker, Margie Gillis, Karen Kain
and Joysanne Sidimus
Moderator–Veronica Tennant

Veronica Tennant offered many insightful comments on her personal experience as a performer. She commented on how a dancer's life is part of a collaborative community involving a collage of different skills such as those of artistic director, teacher and choreographer who are all participating and investing in the dancer's development. She commented on how the dancer can become too obsessed with the specific tool of dance: the body. It is not "the how" but "the what" that should encompass the entire performance.

Peggy Baker suggested looking at choreography as a vocabulary with families or groups of movements. She also recommended looking at the spatial components of the dance, making it a 3-dimensional realm rather than a 2-dimensional surface. The idea is not to give rigid perfectionism.

Joysanne Sidimus offered comments from the coach's perspective. She felt the greatest gift for a dancer who is training for a performance is that of quality. She said dancers should be endlessly curious about the material.

Karen Kain added that as the new Artistic Associate at the National Ballet Company, she was now able to reflect on the spiritual experiences of her performing career.

Margie Gillis said she explores the dance from the inside out. She said she feels her brain working quickly to manifest energy into her movement. She spoke of the "bliss" she experiences in a performance. Twenty-four hours before the performance she asks, What do I care about? What do I desire? Who am I? How am I feeling? Am I miserable? Am I happy? Am I injury bound?

The panel also spoke of the use of imagination pre- and post-performance. Tennant asked, "Are modern dance performances inherently different than ballet?" Gillis felt there wasn't a difference between the two dance styles. "The body does not lie," she said. Kain agreed and added that perhaps the only difference between them is the pointe shoe. She felt that adding this "thing" to the foot added another dimension for the dancer.

The panelists spoke of music as a tool to take a performance to a higher level, leading to a discussion about those very rare moments on stage when "something special happens." Kain commented on the few times in her career when she had experienced this. She felt she didn't make it happen herself but rather that some external force was driving the experience.

Finally, the panelists spoke about many of the personal rituals they engaged in before a performance. Kain said she learned in her career that there were no right or wrong ways to prepare. The pre-performance time was very individual and changed with one's maturity. Gillis said she often sings to see if her body is responding properly with her breath. Baker likes to sit in the house of the theatre and look at the stage from the perspective of the audience which connects her to what the audience will soon experience by watching her.

THE SOCIETAL IMPACT OF DANCE WRITERS AND CRITICS
John Alleyne, Paula Citron, Michael Crabb,
Lindsay Fischer, William Littler, Francia Russell
and Gretchen Warren
Moderator–Richard Philp

Dance writers and critics are writing either for the general public, with some thought to "hooking" people who don't care about dance or for the dance community, even though some dance artists ignore dance writing. There is a need to distinguish between different kinds of dance writing and their purposes and effects, e.g. technical writing, serious criticism, review. This session focused mostly on reviewing because of its obvious impact, with rather brief attention to the damage careless reviewing can do (by omission as well as by rude or unjust fault-finding)–perhaps not surprising since some of the panelists were themselves responsible reviewers.

Dance writers have the power to sell tickets, create reputations, foster (mis)understandings and shape attitudes although one panelist felt they simply witness and report as representative audience members.

Values/Ethics: When does a writer's proximity to dance artists become compromising, however instructive it may be? Allowance should be made for writers' different temperaments, but some general virtues should attach to reviewing: honesty, respect, trust and human decency.

COLLABORATIVE APPROACHES TO TRAINING AT CANADA'S NATIONAL BALLET SCHOOL
Carina Bomers, Elaine Fisher, Ana Jojic, Lori Finklestein and Lindsay Melcher
Moderator–Deborah Bowes

The National Ballet School has a full academic/dance program with physiotherapy/body condition consultants and sister arts to enrich the full needs of the students. The staff, consultants and specialists meet on a bi-weekly basis to achieve their primary goal of working in a healthy environment by exchanging thoughts and discussing problems that might arise in all areas of student life. The exchange of information among staff members is respectful and a very important part of their way of collaborating to create whole, independent persons/dancers/ artists.

BODY WORK I
Karen Bowes-Sewell, Greta von Gavel and Diane Woodruff
Moderator–Sagrario Castilla

This session focused on the necessity of central stabilization in dance. Concepts of imagery, awareness and perception were discussed and demonstrated. Greta von Gavel emphasized the need for techniques to address movement itself, as well as supportive systems such as the respiratory, circulatory, myofascial, neurological and connective tissue systems. Movement was described as based on emotion, cognition, conscious awareness and reflexes.

Diane Woodruff applied neuromuscular patterning to dance through a number of exercises in body awareness. Visual awareness and kinesthetic senses were demonstrated via removal of visual input and observation of peers. Quality of movement was emphasized and substitutions, trick movements and central pelvic control were observed.

Karen Bowes-Sewell completed the session by demonstrating techniques used to develop core support involving somatic and kinesthetic sense, with physical conditioning built on this base. The concept of core support was then linked to ballet and dance classes. Imagery was used throughout to guide participants toward the desired result.

DANCING AND CREATIVITY
Donna Krasnow, Elizabeth Chitty, Anadel Lynton-Snyder, Janet Roseman and Paula Solassaari
Moderator–Norma Sue Fisher-Stitt

Donna Krasnow presented an overview on how the scientific and physical sides can be brought together for more efficient and productive training. She explained the visual, vestibular and proprioceptive systems that develop in childhood and reach a state of working together between ages four and six. It is important to continue to develop each of these systems as training develops to make more fully rounded and holistic performers. She explained and demonstrated how, through improvisation and play, she provides challenge and stimulates growth in each of the systems, whether working with young dancers or adults. These methods enhance both skill development and creative expression.

Elizabeth Chitty spoke of creative process training for nineteen to twenty-five year olds. She believes in the benefits of empowerment and a holistic approach to education and has developed methods to help confront the fear she saw in students about the creative process. Her method, called "say what you see," has students state what they observe without opinion or judgment in order to develop better critical thinking and observation skills, as data from multiple sources is more helpful than being told what to do.

In her presentation, Paula Solassaari was looking to develop the meaning inside the classical ballet vocabulary. In lieu of dancers learning by rote, they must develop interpretive and compositional skills. She introduced imagery as a tool for dancemaking, showing videos of her experiments with dancers performing technical sequences after receiving different motivations. She has found a greater ability to engage in the movement and an expansion of flexibility and compositional skills.

Janet Roseman explored the Dancer as Mystic, examining the parallels between dance and mysticism by citing components that are integrally shared by both realms in relation to "out of ordinary moments" and "communion with the Divine." She cited seven parallels integrating quotes from dancers, artists and writers, as well as excerpts from her forthcoming book, *Dance Masters: Interviews with Legends of the Dance*.

Anadel Lynton-Snyder presented information on her work with communities in Mexico where dance was at the centre of a positive group identity. She provided some historical perspective on dance and art as being for the people and how that aligned with codified Western training. She stated that creativity resides in the local community; that health implies flexibility and pliability. She worked with groups to teach and create meaningful dancers, where spectators were encouraged to witness as co-participants.

Body Work 2
Richard Omel, Jill Pribyl and Joelle Segers
Richard Omel began the session with a discussion of the Mitzvah Technique as applied to the conditioning of dancers outside the realm of dance-specific training. Following the theme of kinesthetic awareness, he outlined the tensegrity model that the Mitzvah Technique centers on: symmetry, synchronicity, body core/torso relationship, relationship of upper extremities to torso and the relationship of lower extremities to torso. The need to understand skeletal relationships to restore balance after dance class, which will eventually flow into dance movement within class, was stressed. This restoration of synchronicity and flow

neutralizes the body. Participants experimented with sitting and posture patterns, gaining synchronicity of the body for proper posture and feeling ease of movement.

Jill Pribyl then introduced Laban Movement Analysis and Bartenieff Fundamentals. Without the ability to coordinate the body in movement, one cannot find expressiveness. The body must be used efficiently in order to accommodate the exploration of emotion in dance. Bartenieff Fundamentals can be incorporated into regular dance class, as a warm-up, for example. Participants experimented with exercises on the floor with Pribyl aiding in the technical execution of the breathing and movement. Individual exercises were then pieced together into combination, illustrating how the fundamentals can be put together for class as a progression.

Joelle Segers then turned the focus to neuromuscular patterning and conditioning. Topics explored included awareness exercises (centering on pressure points, breathing and fluidity), strengthening exercises, and stretching exercises. Conditioning aims to complement classical training, and helps to meet the ever-growing demands of modern day choreography. Segers emphasized the importance of integrating an idea throughout an entire class so concepts are well understood and internalized. Integration of new elements is a slow process, as neuromuscular patterning concepts must first be understood and then applied.

Dance in the Public School System
Judith Alter, Anne Flynn, Robyn Hughes-Ryman, Kathy Lundy, Patti Ross Milne, Ursula Nahatchewitz and Janis Stone
Moderator–Barbara Soren
The discussion of the state of dance in the public school system raised the perceived shortfalls and successes of program development, teaching and learning.

Judith Alter introduced the work of early educators G. Stanley Hall and Luther Gulick who praised folk dance in the schools for its social, psychological, aesthetic and moral benefits. Gulick's philosophy stated that dancing provides a play-like activity where children can enrich their lives with wholesome, interesting and beautiful activities. Dance benefits the whole child,

175

heart, mind and imagination; it also satisfies psychological, physical, emotional and communal needs.

In Canada today, dance is still marginalized in schools and society. In view of raising awareness of dance education, Anne Flynn has developed a video showing the many advantages to implementing dance in the public schools, to encourage parents to advocate dance in their children's schools.

Once dance is included within the program of study, maintaining integrity and excellence are essential in developing a curriculum. Ursula Nahatchewitz, Janis Stone and Kathy Lundy spoke about the dance curricula in Ontario. At the elementary level, dance and drama are integrated into other subject areas and are required of all students; the dance component emphasizes expression and communication of ideas through movement. The secondary school guidelines offer individual dance courses at each grade level, focusing on developing criticism, appreciation and composition skills. Unfortunately, adequate funding is not available for resources such as professional development for teachers and effective use of guest artists.

Robyn Hughes-Ryman noted that the dance curriculum varies from school to school and even where a strong dance program exists, demand often outnumbers available spaces. Furthermore, no qualifications beyond B. Ed. are needed to teach dance in the public education system although some workshops are offered to teachers and the Council of Dance and Drama in Education has been established. Technological resources such as telecommunication, the Internet, computer software, television and video are fairly accessible and supported by various dance advocacy groups.

Performing arts high schools, though limited in number, provide important exposure to dance for many students. The course quality and content have continued to improve, producing knowledgeable dancers and dance audiences. These programs also develop essential life skills including time management and cooperation. Patti Ross Milne has developed a jazz dance program of study, addressing the quality of instruction and providing preparation for a career in dance. She also addresses the needs of teachers by providing workshops on jazz history, technique and style.

Dance in the public school system fills an important need,

broadening the minds of students, encouraging effective personal expression and exposing young people to a rewarding dance experience; however, continued advocacy is necessary to ensure the availability of quality dance programs to all students.

NUTRITIONAL ISSUES FOR DANCERS AND DANCE TEACHERS
Julia Alleyne, Dominique Dumais, Ethan Feldman, Rowena Ridout and Elizabeth Snell
Moderator–Kate Hays

Achieving one's optimal body weight in good health is essential. What we eat fuels our bodies and sustains energy levels for performance. When these needs are not met, bone density, reproduction, psychological health and cardiovascular and gastrointestinal systems can be affected, leading to severe or permanent damage. If all nutritional needs are met through wise, healthy, balanced eating, there is no need for supplements. Dancers should add aerobic exercise (such as swimming and biking) to their day, in order to burn more calories, allowing them to increase their nutritional intake to function at top condition.

Dominique Dumais said education needs have changed and students are now more informed on where and how to get help. Dance is about life, breath and movement, and there is nothing wrong with a female dancer who has breasts and hips on stage. Dancers today must try to stay away from the anorexic look presented by the media. You are what you eat. A healthy person = a healthy dancer.

Who is responsible for a young woman's nutritional health in a dance school or professional dance company? For example, a dancer who exhibits all the signs of the female athlete triad: amenorhea (no menses for three months); eating problems (but not full-fledged eating disorder); and a stress fracture? The panelists agreed that the school should work together with the dancer to help create a healthier life. Lack of proper nutrition, along with genetics, race and hormones can lead to lower bone density, stress factors and osteoporosis, even though a dancer may be aerobically fit. Malnutrition at an early age is irreversible and can lead to osteoporosis later in life. It is essential that dance teachers demonstrate healthy habits themselves, particularly around eating and smoking, as they play a key role model for students.

IDENTIFYING DANCE TALENT

John Alleyne, Annette av Paul, Carole Chadwick, Benjamin Harkarvy, Richard Meen, Penelope Reed Doob, Linda Stearns and Jean-Claude West
Moderator–Gretchen Ward Warren

Identifying dance talent remains an emotional and highly subjective issue. While this panel and participants aimed to answer what is talent and how to recognize it, the definition remained elusive. Gretchen Ward Warren began by stating that talent is rare, intangible, unmistakable and a necessary prerequisite for success. The recognition of talent creates hope and excitement in its potential for greatness.

Psychiatrist Richard Meen dealt with the psychological traits of talented dancers, posing the simple question, "Why do you want to dance?" He referred to Marion Woodman's "divine soul" and Mihaly Csikszentmihalyi's "flow" as the desired bases for responses by young dancers. Teacher and former dancer Annette av Paul discussed the attributes of a world class ballerina. While early immersion in the arts is essential, the presence of an active support system provides the environment for growth and development as an artist. The dancer must also be collaborator and a contributor in the choreographic process and must develop with his or her audience.

Linda Stearns commented on nurturing talent and reinforced that opportunities must be provided by artistic directors and choreographers to bring out the dancer's self-confidence. She also addressed what she looks for when auditioning dancers: certainly the elements of physique, technique, musicality and intelligence are important, but that elusive something inside the dancer which touches the soul is the underlying essence.

Carole Chadwick stressed these same points when identifying talent in young children–it is a process that, over time, allows for talent to be expressed in a safe environment. The combination of an instrument with balletic facility as well as artistic and psychological talents is necessary to face the profession's demands.

John Alleyne united these two themes. When auditioning dancers for his company, he combines some of the subjective elements such as energy, enthusiasm, passion, inquisitiveness, self-imposed discipline, intelligence and instinct with an environment of comfort and respect in order to allow these talents to surface.

Penelope Reed Doob stressed this safe environment when identifying choreographic talent. Her ongoing study of students at the National Ballet School identified certain characteristics of choreographers, as well as the importance of extending training to include all of Howard Gardener's multiple intelligences and nurturing choreographic talent, particularly in girls.

Reiterating the essence of dance talent as the individuality of the dancer taking charge of his or her own expression through movement, Benjamin Harkarvy said late bloomers are imitators who have finally understood what's needed and are doing it to the best of their abilities.

This connection of mind and body was further built on by physiotherapist Jean-Claude West. In order to prevent injuries, the dancer's particular movement signature needs to be identified and the dance needs to be cultivated within this signature. This is the individuality of the dancer that is seen only in performance.

The subjective nature of physical and artistic talent remained unresolved. While all agreed on the recurring themes, several dancers and teachers stressed that it is essential for the passionate dancer to seek a wide range of opportunities and develop the belief in themselves required to deal with the reality of rejection. Talent is but one factor and how we see talent is individual; there is a place for every dancer who has the fire in them.

PREPARING DANCERS FOR PAS DE DEUX

Reginald Amatto, Roberto Campanella, Paul Fiolkowwski, Sylvain Lafortune, Iris Marshall and Betty Tate-Pineau
Moderator–Penny Flemming

Preparation of young dancers, both male and female, for pas de deux and general partnering was discussed by a panel of dancers, ballet teachers, and experts in the field of physical conditioning and injury management. All panelists emphasized the need to begin teaching partnering concepts at an early age. Before students are mature enough for lifting, exercises can develop interpersonal relationships, signaling systems, communication skills and comfort in closeness with other dancers.

Principles of biomechanics and problem solving skills were

identified as building blocks that transfer to all partnering work. The need for males and females to learn both roles in lifting was considered. Training was discussed as an umbrella term encompassing physical, psychosocial, artistic and mental realms. The need for a base of dynamic stability was emphasized and linked to a decreased risk of injury. Once a base of support, general strength and fitness are achieved, specificity of training principles could be implemented to augment performance in specific roles and lifts. More artistically, partners need to learn concepts of bodily interaction, respect and closeness from a young age. Appropriate use of rhythm, musicality and auditory and physical communication could enhance this learning.

Dancers must learn to move through stability and control rather than brute power in partnering. The concept of counterbalance is based on this idea. It was argued that females in particular should be taught to accept their weight and guide it, supporting themselves rather than attempting to resist or aid any movement.

CAREER COUNSELING, PREPARATION AND PLANNING: ANTICIPATING THE FUTURE
Jessica Guillou, Tilman O'Donnell, Rebekah Rimsay, Joysanne Sidimus and Heidi Strauss
Moderator—Lindsay Fischer
This session covered a wide-ranging discussion of how transitions in dancers' lives can be for the good, delayed or stunted according to the dancers' (or dance students') attitude and institutional environment. Several pairs of terms recurred throughout, not as mutually exclusive opposites but as contrasting aspects of a dancer's life that must be brought into balance if the life is to be healthy:
- being goal-orientated versus living in the moment (as both student and dancer);
- devotion to dance versus engagement with the larger world and society;
- individual freedom/independence versus shared commitment/ responsibility;
- what teachers/coaches give and what students/dancers need versus what students/dancers give and what teachers/coaches need;

- childishness yielding to maturity versus adulthood with spontaneity and a sense of wonder.

NON-EUROPEAN DANCE FORMS: ALTERNATIVE INSIGHTS
Mennaka Thakkar and Aminurta Kang
Moderator—Jennifer Bolt
This session included demonstrations of Indian and Chinese dance forms. The history of the individual, the dance, the evolution of the dance form from dancer to teacher, the meaning and place of dance and demonstrations of the stylistic differences within each dance form were covered. The issues and importance of dance seemed to be culturally based. Body image does not appear to have any relevance to either of the presenters. The focus is more on expression and communication than the appearance of the dancer.

Although a dancer usually masters only one style, Mennaka Thakkar presented three of the eight recognized classical Indian dance forms. She felt that the integrity of the dances can be preserved if the dancer understands anatomy and cultural background and nuance, keeping each dance unique and distinct. The dance form began as a ritual form. As the priest mediated between God and people, so did the dancer who communicated with God. The ritual evolved into a theatrical dance form that maintains the spiritual mood. Balance and centre of the body are integral parts. This dance form is a total art involving theatre, music, visual arts and literature.

In India, dance is taught through one-on-one experience rather than explanation, although there are now some larger classes. The dancer finds out what works/doesn't work, what hurts/doesn't hurt through trial and error. It usually takes four years to master the basic movements of the body, steps and rhythms, plus an additional two years to start to learn the dance sequences. The dancer must also be a musician who understands complex rhythms and cycles.

"When you are ill, use dance to cleanse yourself," was a key statement that Aminurta Kang focused on to explain the importance of dance. Western dance has a human-centred focus in its search for a pattern in life (scientific humanism). Eastern dance sees the person as an organic unit and mankind as trying to understand the pattern of the world and the self in it. The body connects to the centre of the earth and always returns to it. This is manifested in the bending, landing and coming full circle movements; in other words the focus is not on leaving the earth in a leap but in coming back.

Western ballet is more scientific and focused on anatomy and gravity; the emphasis is linear, free from gravity. There is a beauty and strength in this. The movement is like a cross/cruciform shape, the focus is horizontal and vertical, and rigid.

Chinese classical dance is based on circles, yin and yang, and balance. Anatomy is used differently: the 8 or "S" shape is used; balance is emphasized and is always recovered by the next step. The eyes convey the emotion and are the window of the spirit. The body is like a flower, opening and closing, up and down, back to the centre, balance, high and low, back to the beginning in order to start again. Meditation and Tai Chi are examples of the holistic nature of Chinese dance. Kang had participants move to focus them on the whole picture, not on specific muscles. The feeling of movement, not the actual physical movement itself, should be the focus: if you concentrate on moving the muscles you will become tired and need a different focus.

Communication is a bridge between teacher and student; it is a relationship. The dance education system needs balance: learn from the past and change the future.

Dance is one of the oldest art forms; whatever its cultural origin, dance is based on our need to continuously adapt to nature. Through scientific technical training and the acquisition of a healthy mind one can achieve a beautiful body and mind. Only when dance can improve one's body, mind and spirit does it have meaning, whether in the past, present or future.

CHALLENGES TO INSTITUTIONAL MODERN DANCE TRAINING
Chantal Cadieux, Robin Colyer, Odette Heyn-Penner, Susan Macpherson, Kathryn Ricketts, Faye Thomson, Tassy Teekman and Dominique Turcotte
Moderator—Pat Fraser

These artistic directors from several private dance institutions across Canada suggested that cross-pollinization—bringing in guest teachers, incorporating working professionals into school programs and engaging in student exchange programs—will become more important as understanding and aesthetics evolve. The quality of the teaching staff and their continuing willingness to learn were also cited as key factors. Everyone lamented that time and money constraints constantly present difficulties in the creation and execution of quality pedagogical programming, and that ingenuity in the face of these obstacles is a daily job requirement. Echoing the sentiments in other sessions, many panelists felt that complementary body works and philosophies were integral to successfully prepare dancers physically and mentally for professional life. All professed devotion to their students and a willingness to do whatever is required to offer them the richest and most fulfilling training possible.

CREATIVITY AND DRAMA IN DANCE AT CANADA'S NATIONAL BALLET SCHOOL
Carina Bomers, Sorella Englund, Deborah Hess, Ana Jojic, Linda Rabin and Veronica Tennant
Moderator—Laurel Toto

Linda Rabin used a video to illustrate the Dance Keys program, a multimedia educational kit that organizes structural elements of dance (space, time, shape, level, direction, flow, force, etc.) into twenty key improvisational movement lessons. The aim of the program is to release creativity through improvisation—stimulating a physical understanding of the concepts and creating a common movement language to enhance artistic growth—and to encourage collaboration and cooperation as well as personal and group creativity. Using the shared language of the keys allows endless invention, interpretation and exposition of movement concepts. Video clips illuminated the honesty, presence and commitment of the students to the process.

National Ballet School (NBS) faculty reported on how they work to develop creativity, artistry and training in classes and workshop settings. Laurel Toto provided the background of Mavis Staines' vision: keep stoking the fire for the next generation instead of guarding the ashes.

Carina Bomers begins teaching creativity to six year olds which she refers to as "the dance of innocence"–movement before any form or falsification. Her training includes the methodology for creative dance developed by Virginia Tanner in which the connection between technique and creativity is structure. "Use enough structure to give freedom." She uses creativity to train musical sense: aiding the child to sense the music and express her/his feelings is one of the greatest gifts you can pass on.

Ana Jojic utilizes the theories of Rudolf Von Laban to encourage creativity. She emphasizes the principles of movement and eye training and doesn't separate ballet class from the creative process, bringing performing time right to the first exercise at the barre. Ana believes that showing passion for what you are doing is a way of living.

Beverly Miller referred to Jirí Kylián's comments about students coming from good homes. "A problem at NBS is that we are their home and their school. They come to us at age ten—we are responsible for them. We need to give them the space to learn and absorb as much as possible." The school uses a team-teaching integrative approach in which courses such as history of dance and history of art reinforce one another and relate to classical art form; what is taught in English is connected with the art class as well as the technique class. The school employs phenomenal support staff who operate as surrogate parents.

Deborah Hess teaches students what they will need to know once they enter a company. They also learn the process of building a character, how to breathe, improvise (again using Laban Principles) and build dialogues for the ballets. Guest artists such as Veronica Tennant also teach at NBS. Drama is an inherent component to the artist and the ability to create the character. Veronica was asked by Mavis Staines to help the shyer students in classical mechanics to understand character development. The dancers would do their barre warm-up in character. Much time was spent preparing the background and context of the character.

Sorella Englund feels she is not an expert in creativity—it is her life. When she stopped dancing, she wanted to coach or direct and asked theatre directors if she could follow them through their process from beginning to end. Sorella uses no method or program other than intuition and instinct. She looks at who and what is in front of her and asks herself, "What do we have here? What is the key?" Her biggest teacher has been her life.

INTERPERSONAL DYNAMICS IN DANCE COMPANIES:
SUPPORTS AND CONSTRAINTS
Anne-Marie Holmes, Christopher House,
Claudia Moore, Mikko Nissinen and Francia Russell-Hill
Moderator–Grant Strate

Grant Strate reasserted a statement made by Jirí Kylián that there is no training for artistic directors; he then asked the panelists, "What is your role as artistic director?" and they responded: choose dancers; embrace creativity to build new classics; teach and develop young talent; write grants; forge, maintain and cherish relationships; bond the company with the community; give students tools and a sense of responsibility; build authority through respect, not fear.

Strate also asked if any of the panelists had difficulties with executive directors. Most of the companies represented placed the artistic director on an equal plane with the executive director, although everyone emphasized that the administrative side must support the artistic side for the company to be successful.

Other questions raised included: How do you terminate dancers' contracts? How do you work with friends? How do you manage a hierarchy in a company? How do you deal with conflict? The panel agreed that communication is essential to solve any interpersonal problems.

BODY WORK 3
Sylvie Fortin, Sondra Fraleigh, Rosemary Jeanes Antze,
Warwick Long and Kista Tucker
Moderator–Pat Miner

Participants were exposed to three different body work experiences in two hours, resulting in a sampling of each rather than a full experience of any one approach.

Matching Not Mastery: Sondra Fraleigh opened with a movement experience that introduced the idea of matching, defined as "a somatic strategy based on kinesthetic attunement to: one's own sensations and movements; the movement patterns and qualities of another; the environment, an idea or an aesthetic process; or change." She defined mastery as "a hierarchical process of overcoming that separates and defines dualisms, such as the dancer's overcoming of gravity (the enemy), mind over matter (the body as controlled by and inferior to mind), or the master/slave dialectic." Standing still, participants were guided to notice where they were, pay attention to sensations in different parts of their body and to match their feelings to the movement. They were encouraged to pay attention to their breath, letting changes happen,and letting that take them deeper into their bodies. The experience was taken into movement, where movers matched their movement to that of others and then to the music.

With participants grounded in the idea and experience of matching, Kista Tucker taught a movement combination, using cues such as, "as you are doing this, what is going on inside your skin? with your breath?" In conclusion, the presenters pointed out that in order to match someone else, we have to be solidly in our own skin. We need to have a strong sense of who we are to be healthy participants in relationships, which certainly could apply to dance class as well as everyday life.

Feldenkrais Method and Dance Teaching: Sylvie Fortin and Warwick Long team-taught the Feldenkrais Method in which rest is important between movements, not because participants are tired from strenuous exertions, but to give the body a chance to process what has occurred. There was one particularly challenging direction–to reach up above the head and put the palm on the floor with the elbow facing the ceiling–which was not demonstrated but just explained verbally. Most participants took several minutes to find the position and one was unable to get it until she looked at her neighbour.

It was interesting to observe the various ways people learn and process, and to reflect on how much of dance teaching is visual and imitative (matching) rather than finding it genuinely in our own bodies (mastery). In conclusion, the challenge of Feldenkrais is to become expert of our own sensations.

Yoga: Rosemary Jeanes Antze who teaches the Viniyoga method to dancers, introduced the topic with a full background to this practice of yoga and observations on working with dancers. She has found that young dancers are overly dependent on external authority, such as letting a teacher define their strengths and weaknesses as a dancer, or letting a doctor define an injury while being unable to describe movements that aggravate it. Yoga can allow a dancer to work around an injury, to study it and keep

using other areas of the body, instead of thinking "since I'm injured, I can't do anything at all." Also, both detachment–being in the moment rather than being attached to the fruits of the activity–and perseverance–learning how to work–are fundamental to yoga. Both principles are also beneficial to the study of dance. An active session followed the theory, where participants experienced several simple postures, always linking the breath and movement. In conclusion, Rosemary said that the "practice feels like a process of removing the extraneous, of returning to a more neutral and natural state where perception and appropriate action become clear and true creativity is freed."

DANCE IN UNIVERSITIES
Karen Duplisea, Norma Sue Fisher-Stitt, Robin Lakes, Susan Lee, Rhonda Ryman and Richard Sias
Moderator–Mary Jane Warner

After the panelists introduced themselves, Susan Lee presented her paper suggesting that higher education in dance should not exist to simply develop dancers and choreographers, but to have an impact on our larger society. Dance departments need to enter into audience preparation and become involved in their local communities. Universities should encourage parent education with conferences that present suggestions for raising a gifted child. They can speak to such issues as "Will dancing make your son gay?" and "How to notice changes in your child's body image."

In response to "What is the main difference between conservatory training and a university education in dance?" Richard Sias suggested that "Education is more integrated, more based in experience, and more founded on a synthesis of ideas." Understanding that "One main difference between the conservatory and the university approach rests with the notion of critical thinking," Richard felt that "Perhaps retirement won't seem so awful if you have ways to contribute to the dance world other than through performance and choreography."

Norma Sue Fisher-Stitt spoke to the question "What is the role of dance in a university?" She stated that "Universities do not 'train' dancers in the narrow sense of the word; they 'educate' future dancers, teachers, researchers and audience members. The ideal result is thinking dancers and dancing thinkers." Fisher-Stitt suggested that eighteen year olds may find it difficult to enter this environment and she encouraged them to dance professionally if they so desire. Then, when they go on to university, they will find that research can be just as exciting as performing. She also indicated that research could help develop and change some practices in the dance studio and that since the white, upper middle class female student body is not reflective of Toronto's demographics, perhaps, a more inclusive group of dance forms should be introduced into the university environment.

Karen Duplisea responded to the query "What professional and academic qualifications are necessary to teach in a conservatory or university setting?" with a single word, "experience." She recalled that one of her most influential teachers had a long and successful performance career. She also spoke of the need for universities to recognize performance-based work as a significant contribution. It was stated from the floor, however, that "life experience" credentials, though significant, do not guarantee good educational practices.

Rhonda Ryman dealt with the question "How can university dance programs meet the needs of a multicultural community interested in dance?" She suggested that "When we look beyond surface differences, we find commonalties that link the dance forms of all societies." Certain themes, such as the need to balance individual desires against social responsibilities, as played out in *Giselle*, are universally recognized. On the other hand, Ryman wondered, with a growing number of non-European students, whether there is a greater need for courses that deal with non-Western dance forms by creating a more open-minded environment? For example, artists from some Asian genres perform well into their seventies and "South Asian attitudes about the dancing body accept a more rounded female form."

PLENARY SESSION: SUMMARIZING THE TORONTO SESSIONS
John Alleyne, Serge Bennathan, Karen Kain,
Annett av Paul, Francia Russell and Grant Strate
Moderator–Michael Crabb
Michael Crabb felt that, because of the broad range and scope of topics addressed over the last two days, it would be difficult for the panelists to proffer succinct summations of the proceedings.

Instead, he asked the panelists for their impressions on how to successfully negotiate what he termed the "trade off" between artistic excellence and health in dancers.

Grant Strate said we are both victims and beneficiaries of our pasts, and as teachers we have a responsibility to grow beyond what we have learned and how we have learned it, so we can responsibly and ethically teach the students of today.

John Alleyne showed excitement for the possibility that this conference offers growth and change within the dance form—an artistic director can give dancers a voice and a platform to use it, and respect between the dancers, choreographers and artistic directors can be mutual.

Serge Bennathan added that instilling curiosity and confidence are other important roles for the artistic director. He also expressed bemusement at suggestions he had overheard that young dancers need help and guidance because it seems they are somehow lost. He does not believe this to be the case.

Although there is absolutely nothing else she would have wanted to do with her life, Karen Kain said there were many challenges in the professional world that she had not been prepared for by her training, for example, knowing how to look after herself and her injuries, and how to deal with the challenges of different choreographers. Obsession with dance is requisite to a career in performance, but so is living a full and complete life.

Dancers today may be more skilled, but they are also more insecure, feels Annette av Paul. She echoed a wish for mutual respect between dancers, teachers and choreographers.

In general, there seemed to be a sense of exasperation when issues of authority in the classroom and the tyranny of hierarchical structure were brought up. Francia Russell suggested that a lot of these attitudes seemed arcane; she wondered if ballet in particular had not already gone beyond them. Good manners, old-fashioned discipline and love of dance must be integrated in the classroom with the new information emerging from the medical and psychological fields.

Audience member Paula Citron asked why some dancers emerging today don't feel they need to pay their dues before rising through the ranks. Kain suggested that artistic directors must be very clear from the start about what their expectations are, so that dancers can look elsewhere if a certain company does not meet their needs. Serge Bennathan felt an understanding of these requirements should be imparted to students in school, so that they are under no illusions when they leave.

Another audience member related a story of his quest for work all around Europe, and how shabbily he and his fellow dancers were treated by certain dance companies they visited. Both John Alleyne and Francia Russell asserted that artistic directors must make it their responsibility to honour the efforts of visiting candidates by going personally to auditions, and speaking to each dancer individually, if possible. Alleyne also acknowledged the reality of small dance companies, and regretted that sometimes, because of time and money constraints, these courtesies are not possible.

Audience member Peggy Baker drew applause when she suggested instead of looking past the few extra pounds a beautiful dancer might be carrying, why not look right at them? Sylvain Lafortune expanded on this theme by reminding us that beauty is arbitrary and that we, as a society, decide what is beautiful to look at. If we decide that a 180° turnout is ugly, for example, then we can halt the relentless drive towards this ideal, thereby circumventing injury. These comments drew wild applause from the audience, and a biting rebuttal from Francia Russell, who said there is nothing wrong with a profession that requires certain standards and facilities from its practitioners even if this means that some people are excluded.

Sara Porter expressed disappointment there was no forum in the Toronto conference to address the challenges of accessing well-rounded training and treatment as an independent dancer. She noted participants in The Hague did have access to a session of this nature.

Margie Gillis made the point that a dancer moves from learning to doing and back to learning his or her whole life. She asserted that it is a phenomenal political and social tool to manifest our spirits in our own bodies. Benjamin Harkarvy rounded out this perspective by saying how lucky we are to be able to come here, learn and pass it on to others, and emphasized that we must take personal responsibility for our own health and well-being.

Where is the wide range of beauty and mastery that should be on stage and could serve as a positive role model for aspiring dancers? asked Donna Krasnow. Serge Bennathan suggested that it is there, and that his company is an example. Mavis Staines agreed that generalizations are not very helpful, and that the dance world continues to move towards greater inclusion.

One of the final audience members at the microphone summed up the feelings of many of the conference attendees. She expressed gratitude to the organizers for taking the initiative to offer an international forum for discussion and for encouraging debate about and within the art form.

APPENDIX TWO
CONTRIBUTORS' BIOGRAPHIES

Anna Aalten is an anthropologist who earned her doctorate in 1991 with a study on femininity and entrepreneurship in The Netherlands. A passionate dancer herself, she has published on dance, femininity and body politics in both popular magazines and academic journals.

Gail Lee Abrams is Associate Professor of Dance at Scripps College, Claremont, California. She is a Certified Laban Movement Analyst and is trained in the Kesterberg Movement Profile. She also performs as a freelance dancer and choreographer.

Gaby Allard has been dancing with De Rotterdamse Dansgroep since 1988. She also works as their teacher/rehearsal director and is currently the chair of the Dutch Dancers' Union.

John Alleyne trained at Canada's National Ballet School and then danced for the Stuttgart Ballet and National Ballet of Canada, where he was resident choreographer. From 1988 to 1991, he choreographed several works for Ballet British Columbia where he has been Artistic Director since 1992.

Julia Alleyne is the Medical Director, Sport CARE, Sunnybrook and Women's College Health Science Centre. She is both a physiotherapist and a medical doctor with a special interest in sports medicine.

Richard Alston choreographed his first work in 1968 as one of the original students at the London School of Contemporary Dance. He formed The Richard Alston Company upon taking up the post of Artistic Director of The Place in 1994.

Judith Alter is an associate professor in dance in the UCLA Department of World Arts and Cultures. She has studied dance and choreographed solos and group works for twenty-two years.

Reginald Amatto trained and danced in his native Romania where he also began teaching in 1966. He has been a teacher at NBS since 1983.

Carol Anderson is a dancer, teacher, choreographer, director, consultant and writer. She holds a BFA in dance and was a member of Dancemakers and the Judy Jarvis Dance Company and Gutherie-Rotante Company.

Rosemary Jeanes Antze trained as a dancer at the Royal Ballet School and Canada's National Ballet School. She has been teaching theory and studio courses at York University since 1981. She has taught Viniyoga in the TKV Desikachar tradition for over twenty-six years.

Annette av Paul was a principal dancer with the Royal Swedish Ballet, the Harkness Ballet, the Royal Winnipeg Ballet and Les Grands Ballets Canadiens. She is presently Associate Program Director of the Professional Dance Program and Director of the Dance Training Program for the Banff Centre for the Arts.

Peggy Baker is a founding member and Artistic Director of Toronto's Dancemakers. She has won international acclaim for performances of her own choreography and as the first artist-in-residence at the National Ballet School she created its modern dance program.

Irén Ballya is a medical doctor who has been the chief physician of the Hungarian National Ballet since 1992.

Carol Beevers joined The National Ballet of Canada as Footwear Specialist in 1967. In 1986, she took on the same job for Canada's National Ballet School, where she became store manager in 1998.

Serge Bennathan is the Artistic Director of Dancemakers. He recently completed a collaboration with opera director Dmitry Bertman of *La Traviata* for the Canadian Opera Company.

Karina Bolger graduated as a ballet teacher from the Rotterdam Dance Academy. She studied Mensendieck Remedial Therapy and started her practice in The Netherlands. Professional dancers are a special patient group of hers.

Jennifer Bolt is a graduate of the NBS Teacher Training Program. She is currently pursuing a Masters in Dance at York University.

Carina Bomers, a graduate of Canada's National Ballet School's Professional Ballet/Academic program, has danced with The National Ballet of Canada and Ballet Y's. She has been a full time teacher at NBS since 1983 and guest teaches around the world.

Kitty Bouten is a physiotherapist, manual therapist and movement scientist who has worked with dancers since 1985.

Deborah Bowes is a Fellow and Examiner of the Imperial Society of Teachers of Dancing, Cecchetti Branch. A graduate of the National Ballet School's Professional Ballet/Academic program, she also has a BA in English and obtained her teacher training by assistant teaching with NBS founder Betty Oliphant.

Karen Bowes-Sewell is an associate professor in the Department of Dance at York University. She was a principal dancer with the National Ballet of Canada where she created roles in numerous original ballets and performed repertory such as John Cranko's *Romeo and Juliet* and Balanchine's *Concerto Barocco*.

Philippe Braunschweig is founder of the International Organization for the Transition of Professional Dancers, which he established in 1992. Following an extensive business career, he has been a prominent member of the Swiss Academy of Technical Sciences since 1981. He has served on the Council of Fine Arts Deans and the board of UNESCO's International Fund for the Promotion of Culture and is currently honorary Chairman of the Prix de Lausanne competition for young dancers which he founded in 1972.

Paul Bronkhorst trained as a career guidance counselor at the Akademie Mens Arbeid in Tilburg and is a specialist in career advice for dancers at the Theater Instituut Nederland. He has been advisor to the Dutch Transition Fund since its founding.

Ann Kipling Brown is a dance educator, performer, and choreographer. She studied dance in the U.K., completing her doctorate in the validity of notation systems. She is currently an associate professor in dance education at the University of Regina.

Julia Buckroyd was student counselor at the London Contemporary Dance School before establishing a private practice. She has written widely on eating disorders and emotional aspects of dance training and the dancer's life.

Roberto Campanella is a graduate of the NBS Teacher Training Program for Professional Dancers and has been a staff member at NBS since 1999.

Hilary Cartwright is co-founder of the White Cloud Studios in New York and teaches yoga and Gyrotonics GXS. She is a former dancer, ballet mistress and international guest teacher in ballet, yoga and Gyrotonics GXS.

Sagrario Castilla is the founder and owner of The Studio in Toronto where she teaches ballet and Pilates. Her professional experience includes Le Ballet de la Jeunesse in Montreal and the National Ballet Company in Mexico City.

Carole Chadwick trained with Mildred Wickson and NBS founder Betty Oliphant. In 1962, she joined NBS where she became Vice Principal of Ballet and developed the Teacher Training Program.

Jasmine Challis is an accredited nutritionist and sports dietician with a particular interest in dance. She is a member of the Dance U.K. Medical Advisory Panel and maintains an interest in clinical work, specializing in eating disorders.

Elizabeth Chitty graduated from the York University Dance Department in 1975 and has been creating unusual and innovative performances ever since. She is active as administrator, board member, technician, writer, curator and producer and offers training in collaborative decision-making and practices as a facilitator, mediator and consultant.

Paula Citron is a freelance arts writer, broadcaster and critic specializing in classical music and dance. She taught in the Theatre department at Claude Watson Arts Program, a performing arts high school.

Gill Clarke studied English and has spent her career as a dancer, teacher, choreographer and advocate. A founding member of the Siobhan Davies Dance Company, she is also on the steering group of Chisenhale Dance Space, the board of Dance U.K. and the British Association of Choreographers.

Michael Crabb is a Toronto-based dance critic, historian, lecturer and editor. He is currently dance critic for *The National Post* newspaper in Canada and prepares a daily Arts Report for CBC Radio 2.

Mihaly Csikszentmihalyi is author of the groundbreaking book *Flow: The Psychology of Optimal Experience* as well as thirteen other books. He is a professor and former chair of the Department of Psychology at the University of Chicago.

Coleen Davis is a principal dancer with The Dutch National Ballet, where she has been for twenty-three seasons.

Patricia de Martelaere studied philosophy at the Catholic University in Leuven where she graduated in 1984 with a thesis on the skepticism of David Hume. She is currently Professor of Modern Philosophy and Philosophical Anthropology at the Catholic University in Brussels as well as Professor of the Philosophy of Language at the Catholic University.

Penelope Reed Doob is Professor of English and Dance at York University. Her current research focuses on the nature and nurture of creativity in ballet.

Susan Drake is Professor in the Graduate Department of the Faculty of Education, Brock University. She focuses on holistic education with research interests in story and interdisciplinary curriculum.

Dominique Dumais graduated from Canada's National Ballet School and joined The National Ballet of Canada first as a member of the corps de ballet and then as Second Soloist. She is now an independent choreographer and teaches ballet and creative dance at NBS.

Karen Duplisea is Assistant Professor in the Theatre School at Ryerson University and senior faculty at the Professional Training Program of The Toronto Dance Theatre. She continues to perform as a freelance dancer.

Nicholas Durand is the consultant foot specialist for Canada's National Ballet School. A former lecturer in physiology, pediatrics and surgery at The Toronto Hospital, he now divides his time between a downtown community clinic and the high risk/vascular clinic at Humber River Regional Hospital in Toronto.

Sorella Englund began her training at the ballet school of the Finnish National Opera. She came to Denmark on a scholarship in 1966 and was soon afterwards engaged by the Royal Danish Ballet, where she danced as principal for many years. She has also been highly prized as a teacher and director at the Royal Danish Ballet and recently staged *Arabian Nights* for the National Ballet of Canada. She is a regular guest teacher at NBS.

Jeroen Fabius teaches Dance History and Dance Anthropology at the School for New Dance Development and the Dance Department of the Theatreschool in Amsterdam.

Ethan Feldman graduated from Life Chiropractic College and holds a BSc in Human Performance with an emphasis on physical rehabilitation. He has extensive experience as a dancer and is a member of the International Association of Dance Medicine.

Chrétien Felser is Director of Studies for SIOO, a Dutch Interuniversity Centre for Organizational Development and Change Management.

Lori Finklestein is a psychiatrist in private practice and a consultant with NBS.

Paul Fiolkowski is a doctoral candidate in the Department of Exercise and Sport Sciences at the University of Florida. His specialization is biomechanics.

Lindsay Fischer, a former principal dancer at the Dutch National Ballet and NYCB, is the Manager of the Dancer Career Planning Program at Canada's National Ballet School. He is responsible for overseeing the transition of all graduating and post secondary students from the school to the professional arena.

Elaine Fisher is a graduate of Canada's National Ballet School Professional Ballet/Academic program. She also studied with Alexander Gavrilov in Miami and was a soloist with The National Ballet of Canada. Ms. Fisher has taught full time at NBS since 1989.

Norma Sue Fisher-Stitt is Chair of the Department of Dance at York University. A graduate of Canada's National Ballet School, she danced with the National Ballet of Canada before attending university. Her research interests include the evolution of ballet technique, dance in Canada in the 20th century, dance and technology and dance/arts education.

Penny Flemming has a Laine Theatre Arts Diploma and degrees in biology, kinesiology and health sciences. She has been the staff physiotherapist at the Sports Medicine Specialists and physiotherapist to

The National Ballet of Canada. She is currently studying at the Canadian College of Osteopathy.

Anne Flynn is Associate Professor of Dance in both the Faculties of Kinesiology and Fine Arts at the University of Calgary where she created the B.A. Dance program.

Ivette Forster studied directing at the Santbergen Media Academy. She now presents the news on the Amsterdam channel AT5 and also covers many stories for Special Report and other programs.

Sylvie Fortin is Assistant Dean of the Faculty of Arts at the University of Quebec at Montreal where she is currently developing a health centre for dancers.

Sondra Fraleigh chairs the Department of Dance at the State University of New York at Brockport. She is the author of *Dance and the Lived Body* and numerous articles on dance and somatics.

Els Frankhuijzen is an advisor on health care in the workplace with Schermer Trommel & de Jong. She advises companies and organizations on how to create optimal working conditions, with a particular interest in helping dancers and actors prevent unnecessary illness, injuries and accidents.

Pat Fraser is the Artistic Director of The School of Toronto Dance Theatre. A graduate of York University's dance program, she studied at the School of London contemporary Dance Theatre, the Martha Graham Company, the Limon Company and Toronto Dance Theatre. She has performed and taught extensively across Canada and in Europe.

Margie Gillis is a solo dance artist, choreographer and performer of more than seventy solo dance works. The year 1995 marked the 20th anniversary of her career, with performances in Toronto, Ottawa, New York, Los Angeles, Montreal and Paris.

Daniela Graca has been dancing professionally throughout Europe since 1985. She teaches dance for various companies in Europe and is a staff teacher at the Theater School Amsterdam.

Danny Grossman began folk dancing in graduate school, studied and performed modern dance with Gloria Unti and danced and toured throughout the world with the Paul Taylor Dance Company. Subsequently, he joined the faculty of York University, worked with the Toronto Dance Theatre and formed his own company. He has cre-ated thirty original works that have toured and performed in seventeen countries.

Jessica Guillou is a graduate of NBS with a particular interest in the exploration of her own choreographic inclinations. She is studying early childhood education at the Montessori Training Centre.

Linda Hamilton is chair of the Board of the Dancers Transition Resource Centre in Toronto. She studied dance in Vancouver and taught ballet for six years at her own studio.

Krishna Lee Hanks is a professional dancer, choreographer and teacher. She also has a Masters degree in kinesiology and is a certified Iyengar Yoga instructor. She is the resident modern dance instructor and choreographer for Arabesque Ballet of Haarlem (The Netherlands) and was involved in a pioneer program teaching yoga and meditation to inmates at the San Francisco State Jail.

Benjamin Harkarvy has been the Director of The Juillard Dance Division since 1992 and has been the Artistic Director and choreographer for the Royal Winnipeg Ballet, The Nederlands Dance Theatre (which he founded), The Dutch National, Harkness and Pennsylvania Ballets.

Kate Hays established a practice in clinical and sport performance psychology in Toronto in 1988 after a twenty-five-year career in psychology in the U.S. With a longstanding interest in the arts, her research, writing and practice involve applications of sport psychology in the performing arts.

Marie Herbert is the training director and staff psychologist at the Santa Clara University Counselling Centre and Assistant Clinical Professor of Medical Psychology at UCSF. She provides direct service to students with depression, anxiety, self-esteem and body image issues, eating disorders and other concerns.

Deborah Hess studied at the American Ballet Theatre School and with Kathleen Crofton. She currently teaches ballet and theatre at NBS and company class at The National Ballet of Canada.

Roger Hobden received his medical degree at the University of Montreal. He has practiced family medicine, work-related medicine, emergency medicine, osteopathic manual medicine, sports medicine and performing arts medicine. His interest in dance has taken him from therapy to choreography; his first dance creation, *Initiation*, was presented recently in Montreal.

Anne-Marie Holmes was trained and coached in Russia. She became Artistic Director of the Boston Ballet in 1997 and also serves as the Dean of Faculty for the Ballet's Centre for Dance Education.

Christopher House has been Artistic Director of Toronto Dance Theatre since 1994, demonstrating remarkable choreography and artistic leadership. His film and television credits include *Dance for Modern Times* and *The Dancemakers* series.

Robyn Hughes-Ryman trained at the Australian Ballet School and danced with Ballet Victoria before studying Benesh Movement Notation at the Benesh Institute in England. She is a choreologist and consultant on computer notation projects.

Suzie Jary is a former Broadway dancer who utilized the Career Transition For Dancers (CTFD) to make her own transition. She is currently CTFD's Director of Client Services for the New York office. She has a range of counseling skills from academic advising and career counseling to psychotherapy and crisis intervention and holds a Masters in Social Work and a B.A. in Psychology.

Ana Jojic is a graduate of the National Ballet School in Belgrade and former soloist of the National Theatre Company, Belgrade. She trained as a teacher at the National Capital Ballet School, Canberra, Australia and is a graduate of the Laban Centre, London and the NBS Teacher Training Program for Professional Dancers. She is on staff at NBS.

Bengt Jörgen is the Artistic Director of the Dance Programs at George Brown College and Artistic Director/Choreographer of Ballet Jörgen.

Deborah Jowitt has been principal dance critic of the *Village Voice* since 1967 and published three books. She has lectured and conducted workshops at universities, festivals, and museums in the U.S. and abroad, and has been on the faculty of New York University's Tisch School of the Arts since 1975.

Allen Kaeja has been creating dances since 1982 following nine years of wrestling and judo. His works have been presented in fifteen countries, and he is co-artistic director/founder of fFIDA (fringe Festival of Independent Dance Artists).

Karen Kain trained at Canada's National Ballet School and enjoyed a long and illustrious career as principal dancer with The National Ballet of Canada, performing every leading role in the classical repertoire. She is now Artistic Associate at The National Ballet of Canada.

Aminurta Kang, choreographer, dancer and instructor, is China's 1998 Gold Lotus Award winner for best dance performance. In 1992 he moved to Toronto where he is creating a new dance style fusing Chinese and Mongolian dances and ballet, as well as contemporary dance gestures and improvisation, with traditional Chinese meditative techniques for maintaining health, physical well-being and fitness.

Ronald Klaassen is a physical education and physiotherapy teacher at the School for Higher Education in Utrecht. He studied jazz dance and now teaches how to use music in training and exercise therapy.

Arthur Kleipool started his career as a physiotherapist working with dancers, rugby players and freestyle skiers. He is a founder of the Dutch Healthcare Foundation for Dancers.

Tom Koch is an actor, singer, dancer and certified teacher of Alexander Technique. He is known for his work integrating the technique with dance movement and training. He also maintains a private teaching practice.

Susan Koff is Assistant Professor and Coordinator of the Dance Education Program at Teachers College, Columbia University. She actively presents, researches and consults in the field of arts education in public education and assessment.

Arie Koops is a trainer and former coach for women's speedskating at the 1992 Olympics. He is now studying to become an exercise physiologist and sports psychologist.

Yiannis Koutedakis is Senior Lecturer at Thessaly University, Greece and Wolverhampton University, U.K. He has attended many dance festivals, sports championships and Olympics as dancer, competitor, national coach and scientific advisor and has published widely in English, Greek, Italian and French.

Donna Krasnow has choreographed and performed for the past twenty-five years across Canada, the U.S. and Japan. She has developed a specialized conditioning and imagery system for dancers called C-I Training. She teaches in the Dance department at York University.

Jiří Kylián was Artistic Director of the Nederlands Dans Theatre (NDT) for twenty-six years and is considered one of the leading choreographers in the world. Over the years, he has created more than fifty ballets. As Artistic Director of NDT, he has built up a unique organizational structure that includes three dimensions of dance. The renowned NDT I has been joined by NDT II (experimental dance performed by dancers aged seventeen to twenty) and NDT III (dancers over forty years who work on a project basis). He continues to play an important role in NDT's development as the house choreographer and artistic advisor.

Sylvain Lafortune has studied and danced in Montreal, Europe and New York where he worked with the Lar Lubovitch Dance Co., Susan Marshall & Co., and Martha Clarke. Returning to Montreal, he has danced with Les Grands Ballets Canadiens as principal dancer, the O'Vertigo Danse and Montreal Danse.

Robin Lakes is a member of the Dance faculty at Northwestern University who has studied with teachers of Graham, Limon, Cunningham and Holm.

Barbara Leach danced with The Dutch National Ballet from 1979 to 1991. She is now pursuing a degree in law.

Susan Lee has published extensively in the area of dance education, psychology and dance, and the development of the artist.

Nanine Linning is considered, at twenty-two, one of the most promising Dutch choreographic talents. She recently graduated from the Rotterdamse Dansacademie and is currently choreographing an ensemble piece for Scapino Ballet.

William Littler is music and dance critic for *The Toronto Star*. He is currently a lecturer at the Royal Conservatory of Music of Toronto.

Jane Lord graduated from Canada's National Ballet School and has been first soloist for many years with the Dutch National Ballet. She is also Chairperson of the Worker's Council and active with the Education Program of Het Muziektheatre.

Kathy Lundy is District Coordinator of Dramatic Arts and Dance for the Toronto School Board where she oversees drama and dance programs for primary and secondary students.

Brian Macdonald is currently Artistic Director of the Banff Centre for the Performing Arts. He is internationally known as a choreographer and director of ballet, opera and musical theatre.

Susan Macpherson has a degree in languages and has taught dance at York University and the University of Quebec at Montreal. She continues to perform and was appointed Artistic Associate at the School of Toronto Dance Theatre in 1997.

Ferenc Mády is a specialist of orthopedics, traumatology and hand surgery and works in the Semmelweis Medical University Budapest as chief surgeon of the foot and ankle.

Jean-Christophe Maillot studied at Rosella Hightower's Centre Internationale de Danse in Cannes. He is now Artistic Director of Les Ballets de Monte Carlo where he has achieved remarkable critical acclaim.

Iris Marshall is a sport medicine physician skilled in osteopathic assessment and treatment. In Toronto, she holds weekly clinics at the National Ballet School as well as at The Child and Adolescent Health Unit at the Toronto Western Hospital and at the MacIntosh Sport Medicine Clinic at the University of Toronto.

Jane Marsland was General Manager of the Danny Grossman Dance Company from 1983 to 1999. She is currently co-leader of ARTS 4 Change, a program designed to create positive change for and by Toronto arts professionals.

Moira McCormack was trained at the Royal Ballet School and went on to dance with the Sadlers Wells Royal Ballet, the National Ballet of Canada and the London Festival Ballet. Currently she is working as physiotherapist for the Royal Ballet School in London.

Sarah McCutcheon has been on staff at Canada's National Ballet School as a physiotherapist and is currently pursuing her Masters with a study of cardiovascular profiles of professional dance students and dancers.

Darcy McGehee incorporates training in theatre, voice, anatomy, kineseology BMC, cranio sacral therapy and massage therapy in her approach to dancing, choreographing and teaching. She is currently researching the application of somatic therapies in the diagnosis and treatment of autism and PDD.

Lindsay Melcher is Manager of Physiotherapy and Health Services at Canada's National Ballet School where she supervises the health and body conditioning team and collaborates with ballet staff.

Richard Meen is Clinical Director and Chief Psychiatrist at the Thistletown Regional Centre as well as psychiatric consultant to many facilities including Canada's National Ballet School. He is an expert in the field of antisocial youth.

Patti Ross Milne founded the dance program in the first performing arts high school in Mississauga. With over twenty years teaching, performing and choreographic experience, she continues to work as a freelance educator.

Pat Miner is a respected teacher of Modern Dance in the Toronto community and at Toronto Dance Theatre. She is also on staff at NBS with the Teacher Training Program.

Claudia Moore has created over thirty dance works and collaborated with other performing artists and companies including multimedia productions, contemporary theatre, musical theatre and contemporary opera. In 1997, she launched her own company, MOonhORsE Dance Theatre.

Ursula Nahatchewitz has pioneered three dance programs at both the elementary and secondary level in Ontario. She also acts and performs in rock videos.

Mikko Nissinen began his training at eleven at The Finnish National Ballet School and completed his studies in Russia at The Kirov Ballet School. At fifteen, he joined the Finnish National Ballet and a year later was dancing principal roles. After retirement, he began teaching and directing and is now Artistic Director for Alberta Ballet.

Tilman O'Donnell recently graduated from the full-time professional ballet/academic program at the National Ballet School following formal training at the Boston Ballet School. During his training, he danced works by Balanchine, Peter Martins, Ralph Lemons, John Neumeier, Rudi van Dantzig and James Kudelka.

Darryl Ogilvie-Harris, a Liverpool University medical school graduate, currently teaches at the University of Toronto and the Toronto Hospital. He is Chief of Orthopaedic Surgery at Toronto Western Hospital and Toronto Hospital and Orthopaedic Consultant to the Toronto Maple Leafs hockey club and the National Ballet of Canada.

Tom J. O'Hara is a clinical consulting and sport psychologist. He has prepared individual and team athletes for six Olympiads and fifteen World Championships.

Richard Omel is a chiropractor who has studied the Mitzvah Technique for over fifteen years with its founder, Nehemia Cohen. He was a faculty member of the Shiatsu School of Canada, Sutherland-Chan School of Massage Therapy and Fanshawe College where he taught human anatomy and basic human biomechanics-kinesiology.

Naomi Perlov studied dance at Bat Dor School in Tel Aviv, Schola Cantorum in Paris, and with Milton Myers in New York. She currently assists Barak Marshal + Mayumana Group, teaches at the Suzanne Dellal Centre and recently restated *Casanova* and *Le Parc* at the Paris and Berlin Operas.

Tim Persent trained at the Rambert Ballet School and has performed works by Martha Clarke, Merce Cunningham, Ton Simons and others. He is now a freelancer, working with Johan Greben.

Richard Philp is a writer, editor and journalist and is currently the Executive Editor of *Dance Magazine* in New York City where his association dates back many years. He has authored or edited several books in the dance field, including *To Move, To Learn; Danseur: The Male in Ballet;* and *Memoirs of a Dance*.

Niva Piran is Professor of Education at the University of Toronto and a practicing clinical psychologist writing and consulting on body image and eating disorders who has implemented a prevention program for eating disorders at Canada's National Ballet School.

Walter Pitman has been President of Ryerson Polytechnic University, Director of the Ontario Institute for Studies in Education and Executive Director of the Ontario Arts Council. He is the author of *Learning the Arts in an Age of Uncertainty*.

David Popalisky directs the Dance program at Santa Clara University where he teaches dance history, modern dance and choreography.

Sara Porter is a choreographer, performer, teacher, writer and lecturer who has worked in Canada, the U.K. and Spain and now teaches at York University in Toronto.

Jill Pribyl, a certified Laban Movement Analyst, has danced and choreographed in New Mexico for over fourteen years.

Kathleen Rea trained at Canada's National Ballet School and has danced and choreographed with The National Ballet of Canada and Ballet Jörgen. She is currently studying Expressive Art Therapy as well as dancing, teaching dance and choreographing. In 1996, she choreographed *Frames of Control*, a dance and theatre piece that dealt with her experiences with an eating disorder.

Dwight Rhoden began dancing at seventeen while studying acting. He has dedicated the last several years to the development of Complexions Inc., which he co-directs with Desmond Richardson. He is working on commissions for the Dance Theatre of Harlem, the Washington Ballet and the Alvin Ailey American Dance Theatre.

Rowena Ridout is a staff endocrinologist at Women's Health Sciences Centre in Toronto, whose interest is osteoporosis.

Rebekah Rimsay was an award-winning student at Canada's National Ballet School. She joined The National Ballet of Canada in 1990 and became First Soloist in 1998.

Rachel-Anne Rist is the Director of Dance at the Art Educational School, Tring Park, U.K. She is the author of many books and articles on dance and is engaged in research on safe dance techniques.

Margot Rijven started her career as dance teacher in 1979 and became a certified Body-Mind Centering practitioner in 1989. She teaches at the 5 Dance Departments of the Theatreschool, Amsterdam School of the Arts where she is co-ordinator of the Health Care program. She is co-founder and chair of the Dutch Healthcare Foundation for Dancers (Stichting Gezondheidszorg voor Dansers).

Anuschka Roes is Head of Teacher Training at the National Ballet School in Toronto, Canada. She also works as an examiner for the Royal Academy of Dancing and for the Imperial Society of Teachers of Dancing, National Dance Branch.

Janet Roseman is a dance critic and author who is currently writing a book called *Dance Masters: Interviews with Legends of the Dance.*

Francia Russell, one of the first ballet masters chosen by Balanchine to stage his works, has staged over one hundred of his ballets throughout the world. Since 1977, she has been Pacific Northwest Ballet's Artistic Director and Director of its school.

Rhonda Ryman has taught courses on Dance Appreciation, Notation and Reconstruction and Principles of Dance Technique for over 20 years at York University. She is currently developing a system for animating classical ballet using the Life Forms computer application.

Roland Schankula danced for several years but had to stop due to injury. Today he is a dance-movement therapist in a psychiatric clinic, as well as a choreographer.

Toine Schermer is a physician with a special interest in healthy workplaces. His clients include the National Opera, the Royal Concertgebouw Orchestra and the International Dance Theatre. He is a charter member of the Dutch Health Care Foundation for Dancers.

Marianne Schultz is both a performer and a teacher of contemporary dance. In 1992 she choreographed Jane Campion's film, *The Piano.*

Michael Schumacher has danced with Ballet Frankfurt, Twyla Tharp Dance, Feld Ballet and the Pretty Ugly Dance Company. As a choreographer, he collaborated with Ballet Frankfurt and GRIP and has also conducted workshops in movement and improvisation techniques.

Joelle Segers is a physiotherapist, with a background as a dancer and dance teacher, who has been dealing with dance injuries for many years. She created a program of dance injuries prevention, Balance, which is now used in pre-professional dance schools in Ottawa.

Guido Severien is a former dancer, teacher and choreographer who now works as a dance consultant and project manager at the Dutch National Arts Employment Office where he is concerned with improving the dancer's position in the labour market and stimulating employment in the arts.

Richard Sias is Coordinator of the Ballet Division at Florida State University where he is working on CORPS, an international organization to provide a forum for ballet faculty to move their art form forward, preserve the tradition and further examine and enhance the care and training of young dancers.

Joysanne Sidimus is the Executive Director/Founder of the Dancer Transition Resource Centre in Toronto. A former pupil of George Balanchine and former principal dancer with The National Ballet, she is also now Balanchine Repetiteur for the National Ballet of Canada.

Ton Simons is currently the resident choreographer and Artistic Director of The Rotterdam Dance Company.

Robert Sirman has been Administrative Director of Canada's National Ballet School since 1991. Previously he spent twenty-three years in the Ontario public service, including five years as a policy advisor in the Ministry of Culture and Recreation and ten years in the Ontario Arts Council as Director of Operations and Director of Research and Policy Planning. He has an MA in sociology and serves as president of Peggy Baker Dance Projects.

Clyde Smith is a doctoral candidate in Cultural Studies in Education at Ohio State University with his BFA and MA in dance studies.

Elizabeth Snell is a consulting dietition/nutritionist and President of Snell Associates Nutrition Consultants Inc. She counsels competitive and recreational athletes in a wide variety of sports and is a consultant to a variety of schools, including Canada's National Ballet School.

Anadel Lynton Snyder is a researcher at Mexico's Jose Limon National Centre for Dance Research located in the National Centre for the Arts and is a doctoral candidate in the Dance department of Temple University.

Paula Solassaari is presently teaching ballet and dance analysis at the Theatre Academy of Finland, Dance and Theatre Pedagogy Department. She is preparing a doctoral dissertation on enhancing creativity in teaching and learning ballet.

Barbara Soren is an educator who has been working with schools, community organizations, museums, science centres and performing arts organizations since the mid-1970s.

Mavis Staines, graduate of Canada's National Ballet School and former soloist with The National Ballet of Canada and Dutch National Ballet, has been Artistic Director of NBS since 1989. During the past decade, she has kept NBS at the forefront of dance teaching by advocating the advancement of excellence and health in tandem. Regarded as a pioneer in the evolution of classical ballet training, she has presented papers on this subject in Europe and North America and serves regularly as a juror at the Prix de Lausanne.

Linda Stearns began her training in Toronto with Bettina Byers and continued in London, England before enrolling at the School of American Ballet. She held a variety of positions with Les Grands Ballets Canadiens including dancer, soloist, ballet mistress and artistic director. Since leaving the company, she has worked on operas and with British ice dance champions Jayne Torvill and Christopher Dean. She currently coaches and teaches ballet and movement to figure skaters.

Janis Stone is currently a secondary school teacher of dance and program administrator. She is the founding director/choreographer for Kinesis Dance Company.

Heidi Strauss trained in Winnipeg, New York and Vienna and the School of Toronto Dance Theatre. Roles have been created for her by Murray Darroch, Julia Aplin, Mitch Kirsch and others. She has also performed in works by James Kudelka, David Earle and Bill James.

Grant Strate is a dance educator, administrator, choreographer and writer. After a career with the National Ballet of Canada, he went on to found Canada's first university dance degree program at York University in Toronto and later joined the faculty of Simon Fraser University in Vancouver.

Mark Suffolk joined Freed of London, a leading shoe manufacturer, as a pointe shoe maker in 1982. His engineering background was put to good use as his skills in developing new pointe shoe innovations have been actively encouraged resulting in several new shoe designs.

Britt Tajet-Foxell is psychologist to elite athletes and professional ballet dancers at the Royal Ballet Company, the Royal Opera House, Covent Garden and the British Olympic Medical Centre. Her special area of expertise is the psychological effect of injuries on performance.

Betty Tate-Pineau joined Canada's National Ballet School as Body Conditioning Coordinator in 1988. She is a Course Conductor with the National Coaching Certification Program and owns and operates her own gymnastics training facility.

Veronica Tennant was a principal dancer with the National Ballet of Canada. She has continued as a performer in theatre and film, and as a director and producer/writer of profiles of Margie Gillis, Karen Kain and James Kudelka for CBC television.

Mennaka Thakkar is an internationally renowned dancer, choreographer and teacher working in three forms of classical Indian dance. She is adjunct professor of dance at York University and Artistic Director of Mennaka Thakkar Dance Company.

George Thorn has conducted action research projects for institutions such as the Kennedy Center, the Association of Performing Arts Presenters, the Lower Manhattan Cultural Council and the Society of Stage Directors and Choreographers.

Laurel Toto studied at New York's High School of the Performing Arts and the Joffrey School of Ballet. Following her career as a performer, she graduated from the National Ballet School's Teacher Training Program. She has been a full member of NBS faculty since 1982 and also regularly teaches master classes across Canada and rehearses NBS students for National Ballet of Canada productions.

Kista Tucker is the Founder and Artistic Director of the Kista Tucker Dance Company. She has been guest artist in universities and other educational institutions throughout the U.S.

Cisca van Dijk-de Bloeme is currently Director of the Rotterdamse Dansacademie. She worked as a dancer and rehearsal director with companies in The Netherlands and the U.K. before dedicating herself to dance education, and more specifically vocational dance training.

Bianca van Dillen studied classical ballet at Scapino in Amsterdam and modern dance in New York, Cologne and London. In 1993, she founded Stamina, a choreographical computer company that conducts research and educational projects.

Robbart van Linschoten is a registered sports physician and researcher in The Netherlands. He is now head of the Sportsmedical Centre Rotterdam, where dancers get medical counselling, physical therapy and rehabilitation.

Jacques van Rossum is a staff member of the Faculty of Human Movement Science with interests in motor learning and performance-determining factors in sport and physical education.

Lucia van Westerlaak has been a guitar teacher and a singer. She has worked for the Dutch society of gays and lesbians, ABVAKABO FNV, the Dutch union for public services and FNV KIEM, the union for Arts, Information Services and Media.

Cees Vervoorn competed in three consecutive Olympics as a swimmer. He has a Masters in Physiology of Exercise and Sports Psychology and has a research interest in the neuro-endocrine aspects of exercise and training and overtraining of elite athletes.

Greta von Gavel melds extensive physiotherapy practice and study with a strong background and interest in dance and fitness. She has focused her work on the growing demand for an integrated approach to health and well-being.

Paul Waarts spent the most important part of his modern dance career with Dansgroep Krisztina de Chatel. He is now studying law at the Vrije Universiteit in Amsterdam.

Eileen Wanke is a surgeon of plastic and hand surgery at Bassum Hospital where she established the Centre of Dance Medicine in 1997. She is consultant to ballet companies and dance academies in Northern Germany and has done extensive research in the field of Dance Medicine with the Universities of Kiel and Bremen.

Mary Jane Warner is the Graduate Program Director in Dance at York University. She teaches courses in dance education, Canadian dance history, reconstruction and movement analysis.

Gretchen Warren is Professor of Dance in the College of Fine Arts of the University of South Florida. She has studied ballet pedagogy in England and the former U.S.S.R., conducted teaching seminars throughout the U.S., Canada and Europe, choreographed and danced as a soloist, in addition to writing a number of books.

Myles Warren, Executive Director of the Dance Umbrella of Ontario since 1992, is a theatre/dance researcher and Co-Leader of Arts 4 Change, a program designed to create positive change for and by Toronto arts professionals.

Jean-Claude West is a master teacher, clinician and inventor who concentrates on restoring functional movement patterns in the dance-specific population. His functional anatomy courses have been taught to physical therapists, osteopaths, chiropractors and other movement specialists.

Francis Weyts graduated from the Antwerp School for Physiotherapy and has completed courses in Manual Therapy, Osteopathy and Muscular Chain Therapy. Running his own practice in Antwerp, he has worked with dancers from The Flanders Royal Ballet, Frankfurter Ballet and the Pina Bausch Dance Company.

Valerie Wilder studied ballet in Japan, and at the Royal Ballet School, Butler University and Canada's National Ballet School and joined The National Ballet of Canada in 1970. She then studied business management at the University of Toronto and worked as an independent business manager and tax adviser for dancers and choreographers. She is now the Executive Director of The National Ballet of Canada.

Ted Willemsen has been working as a physical and manual therapist in Amsterdam since 1981. He also teaches anatomy and injury prevention and, since 1995, has been a clinical instructor for the American Stream Physical Therapy project at the Academy for Physical Therapy at the Hogeschool van Amsterdam.

Marion Woodman is a Jungian analyst and author of *Addiction to Perfection: The Still Unravished Bride*. A pioneer in the study of eating disorders and compulsive behaviors, she is a renowned lecturer and workshop leader affiliated with the University of Southern California (Berkeley).

Diane Woodruff has a Ph.D. in Somatic Education and wrote her dissertation on Bartenieff Fundamentals of Movement. She is a certified

Laban Movement Analyst, a registered Movement Therapist and a cranio-sacral therapist in private practice.

Claire Wootten received her dance training with the Royal Winnipeg Ballet. She has taught and adjudicated extensively throughout Canada and has been on Faculty at the department of Dance, York University where she is currently completing a Masters in Dance.

Samuel Wuersten is a dancer, teacher and choreographer, and the Artistic Director of the Holland Dance Festival. As a teacher he works internationally with many different schools and companies including the London Contemporary Dance School, the Batsheva Dance Company, Charleroi Danses, Geneva Ballet, and the Prix de Lausanne. He regularly conducts guest residences in Japan. He is currently Artistic Director of the Dance department of the Hogeschool voor Muziek en Dans Rotterdam

Linda Yates is Executive Director of The Dance Companies Resettlement Fund and The Dancers Trust.

Maurits Ypma started working as a physical therapist ten years ago at Scapino Ballet. His interests are sport injuries, posture correction and podokinesiologie (Bourdiol method).